Eternity Today

ON THE LITURGICAL YEAR

Volume 1

Eternity Today

ON THE LITURGICAL YEAR

Volume 1

ON GOD AND TIME,
ADVENT, CHRISTMAS,
EPIPHANY, CANDLEMAS

Martin Connell

continuum

NEW YORK • LONDON

2006

The Continuum International Publishing Group Inc
80 Maiden Lane, New York, NY 10038

The Continuum International Publishing Group Ltd
The Tower Building, 11 York Road, London SE1 7NX

Printed in the United States of America on Recycled Paper

Library of Congress Cataloging-in-Publication Data

Connell, Martin F.
    Eternity today : on the liturgical year / Martin Connell.
      v. cm.
    Includes bibliographical references and index.
    Contents: v. 1. On God and time – Advent – Christmas – Epiphany – Candlemas.
      ISBN-13: 978-0-8264-1870-8 (v. 1 : hardcover : alk. paper)
      ISBN-10: 0-8264-1870-8 (v. 1 : hardcover : alk. paper)
      ISBN-13: 978-0-8264-1871-5 (v. 1 : pbk. : alk. paper)
      ISBN-10: 0-8264-1871-6 (v. 1 : pbk. : alk. paper)
      1. Church year.   I. Title.
  BV30.C598 2006
  263'.909 – dc22

                                        2006030812

I dedicate this book to my mom, Rose Marie,
who brought God's gift of life,

And to the memory of my dad, Bill (+1996),
who brought the church's gift of faith.

CONTENTS

PREFACE

Conceptions, Births, and Deaths

The two poles of the liturgical year — Christmas and its seasons, Easter and its seasons — reflect the two poles of all human life, its beginning and end, its birth and death. Some fathers of the early church preached that God's plan for the salvation of the world in the incarnation of Jesus of Nazareth was manifested by his conception and death having happened on the same calendrical date, though the New Testament does not make such a claim about God's timing or about the calendar. By their reckoning the coincident day was *pascha*, the Greek word for "Passover" among Jews and eventually for "Easter" among Christians, after the latter faith broke away from the former. In such a theology of the Christian liturgical year with Jesus' conception and death at Passover, there was at first only one main pole, in the spring, after which the reckoning of the span of the Savior's gestation occasioned the emergence of the second pole, the nativity.[1]

In the New Testament, only the dates of the last few days of Jesus' life are supplied, not those of his conception or birth, which were added to the calendar — after debate and wrangling among communities with different theologies and time-reckonings — between the writing of the New Testament and the middle of the fourth century. Now, many centuries later, these two poles of Christmas and Easter are still the pivots of the liturgical year for most churches, the former immutable in its date (December 25) and the latter a moveable feast according to the complex formula for its assignation for almost seventeen centuries.[2]

As with the poles of time in the life of Jesus of Nazareth, so with the incarnate life of the risen Christ in the church, with the life of

---

1. Passover is on a spring date of the Jewish lunar calendar. A remnant of the conception's early date is still on the Christian calendar, with the Solemnity of the Annunciation (or Incarnation) on March 25. The reckonings of these dates are taken up at length in Volume 1, Chapter 3, "Christmas," for the winter pole, and in Volume 2, Chapter 3, "The Three Days," for the spring pole.

2. The formula differs in the Eastern (Orthodox) and Western churches, with the result that in some years they celebrate Easter on the same Sunday and in others on different Sundays.

humanity as a species, and with each person's life: Each had or will have a specific moment of life's beginning and another of life's end. How much God's providence plays into when the beginning and end of human life take place is itself a matter of faith. Some believers and communities feel that God is closely and actively involved in the unfolding of each individual's and each community's life, indeed, even of every event in those lives, while others believe that, while God's love is constant, divine involvement in the close details of timing and coincidence is less certain. However God's involvement is reckoned, what is clear — at least from the witness of the saints — is that providence does not make holier lives longer or sinful lives shorter, for some of the most sanctified of communities and holiest of human lives end at young ages and some of the most energetic, fervent sinners and less than exemplary church communities endure well into ripened old age.

Culture and Calendar

In the general culture of the United States the nativity pole of the Christian calendar, spanning ahead of and after Christmas, is more manifest than the Easter pole of the year, a fact surely related to the natural and spontaneous joy that usually accompanies birth, but also likely a reflection of the American aversion to the sick, the dying, and the dead. Many churches in the United States follow the culture's lead in this, for unlike many of the churches of Europe, Christian communities in America keep the bodies of the dying and the dead far from everyday life, with populations of the elderly peripherally away from families and concentrated accumulations of buried corpses sidelined in cemeteries far removed from concentrated populations of the living. Though cemeteries are often lush and verdant, the dead in them are often forgotten, their burial plots remembered only by paid lawnmowers and landscapers; out of sight, out of mind, and, I suppose, out of belief also, kept up with perpetual-care stipends for the comfort of believers. U.S. Christians prefer the shining star over Bethlehem to the blood and guts of Gethsemane and Calvary, and in the springtime nexus of feasts, American Christians celebrate the Sunday of the resurrection more fervently than the Friday of the death. American anthropology is reflected in how its churches keep time.

How believers face and celebrate the ingredients of the two poles of the liturgical year is influenced by the families, societies, and cultures in which they live out their faith, and the culture's mania at Christmas is, at least in part, reflective of a bright-eyed piety that weighs heavier in the balance than American sobriety in the face of weakness, fragility, and death. Believers' appropriation of the calendar is also influenced by their own personal life experience, by how much they pass time with the sick and dying, by how soberly they face the inevitability of their own death, and by how they imagine the impermanence of human life in relation to the eternity predicated on the life of God.[3]

Faith provides consolation and support to the living, and the liturgical year coordinates occasions for remembering, celebrating, and anticipating conceptions, births, and deaths. In the uncertainty about when the second pole of life will come, the liturgical year coordinates the ingredients and time frame for embracing God's presence and providence in the many moments of life between humanity's conception and death.

As the church celebrates the liturgical year, may it attend to its own address to God as on the Solemnity of All Saints:

> Around your throne
> the saints, our brothers and sisters,
> sing your praise for ever.
> Their glory fills us with joy,
> and their communion with us in your Church
> gives us inspiration and strength
> as we hasten on our pilgrimage of faith,
> eager to meet them.
> With their great company and all the angels
> we praise your glory
> as we cry out with one voice:
> Holy, holy, holy Lord, God of power and might . . .

Acknowledgments

I thank the staff of the Clemens and Alcuin libraries — Reference Desks, Circulation, Interlibrary Loan, and student workers — for the many times when you rescued me and helped me track down an obscure source.

I thank the Hill Museum and Manuscript Library, and Alan Reed, OSB, in particular, for the use of the images from the fifteenth-century *Codex Gottwicensis* for the covers.

---

3. Other ways in which time-keeping has been shaped in the history of the United States are taken up in Volume 1, Chapter 1, "On God and Time."

I thank my colleagues and students in the Department and School of Theology at the College of Saint Benedict and Saint John's University, particularly my colleagues and friends who offer insight at the lunch table and students who read the manuscript at various stages in Liturgical Year 421 and offered critical questions and corrections. In particular I thank Cody Unterseher, whose keen editorial eye and intelligence were outdone only by his humor.

I thank my teachers at Our Lady of Fatima Grade School, Cardinal O'Hara High School, Saint Charles Seminary, Villanova University, and the University of Notre Dame for the great education and generous scholarship assistance. I also thank my colleagues in the Early Liturgy Seminar at the North American Academy of Liturgy.

Among those whose experience and insight enriched my study and celebration of God's presence in time — and whose critical questions, insight, affection, friendship, and love strengthened me and the work — I thank Jean Louise Bachetti, IHM, Gian F. Baldovin, SJ, Allen Boykins, Paul F. Bradshaw, Harald Buchinger, Kristi Butler, Nancy and John Cavadini, Andrew D. Ciferni, OPraem, Jill Burnett Comings, Victoria Costa, Donna Cushing, Robert J. Dahlke, Mary Rose D'Angelo, Bernard E. DeLury, Jr., Megan Duffy, Delores Dufner, OSB, Richard Fabian, Mark Foster, Mark Francis, CSV, Joshua Gert, Karen Gibson, Ronald Goba, Sergio Gomez, Angelo Haspert, OSB, David Hoyt, Gabe Huck, Jeffrey Hutson, Paul Janowiak, SJ, Fenton Johnson, Maxwell E. Johnson, Marie, Mary Joy, and Madeline Kozak, Heinz Kuehn, Ruth Langer, John Leonard, Fabian Lochner, Kurt Mather, E. Ann Matter, Mark Morozovich, Vicki Murray, Hernan Noblega, Melissa Nussbaum, Lisa Opdenaker, L. Edward Phillips, Jim Price, Marc Radell, Chetty Ramanathan, Prabakar T. Rajan, Dietrich Reinhardt, OSB, Bradley Reusch, Timothy C. Senior, Kyle Smith, Robert F. Taft, SJ, Nicole Terez, Johan van Parys, Artur Waibel, Patty Weishaar, Barry Yeoman, and Laurence Zoeckler.

I thank God as I remember Christian Hernan Saavedra (who died in 2004), Mark Searle (1992), Tom Struhs (1998), James F. White (2004), and Thomas Talley (2005).

The book and my research and writing are much stronger for the patience and encouragement of Frank Oveis, of Continuum International. I could not have imagined that — on becoming friends long ago at the American Academy of Religion — we would later cooperate on such a book. I thank Frank for his humor, encouragement, and direct suggestions, as I also remember, too, the hospitality (and patience) of his partner, Tom, as Frank and I waxed for too long about too many religion books.

I thank my godparents, my dad's siblings Marcella Houck and Joseph Connell (1985), and my godchildren, Mary Rose Cavadini and Kevin Prandeski.

As a family, we Connells lived just a few minutes' walk to church. My dad always got there before the start of Mass, while we three kids darted out with Mom to make it in time for the gospel reading. Arriving late called for reading the ritual's data to figure out the season or feast, giving birth to my awareness of the liturgical year. We still tend to a back-pew, arrive-late/leave-early, Monday-to-Saturday piety, revealing an innate affinity for rite and a shirking of authority by ignoring the obligatory day, when the rite was often too long and the church too crowded. I dedicate this work to my parents, Bill (1996) and Rose Marie, for having formed me in a life of faith and thanksgiving.

Contents

The two poles of the liturgical year are generally those that determine the content of the two volumes of *Eternity Today*. Each volume opens with an introductory chapter; for Volume 1 this chapter is "On God and Time," reflecting the interaction of theology and time-keeping in the history of the church; for Volume 2 it is "Sunday," the foundation of the liturgical year throughout the year, whatever the time or season.

The order of each volume after the introductory chapter was determined primarily according to how the feasts and seasons unfold in the course of the liturgical year. Chapter 2 of Volume 1, therefore, begins at the start of the liturgical year, "Advent," and continues to "Christmas" (Chapter 3), "Epiphany" (Chapter 4), and "Candlemas," also called the Presentation of the Lord (Chapter 5).

After "Sunday," Chapter 1 of Volume 2, are "Lent" (Chapter 2), "The Three Days" (Chapter 3), "The Easter Season" (Chapter 4), and "Ordinary Time" (Chapter 5), which has two spans in each year, a shorter one between the Christmas season and Mardi Gras, and a longer one between the end of the Easter season and the beginning of the next Advent. This order of the liturgical year would facilitate reading in a church context as members follow the chapters as the liturgical year itself unfolds.

For classroom use, however, the ten chapters of the two volumes might more fruitfully be read according to the order that the feasts emerged in the development of the liturgical year, with "On God and Time" (Volume 1, Chapter 1) as the introductory chapter, followed by "Sunday" (Volume 2, Chapter 1), "The Three Days" (Volume 2,

Chapter 3), the "Easter Season" (Volume 2, Chapter 4), and "Lent" (Volume 2, Chapter 2). These would be followed by the chapters on the other pole of the year, with "Epiphany" (Volume 1, Chapter 4), "Christmas" (Volume 1, Chapter 3), "Candlemas" (Volume 1, Chapter 5), and "Advent" (Volume 1, Chapter 2). "Ordinary Time" (Volume 2, Chapter 5) — considering the history of lectionaries generally and the reform of the Lectionary after Vatican II — is the last chapter for parish or classroom reading.

ABBREVIATIONS

AAS	*Acta Apostolicae Sedis* (periodical)
ACW	Ancient Christian Writers (collection)
ANF	Ante-Nicene Fathers (collection)
CCSG	*Corpus Christianorum, Series Graeca* (collection)
CCSL	*Corpus Christianorum, Series Latina* (collection)
CCT	Consultation on Common Texts
CPG	*Clavis Patrum Graecorum* (reference work)
CSEL	*Corpus Scriptorum Ecclesiasticorum Latinorum* (collection)
CWS	Classics of Western Spirituality (series)
DACL	*Dictionnaire d'archéologie chrétienne et de liturgie*
FC	Fathers of the Church (collection)
Mansi	J. D. Mansi, *Sacrorum conciliorum nova et amplissima collectio* (collection)
NPNF	Nicene and Post-Nicene Fathers (series)
NRSV	New Revised Standard Version
OR	*Ordines romani*
PG	*Patrologia Graeca*
PL	*Patrologia Latina*
RSV	Revised Standard Version
SC	*Sources chrétiennes*
UP	University Press

Unless otherwise noted, all quotations from scripture are taken from the Revised Standard Version of the Bible (RSV), New Testament copyright © 1946, Old Testament copyright © 1952; second edition © 1971 by the Division of Christian Education of the National Council of Churches of Christ in the U.S.A. and are used by permission. All rights reserved

Texts marked DCT are from The Holy Bible, Old Testament in the Douay-Challoner Text, New Testament and Psalms in the Confraternity Text, ed. John P. O'Connell (Chicago: The Catholic Press, 1950).

Texts marked NRSV are from the New Revised Standard Version Bible, copyright © 1989 by the Division of Christian Education of the National Council of Churches of Christ in the U.S.A. and are used by permission. All rights reserved.

Chapter 1

ON GOD AND TIME

Heaven Here and Eternity Today

This book derives its title from the *Confessions* of St. Augustine (354–430), an early bishop in North Africa whose prolific writings have shaped Christian theology in the West — Roman Catholic and Protestant — more than any other theologian of the Latin tradition. Yet the gregarious and prolific Augustine had something of a complement in an American saint, the shy and reclusive Emily Dickinson (1830–1886). Dickinson's work is so powerful and assertive in its theology that her elected seclusion is sometimes hard to comprehend in balance with the universal appeal of her message. Yet for both saints, of Africa and Amherst, one thing was clear: today is eternity, and eternity today.

Emily Dickinson's Poem #624 — her poems were not titled, merely numbered posthumously by editors of her work — transplanted Augustine's theological mien to North American Christianity and culture:

> Forever – is composed of Nows –
> 'Tis not a different time –
> Except for Infiniteness –
> And Latitude of Home –
>
> From this – experienced Here –
> Remove the Dates – to These –
> Let Months dissolve in further Months –
> And Years – exhale in Years –
>
> Without Debate – or Pause –
> Or Celebrated Days –
> No different Our Years would be
> From Anno Domini's –

Emily Dickinson's work teaches with a courageous assurance, complementing the identity of time in the theology of Augustine, *"Today,"*

1

with the identity of place, "this – experienced *Here.*"[1] Though never easy to read, her verses nudge the reader or hearer into realizing that — if one erased from the experience of "this" and "Here" as well as the time increments of "Dates" and "Months," and "Years" — "Our Years" would indeed be the time of Jesus Christ, the *Anno Domini.*

The poem was written in 1862, during the three-year span of her most fruitful, perhaps even manic, creativity. Examining the foundation stones of older buildings, one sees the abbreviation "A.D.," an abbreviation of the Latin phrase that appears in the last line of her poem, *Anno Domini.* This phrase denotes a relationship of time, with *anno* meaning "in the year," and of possession or identification, with *domini* meaning "of the Lord." This abbreviation was omnipresent in cornerstones for a long time, and surely on the public buildings Dickinson had seen in her life-long hometown of Amherst, Massachusetts.

The bearing of the Latin idiom, in her words and in its use on edifices of stone, captures the gravity of the life of Christ the Lord; yet she juxtaposed that bearing to "our years" and "celebrated days," her regard lifting up human life now as comparably valued to the life of Jesus of Nazareth. In American culture, the length of one's life is held up as a reward for having lived a worthy, good, productive, or holy life. In stark contradiction, the Christian tradition does not value a long life as such a reward, one of many examples of the rubs between U.S. culture and the Christian faith that the culture too stalwartly claims as its own.

The genius of Dickinson's poem is her nineteenth-century insight that the chronicling or quantifying of time is of no consequence in God's eyes. The marking of time, while perhaps an aid in coordinating the social matters of daily life, is often an impediment to the realization of God's presence. Fundamentally, time does not separate human beings from God — a truth captured in the work of both saints, Augustine and Emily. Their collective word veers sharply away from the common Christian inclination to consider the present, that is, the time between the life of Jesus and Nazareth and the end of the world, as impoverished in comparison with the heightened realization of God's presence in the incarnation of Jesus and in the final kingdom to come.

Emily Dickinson's words reflect the immediacy of St. Paul's exclamation, "now is the day of salvation." Paul's theology of time, as considered below, introduces a critical reflection on the relation of

---

1. Emily Dickinson, *The Complete Poems of Emily Dickinson,* ed. Thomas H. Johnson (Boston: Little, Brown, 1960): #624. (Italics added.)

time-keeping and theology throughout Christian history. St. Augustine's *"Hodiernus tuus aeternitas,"* that eternity in God is the daily experience of humanity,[2] is echoed centuries later in Emily Dickinson's "Forever — is composed of Nows," and together these two bellow with St. Paul's "behold, now is the acceptable time; behold, now is the day of salvation" (2 Corinthians 6:2b).

Paul's impetuosity is apt at the start of a study of the liturgical year, for, asked why the church maintains a liturgical year, many Christians would respond that it gives opportunities to remember events of the life of Jesus: when he was born and baptized; when he ministered to the sick, broken, marginalized, and possessed; when he was "tested as we are, yet without sin" (Hebrews 4:15), suffered, and died. This assessment is true if one considers the shape of the year as established by the fourth and fifth centuries; yet merely looking back at any event of salvation does not capture the fullness of the mystery of salvation wrought by proclaiming and hearing the scriptures, among which, complemented by narratives of the Old Testament, the community hears about the life of God incarnate as a human being in the historical person Jesus of Nazareth. Though remembering as a community is fundamental and irreplaceable in the experience of Christian faith and worship, the efficacy of the life of Jesus for human salvation, as the church teaches, continues until the end of time. Life in the present does not weigh less in God's balance than life in the past or the future.

Memory and the Liturgical Year

Little new is revealed to the assembled church in the remembrances of the liturgical year or in the three-year cycle of readings built on the synoptic Gospels.[3] The patterns of worship and the sequence of readings continue inexorably, as ever, with the prayers and readings nearly the same as the last time they were proclaimed and heard a year ago, three years ago, a century or a millennium ago. The repetitious pattern of the liturgical year — starting with Advent and the Christmas season; through the Forty Days of Lent, the Three Days, and the Fifty Days of the Easter Season; and over the Sundays in the two spans of Ordinary Time — brings the life of God, the risen Christ, and the Holy Spirit to believers in the church today. Yet the manifestation of God's gifts of life and grace do not depend on anything new being taught or learned in the liturgy's annual cycle. The communal and sensory

---

2. Augustine, *Confessions* 11.13.

3. For more on the Sunday Lectionary and its three-year cycle, see Volume 2, Chapter 5, "Ordinary Time."

experience of people at worship always reveals God's love for creation and humanity, and how this love is mediated in the present experience of the rites and also in life apart from the church.

These gifts of God are not confined to the baptized or their rites; but for the baptized the sacraments — and the liturgical year during which the rites unfold — are the privileged and familiar moments when God's presence shows forth and human beings are knitted together in the name of Christ. "Where two or three are gathered in my name, there am I in the midst of them" (Matthew 18:20). The narratives proclaimed in the taxonomy of the calendar are a gift wrought by the inspiration of the Holy Spirit and realized in the church's vocation to bring the people of God together. In that process remembering is a constitutive element, but fruitless if it languishes as mere memorial.

The biblical narratives in the shape of the liturgical year have not changed significantly for a very long time, but — because the stories are elastic in human imaginations and often spare in descriptive details — faith supplies contexts as the narratives are unfolded from parish to parish. The bonding of imaginations in the church through the proclamations (and, perhaps, the preaching) brings people together toward sanctity and salvation. In this fundament of worship, human lives are made one in the sacraments, most frequently at the Lord's Supper on Sundays.

Year after year church-goers hear that the newborn Jesus was laid in an animals' feeding trough in Bethlehem, the same as they heard the year before. Year after year that he ministered to the forsaken and the dead; that he was crucified, died, buried, and rose, again, just like last year. Proclamation is rarely effective in revealing new insights about Jesus; rather, the efficacy of telling the familiar stories is realized through the local community's ordering and experience of proclaiming and hearing the narratives in the Liturgy of the Word, and in giving and receiving the body and blood of Christ. The Liturgy of the Word is not an educational opportunity, but a phenomenal, transformative, *saving* experience that unites reclusive, manic, depressed, erratic, possessed, infirm, lunatic, and dead people and makes of them a church. (The sane need not apply or inquire!) Memory is a necessary medium, but the end of worship — as of all human and cosmic existence — is the revelation and realization of God's love in Christ.

Experience confirms this, for believers return to worship not to learn, but to discover in the seasons and feasts a rich context for discovering God present in and through the community of faith. The present lives of believers are changed by the phenomena of the liturgy, its proclamation of the narratives and the experience of remembering the stories — historically true or not — and its rites. Although the Liturgy of the Word focuses on the proclamation or animation of texts mostly about *past* events, the liturgical event itself, in which these events are proclaimed and heard in the gathered community of faith, is a *present* and *sensory* experience that enables human lives to be wedded, reimagined, and transformed.

By baptism the church is the body of Christ, and as such it is the ever incarnate Christ realized by God's promise Sunday after Sunday. By the power of the Holy Spirit, baptism is the occasion for uniting each person's story to the stories of the tradition and for revealing "the measure of the stature of the fullness of Christ" (Ephesians 4:13b), in the word made flesh, in the body and the blood, and in the church and its ministers. Even before baptism, the Holy Spirit redirects the narrative of a person's life, and by that rite — in infancy or adulthood — the story of the individual takes on new possibilities and interpretations, new starts and endings from the time of that salvific bath forward, as the narrative of that person is grafted onto the single and infinitely complex narrative of God's people. The incredible mystery of God's grace is not only that Jesus lived and moved and had his being in first-century Palestine, but that, by rites punctuated with ancient stories, "we live and move and have our being" (Acts 17:28) in his risen presence, accessible and perceptible to believers in the liturgical year two millennia later.

Theology and Time-Keeping

This book takes up the main days, feasts, and spans of the liturgical year. Yet there have been many whose work contributed to the development of the year, not in terms of fasts and feasts and seasons, but in terms of the interaction between creed (what the church believed) and chronometry (how the church kept or measured time). Awareness of this interaction helps one to see that calendar and faith shape and inform one another. Thus, this book on the liturgical year begins by introducing the protagonists of this interaction between creed and chronometry in Christian history.

Calendars interact also with theologies of time, with humanity's understanding of how God's nature is manifest in present, past, and future; with how the historical Jesus and the risen Christ are revealed and perceived in time; and in the relation of time-keeping and church-building. This chapter presents some of the people whose ministry, mission, teaching, or experience reflects how the church's understanding of time changed as theologies of revelation and the church's self-understanding developed. Each character contributed to how time itself was understood, even though her or his role did not always directly influence decisions about the calendar. Their theologies and experiences of time can be juxtaposed to the historical development of the Christian understanding of the liturgical year and of the life of Jesus proclaimed and celebrated in the calendar's feasts and seasons. Some reappear again in later chapters, some do not; either way, appreciating their contributions helps both theologians and worshipers recognize how the study of the interactions of time and faith — of chronometry and creed — are related to what became the liturgical year. The characters are presented in historical order, in four sections:

1. Time in the Early Church
2. Time in the Middle Ages
3. Time in the Reformation and the French Revolution
4. Time in the United States

Part One:
Time in the Early Church

Paul

Like Jesus of Nazareth, Paul of Tarsus was born a Jew. Unlike Jesus, Paul did not die a Jew, but a Christian, an advocate of that new faith emerging from the older tradition. His letters (dated to the years ca. 50–60) are the earliest writings of the nascent faith as it distinguished itself from the Judaism from which it was born. In one of his missives, the Letter to the Galatians, he wrote about his life as a Jew and about his conversion:

> you have heard of my former life in Judaism, how I persecuted the church of God violently and tried to destroy it; and I advanced in Judaism beyond many of my own age among my people, so extremely zealous was I for the traditions of my fathers. (1:13–14)

By his own account, Paul described himself as a dedicated, Law-abiding Jew and a persecutor of those who were part of the Christian movement when it was still predominantly within Judaism. The apostle's conversion brought the church its most vociferous advocate for the admission of non-Jews, as Paul vied against the apostle Peter, who sought to keep the Jewish Law integral to Christian faith and practice. Peter's proposal would have excluded non-Jewish converts and circumscribed in both place and calendar how much the new faith would grow.

Paul's letters (and the second half of the Acts of the Apostles) mention many places in which the new faith was coming into being. Indeed the letters were addressed to members of new Christian societies along the northern edge of the Mediterranean basin: Galatia, Philippi, Thessalonica, Corinth, Rome. Less numerous in his letters are references to time and calendar. Perhaps because of the success of his advocacy on behalf of the Gentiles, the apostle foresaw that the imminent wave of Gentiles seeking membership signaled the diminishing importance of the Jewish calendar of feasts in the new faith.

The winnowing of the weekly, monthly, and yearly components of the Jewish calendar — components that themselves varied from one Jewish community to the next in antiquity — was not complete. For in First Corinthians (5:7) he proclaimed that "Christ, our Passover, has been sacrificed," drawing from the Jewish year a significant metaphor of time for the new Christian tradition.[4] In other places of his correspondence, time-references are perhaps less theologically freighted, as, for example, at the end of the First Letter to the Corinthians, where he wrote that "I will stay in Ephesus until Pentecost" (16:8), more likely a familiar point of reference than one with theological bearing.

The few time-references in Paul's letters might have been because the new faith was beginning to distance itself from Judaism, even just a generation after the death of Jesus; but also because the apostle encouraged those of pagan background to resist those who, like Peter, wanted Christians to observe the Law and its feasts. Paul coaxed the community at Galatia to give up its former time-keeping observances, else he would have wasted his time in bringing the gospel to them:

> Formerly, when you did not know God, you were in bondage to beings that by nature are no gods; but now that you have come to know God, or rather to be known by God, how can you turn back again to the weak and beggarly elemental spirits, whose slaves you want to be once more? You observe days, and months, and seasons, and years! I am afraid I have labored over you in vain. (4:8–11)

For Paul the observing of special "days, and months, and seasons, and years" was a characteristic of those who "were in bondage to beings that by nature are no gods," that is, as the Galatians had been before they came to the faith — before they had come to know the one true God of Jesus Christ.

---

4. *kai gar to pascha hēmōn etuthē Christos;* trans. Connell.

Commentators have been divided in trying to explain why the apostle used generic words of time-keeping, "days, months, seasons, and years," rather than Jewish references such as "Sabbaths," "New Moons," "Days of Atonement," and "Passovers."[5] Some have supposed that he did so because the community at Galatia, made up mostly of Gentiles, was inclined to regress into pagan practices of reading the stars and seasons as indicators of divine will. Paul thus employed terms pointing to that persuasion. Others assume that the Galatians were under the influence of teachers who still believed that the new religion should follow Jewish observances, and that the "days" was linked to the "sabbaths" of the Jews, "months" to the appearances of the "new moon," "seasons" to Jewish spans like Passover and Tabernacles, and "years" to sabbatical years or other years of significance for Jews, such as the Jubilee Year. But the main message of Paul — whether he was intent on discouraging the Galatians from keeping Jewish or pagan feasts — was that such observances were impediments to the true faith and were to be discarded, signs that they had returned once again to enslavement by "weak and beggarly elemental spirits" (4:9).

the church heeded Paul's admonition that enslavement, you would be much closer to ginning!)

The First Day of the Week and the Christian Passover

While some suppose that the church maintained Jewish observances of time after the death of Jesus for a few decades — at least until the time of the Council of Jerusalem (ca. 50) — by the middle of the century there were advocates, like Paul himself, that the church should welcome Gentiles and that they should not have to be circumcised or follow the dietary laws and other religious prescriptions of the Law. In the chapters to come, the argument is made that there are moments in the history of the church when changes in the liturgical-year reflected changes in the church's understanding of itself. The change of the weekly holy day from Jewish Sabbath, "seventh day," to Christian Sunday, "first day of the week," was the first observable change of how time-keeping reflected a perceptible change in the church's population and self-understanding. As Gentiles increased in the church's fold, the Jewish Sabbath decreased in importance, and the uniquely

---

5. See, for example, Richard N. Longenecker, *Galatians*, Word Biblical Commentary 41 (Dallas: Word Books, 1990): 178–183, especially 182–183; or J. Louis Martin, *Galatians: A New Translation with Introduction and Commentary* (New York: Doubleday, 1997): 409–418.

Christian Sunday became the church's manifestation of distinguishing itself from the Temple and the Law.

The correspondence of Paul provides the first extant remnant of this change in the week, though the remnant is brief.[6] In churches with stronger ties to their Jewish roots or with more members of Jewish origins, the communities still celebrated the Sabbath as the weekly time for assembly. But at the end of Paul's First Letter to the Corinthians, as he is leaving them with final instructions and greetings, he wrote: "Now concerning the contribution for the saints: as I directed the churches of Galatia, so you also are to do. On the first day of every week, each of you is to put something aside and store it up, as he may prosper, so that contributions need not be made when I come" (16:1–2).

How much the church forsook Jewish elements in the calendar is not fully appreciable in Paul's writings, for, as mentioned above, Paul did write of Christ as "our Passover," and the Greek word for the day, *pascha*, was merely a transliteration of the Hebrew word for the Jewish Passover, *pesach*. The references to the assembly on "the first day of every week" (1 Corinthians 16:2) and to Christ as the "Passover" (1 Corinthians 5:7) reveal that in the middle of the first century the church was both maintaining some Jewish elements and discarding others, and this probably reflects the moment of transition from the church's early ties to the faith from which it sprung and its nascent inclination to break away from Law, Jerusalem, Temple, and Sabbath.

Gospels

The Week

In the four Gospels, written in Greek in the span of years from 70 to 100, time references are more plentiful than in Paul's letters. They reflect how the church was changing in the late first century, how Christian communities were distinguishing themselves from others by how they kept time, and how time-references were being used for theological carriage. Deep in the Christian imagination are the many Gospel narratives in which the Pharisees confront Jesus about breaking the proscriptions of activity on the Sabbath, as in this familiar story:

One sabbath he was going through the grainfields; and as they made their way his disciples began to pluck heads of grain. And the Pharisees said to him, "Look, why are they doing what is not lawful on the sabbath?" And he said to them, "Have you never

---

6. See Volume 2, Chapter 1, "Sunday."

read what David did, when he was in need and was hungry, he and those who were with him: how he entered the house of God, when Abiathar was high priest, and ate the bread of the Presence, which it is not lawful for any but the priests to eat, and also gave it to those who were with him?" And he said to them, "The sabbath was made for man, not man for the sabbath; so the Son of man is lord even of the sabbath." (Mark 2:23–28; parallels at Matthew 12:1–8 and Luke 6:1–5)

Although Jesus and the Pharisees are the main antagonists here, the story is most likely a reflection of the antagonism between Jewish and Gentiles Christians in the community of the Gospel of Mark decades after the death of Jesus. The historical circumstance that signals the change in Christian time-keeping between the letters of Paul and the synoptic Gospels is the heightened aggression of the Roman Empire against Jews in Palestine, and the catastrophic finale of that aggression was the destruction of the Temple (in the years 66 to 70), the locative center of Jewish life and faith. Throughout the Gospels conflicts between Jesus and the Jewish authorities reflected, among other things, conflicts between the Jewish and Gentile adherents to the new Christian cult. The "first day of the week" had already started to become the day of the weekly assembly, but Paul's mention of it was positive and indicative, that is, not coupled with a denunciation of the Sabbath, the sacred day of the Law, which appeared in the writing of the Gospels as the evangelists put anti-Sabbath rhetoric in the mouth of Jesus.

Written more than a decade and a half after Paul, the Gospel of Mark contains no positive advocacy for the first day, Sunday, but simply a single if weighty mention of the "first day of the week" in the empty-tomb narrative (16:2);[7] but the Gospel does have a heated antipathy toward the sabbath, the seventh day. The repetition of the word "sabbath" five times in the short narrative above makes clear the significance of the conflicts over the weekly day of observance in the Marcan community when the Gospel was written. Although the acceptance of the Gentiles was twenty years earlier than its writing, the Gospel of Mark reveals the calendrical reshaping occasioned by their admission, as the first day emerges while the Jewish week is still vibrant in the church's practice and memory. As before, time-keeping reflects values and social affiliation, as the early communities distanced themselves from the Law and gradually developed their unique chronologies of the life of Jesus and taxonomies of the calendar.

---

7. The synoptic parallels are Matthew 28:1 and Luke 24:1, though in the Gospel of Luke the mention of Sunday at the empty-tomb account is not the only one; see 24:13.

The Year

While the literature about the date of the death of Jesus is too complex to delve into in great detail, the simple fact of a difference in the date of Jesus' death in the Synoptic and Johannine traditions reveals that, as church and time-keeping were linked above, Christology and time-keeping also influenced one another. What the church believed about Jesus of Nazareth and how it marked time resulted in different dates for the same event.[8] In the synoptic Gospels, the death of Jesus happens on the first full Day of Passover, while in the Gospel of John on the Day of Preparation for Passover, that is, the day before Passover, when Jews sacrifice lambs in anticipation of the domestic rite of the Passover meal, according to the prescriptions for the meal, as in Deuteronomy 12:1–20.[9]

In reality — save for the Book of Revelation, in which it appears almost thirty times — the word "lamb" appears only four times in the New Testament: twice in the Gospel of John, once in Acts (8:32) and once in 1 Peter (1:19). "Lamb" does not appear at all in the Gospels of Matthew, Mark, and Luke. So the Christologies of the two dominant Gospel traditions, Synoptic and Johannine, influenced the evangelists' choices about dates, even for so key a time as the death of Jesus. Yet the discrepancy is appreciable when one is aware that the Gospel of John is the one that refers to Jesus as the "Lamb of God" (at 1:29 and 1:36), so it is then fitting that its author constructed the chronology of the death of Jesus by temporally locating the death of Jesus on the Day of Preparation, at the time of the sacrifice of the lambs, even if he might have been aware that other Gospel traditions had already ascribed the event to the following day, Passover. The community of the Gospel of John was familiar with the image of the lamb for Jesus, and therefore the Christology of the community was more important than historical accuracy or even calendrical agreement. The Christology of the community and its evangelist was matched with the Gospel's unique date for the crucifixion.

Tertullian

In his work "On Fasting," the North African theologian Tertullian (ca. 160–225) took up Paul's critical position regarding time-keeping

---

8. For an accessible and detailed presentation of the complexity of matters on this topic, see "Appendix II: Dating the Crucifixion (Day, Monthly Date, Year)," in Raymond Brown, *The Death of the Messiah* (New York: Doubleday, 1994): 1350–1378.

9. On the emergence of Easter and its meaning in the early church, see Volume 2, Chapter 3, "The Three Days."

against the Galatians. The polemicist of Carthage reflected on time-keeping in the Christian tradition of the early third century:

> As keepers of the seasons and days and months and years, we also act like Galatians.[10] Certainly we keep Jewish ceremonies and solemnities of the Law, even though the apostle erased them, suppressing the Old Testament that was buried in Christ and establishing the New. If in Christ there is a new creation, they [ceremonies and solemnities] too must be new and solemn.[11]

A century and a half had passed between Paul and Tertullian, and Tertullian's treatise demonstrates that a skeleton of the church year had begun to emerge in this period in North Africa. In this work "On Fasting" Tertullian raised questions drawing from Paul's observations to the Galatians: "If the apostle erased completely the seasons and days and months and years, then why do we celebrate Easter each year in the first month [spring]?" He continues with other examples of North African practice that countered Paul's aversion to time-keeping as a sign of regression: "Why in the fifty days following [Easter] do we spend fifty days in complete rejoicing?" And, finally, he asked a question that has led to misinterpretations about the fast before Easter: "Why do we dedicate the fourth-day [Wednesday] and the sixth-day [Friday] to stations, and Preparation Day [the day before Easter] to fasts? You sometimes continue [fasting] to Sabbath-day [Saturday], a day never for fasting except at Easter."[12]

Much had changed between Paul's first century and Tertullian's early third, and, as before, the way local churches are keeping time reflects their values and priorities. Tertullian was one of the earliest fathers of the church to write in Latin, and his "On Fasting" is the

---

10. *De ieiunio* (On Fasting), 14. The Latin verb that Tertullian employed here, *galaticamur*, is his own invention, used to accuse his people of too much attention to time and seasons as had Paul accused the Galatians. In this translation I have employed the phrase "act like Galatians" instead of "Galaticize," even though the latter is grammatically more accurate because it is one word and that word a verb, as it was in Tertullian's rhetoric against the Psychics.

The Latin original of "On Fasting" is in the critical edition, August Reifferscheid and Georg Wissowa, eds., *Quinti Septimi Florentis Tertulliani Opera*, CSEL 20 (Vienna: Corpus Scriptorum Ecclesiasticorum Latinorum, 1890): 274–297.

11. *Horum igitur tempora obseruantes et dies et menses et annos galaticamur! Plane, si Iudaicarum caeremoniarum, si legalium sollemnitatum obseruantes sumus; illas enim apostolus dedocet compescens ueteris testamenti in Christo sepulti perseuerantiam et noui sistens. Quod si noua conditio in Christo, noua et sollemnia esse debebunt* (IV.1–2); trans. Connell.

12. *Cur stationibus quartam et sextam sabbati dicamus et ieiuniis parasceuen! XIV.2. Quamquam uos etiam sabbatum, si quando, coninuatis, numquam nisi in pascha ieiunandum* (XIV.3); trans. Connell. This is taken up in Volume 2, Chapter 2, "Lent."

oldest complete work on the topic. The entire work on fasts was a polemic, and among the many reasons Tertullian indicted his readers was their imitation of the errors of the Galatians by keeping special days and feasts.

The Year in the Age of Tertullian

In the questions Tertullian posed after his indictment of "Galaticizers," he reveals that a number of elements had been added to the liturgical year by the early third century. He mentions the "fifty days following Easter," those days of "complete rejoicing." Although this is clear evidence that the "Fifty Days" were observed in the early third century, interpreters often take his indication as evidence that such an element was universal in the calendar — though little about the calendar was universal in the third century.[13]

Tertullian also wrote of the fast on the Saturday of the Easter Vigil. Though this is a very early precedent for what will become an ascetic span leading up to Easter, this should not be readily seen as an early indication of Lent; more likely, this is an early indication of the gravity of the span immediately before Easter itself — more a precedent for the span of the Three Days before Easter than for the forty days of Lent. (That the church does not celebrate the Eucharist on Good Friday, for example, is a better example of what Tertullian points to than Lent.[14])

Finally, although Tertullian's work does not reflect it, the earliest evidence for the solemnity of Epiphany appears close to the end of Tertullian's life. In the year 215 Epiphany appears for the first time in Egypt in the correspondence of Clement of Alexandria. Although Easter and Christmas are the best known annual Christian feasts today, the first two to emerge in the tradition are not Easter and Christmas but Easter and Epiphany. It would be another century and a half after Tertullian before the next piece of evidence on Epiphany would appear, but that early datum about Epiphany from Egypt, worlds away from the Latinized North Africa of Tertullian, was coincident with the end of his days.

St. Helena

As the emperor Constantine — the first Christian emperor, who died in 337 — faced his enemies in the year 312 at the Battle of the Milvian

---

13. On the different spans, configurations, and theologies of the season after Easter Sunday, see Volume 2, Chapter 4, "The Easter Season."

14. On the various origins and spans of Lent, see Chapter 5, on Lent. On the Roman church's suspension of the sacraments on Good Friday, see my *Church and Worship in Fifth-Century Rome: The Letter of Innocent I to Decentius of Gubbio*, Alcuin Club 52 (Cambridge: Grove, 2002): 34–38.

Bridge, the place of the newly emerging religion in the empire was about to be elevated to imperial status. In a dream the night before the battle, Constantine saw the cross of Jesus as a sign of his proximate victory, and, according to tradition, he marked his shield and those of his soldiers with the sign of the cross, the symbol of Christ, the victor under whom Constantine thought his battle had been won.[15]

In addition to this thirst for victory in battle, the dedication of his mother, Helena (who died in 330), contributed to his conversion. Once her son found favor from the Christian God, the imperial mother, who made one of the first pilgrimages to the Holy Land in the year 324, lobbied her son for money to undertake a building campaign in the places of Palestine where Jesus of Nazareth had, according to the Gospels, been born, ministered, died, and rose.[16] The Church of the Nativity in Bethlehem and the Church of the Holy Sepulchre in Jerusalem still stand in the places where Helen's campaign led to their first construction, almost seventeen centuries ago.

The building program of the Roman Empire in the Holy Land is usually studied for the places and the physical shape of the terrain where Christian pilgrims would go to see the land where their Savior once lived. Yet under the same emperor, and his mother, the shape of the liturgical year was also given a boost by that project, for the specificity sought by pilgrims regarding the *places* of the life of Jesus was complemented by their thirst for knowing and marking the *times* of his life.

Moreover, Constantine knew that the unity of the Christian cult would lead to a more peaceful empire. So in 321, just a few years before he would convene the Council of Nicea, he mandated Sunday as the day when all citizens would abstain from work. This edict was met with resistance because both Jews and Roman pagans observed the planet Saturn's day, Saturday, as the day of rest. The emperor's edict is clearly a sign of the ascendancy of Christian faith in the empire.

The other major change in the calendar advocated by Constantine was his demand for consensus on a common date for the Christian Easter. This supreme annual celebration — not yet a span of Three Days — was a cause of much contention and acrimony in the second, third, and beginning of the fourth centuries. The emperor did not care what time-reckoning was employed for Easter, but he wanted the matter settled. Various factions were at odds with one another about this basic issue. Some believers still used the date of the Jewish Passover,

---

15. See Eusebius, *Vita Constantini:* 28–32.
16. Ibid.: 41–47.

based on lunar cycles. Others used the dates of the solar calendar of the Roman government for time-keeping. Still others looked not for a particular date but for a day of the week, advocating that Easter be on a Sunday, since the first day of the week was already the day of assembly for Christians. A common date for Easter would signify the unity of the church, and — though still not yet achieved these seventeen centuries later — the emperor wanted the church to agree on a formula for determining the date.

The complex formula for the day of Easter was the church's medium for bringing together various sectors of the church in the early fourth century: those who maintained Jewish traditions more strongly (which begot the "after the full moon" of the prescription, from the Jewish lunar calendar), those who followed the solar calendar of the Roman Empire (which begot the "after the spring equinox" of the prescription), and those who wanted the highest annual feast to be on the day of the weekly assembly (which begot the "Sunday" ingredient of the prescription).[17]

Though there are still periodic calls for agreement on the date of Easter,[18] this divergence is similar to that of the two dates of the crucifixion in the Synoptic and Johannine chronologies. The differences in time-keeping reflect different theologies and social values in Christian churches of the Eastern and Western traditions. As ever, divisions in time-keeping reflect divisions in the church.

Christmas

Noted above is that near the end of Tertullian's life, and on the other side of the Christian world, the feast of Epiphany had emerged. So here, just after the death of Helena, in 330, and just before the death of her imperial son, in 337, Christmas appeared, but on the other side of the Mediterranean world in the church at Rome. The earliest evidence for Christmas appears at Rome in 336, far from the realm of the building program in Palestine, though it would eventually echo to that part of the church. The desire to discern the places and times of the life of Jesus began at the beginning of the fourth century, but consensus about the times was not immediate, and one of the more acrimonious disputes was about whether the nativity would be reckoned according to the traditions of the East (and of most of the churches of the West) or the tradition of Rome.[19]

---

17. For more on the date of Easter, see Volume 2, Chapter 3, "The Three Days."

18. See the Appendix to the *Constitution on the Sacred Liturgy*, promulgated at Vatican II (1963).

19. On the origins of Christmas, see Volume 1, Chapter 3, "Christmas."

Egeria

At the end of the same century in which the emperor's mother prompted her son to launch the building campaign in Jerusalem, many pilgrims began to flock to the sites of the lives of the patriarchs of the Old Testament and the life of Jesus, and one of these pilgrims left an incomparable record of her journey. Though traveling in places where Latin was not the common tongue, the pilgrim came from a community of women back in the Western part of the empire, and so she wrote a diary kept for her community in Latin, called *Itinerarium* or sometimes *Peregrinatio,* in English the "Diary of a Pilgrimage." The work reveals an enormous amount about what had appeared in terms of buildings and rites during the course of the fourth century.

The pilgrim was Egeria.[20] At one point in her chronicle, as she begins to describe the décor of a scene, she mentions the former emperor and the influence of his mother:

> You see nothing there but gold and gems and silk. If you look at the hangings, they are made of silk with gold stripes; if you look at the curtains, they are also made of silk with gold stripes. Every kind of sacred vessel brought out on that day is of gold inlaid with precious stones. How could the number and weight of the candle holders, the candelabra, the lamps, and the various sacred vessels be in any way estimated and noted down? And what can I say about the decoration of this building that Constantine, with his mother on hand, had embellished with as much gold, mosaics, and marble as the resources of his empire permitted?[21]

This description brings forward the imperial building program of Helena's initiative to the later fourth century, and one sees from Egeria's chronicle that the excavations and building had continued.

Her travelogue is a wonderful late fourth-century complement to the histories of the building campaign,[22] for this pilgrim to Jerusalem —

---

20. Over time, sources have given the name variously as Etheria (or Aetheria), Eutheria, or Sylvia.

21. Egeria, *Peregrinatio,* 25.8–9: *Ubi extra aurum et gammas aut sirico nichil aliud uides; nam et si uela uides, auroclaua oleserica sunt, si cortinas uides, similiter auroclaue oleserica sunt. Ministerium autem omne genus aureum gemmatum profertur illa die. Numerus autem uel ponderatio de ceriofalis uel cicindelis aut lucernis uel diverso ministerio nunquid uel extimari aut scribi potest?*

Nam quid dicam de ornatu fabricate ipsius, quam Constantinus sub praesentia matris suae, in quantum uires regni sui habuit, honorauit auro, musiuo et marmore pretioso?

22. On the mother's influence on her son, and on her invention of the true cross of Jesus, see Eusebius of Caesarea, *Vita Constantini,* and Zosimus of Constantinople (later fifth century), *New History,* 2.8. English translation in J. J. Buchanan and H. T. Davis, *Zosimus: Historia Nova; The Decline of Rome* (San Antonio: Trinity, 1967).

the trip is usually dated between 381 and 383 — wrote to members of her community who would not see the sites themselves, so at times she described sites in detail. In addition to descriptions of the context, like the one above, Egeria also wrote in some detail about the liturgies that were celebrated at those sites.

Although most of the itinerant's records for her community attended to places of biblical narratives, concentrating on the Gospels in particular, she also attends to time, the liturgical year, and its seasons. A phrase repeated often by the pilgrim, particularly in the second half of her account, is *omnia apta ipsi diei et loco*, "everything was fitting for the day and place." The phrase appears as she wrote about hymns, psalms, antiphons, prayers, and sermons, which, in the account, are always "suited to the day and the place." The late fourth century is still relatively early in the development of the calendar, but the concentrated attention Egeria gave to the particularities of the locations — because it was very important to her when she was in the very place at which tradition held that a biblical event had taken place — suggests that the "appropriateness" to the day was also in keeping with the Biblical chronicle of events as well. Her account gives early witness to Holy Week, that is, to the liturgies of the week before Easter and to the dedication of the local church of Jerusalem to worshiping at the very sites on the very days and at the very hours when the events took place.

Lent and Candlemas

The fourth-century span covered by the life of Helena and the itinerancy of Egeria reveals a fervor for recovering the places and times of the life of Jesus as they contributed to the basic shape of the liturgical year. It does not seem to be merely coincidence that the shape of the year was established in the very span when the life of Jesus shaped the terrain for pilgrims to the Holy Land. The fourth century was a critical time regarding the development of the year, particularly regarding the nativity cycle of feasts, Christmas, Epiphany, and Candlemas. By the start of the fifth century most churches had accepted the Roman date for the nativity of Jesus, December 25, and most churches of the Latin tradition had circumscribed the variety of narratives of Epiphany to only one, the visit of the magi.[23]

Egeria gives witness to two particular observances in the calendar of the Holy Land that reveal how much the liturgical year had developed

---

23. Egeria, *Peregrinatio*, chapter 27. On the origins and development of Epiphany, see Volume 1, Chapter 4, "Epiphany."

by this time. Of Lent, she mentions that in Jerusalem the church observed the Forty Days, but that, because Saturdays and Sundays were never fast days there, the span of Lent was eight weeks in length.[24] (Tertullian, above, also noted that Saturdays were never to be fast days, except earlier in the day of the Easter Vigil.) The other novelty revealed in the diary is that Egeria supplies the very earliest evidence for a celebration of the Presentation of the Lord in the Temple, or "Candlemas," as it is known and will be called in this book.[25] Rather than the date of February 2 for the Presentation, which was (and is) forty days after Christmas, the date of Candlemas in the Jerusalem of Egeria's journey was February 14, forty days after Epiphany (January 6), when the birth of Jesus was celebrated as one of the variety of epiphanies remembered on that day.[26]

Part Two:
Time in the Middle Ages

Augustine

Bishop Augustine of Hippo in North Africa is a monumental figure in the church's understanding of time and its theological foundations, as he is with so many things in the history of the Latin church and its theological and liturgical traditions. Although he appears intermittently throughout this book as a witness to the history of the liturgical year, he is highlighted here because he was the first Christian philosopher to dissertate theologically on the significance of memory and time in both human and Christian experience. While his contributions on the calendar are important, his theology of time gives a valuable foundation to the Christian understanding of time and worship in all ages and places.

Augustine was nothing less than a genius who wrote many, many works addressing fundamental and perennial issues of human life in general and of Christian life in particular. His life coincided with a period of significant change in the church, its theology, and its calendar. In addition to borrowing Augustine's words for its title, this book

---

24. On Egeria's witness in the context of other spans for observing Lent, see Volume 2, Chapter 2, "Lent."

25. On the origins of Candlemas as evident in Egeria, and on the development of Candlemas through history, see Volume 1, Chapter 5, "Candlemas."

26. Once the date of Christmas was accepted by the churches of the East, the date of the Presentation was moved back twelve days, to February 2, where it has remained. See Volume 1, Chapter 3, "Christmas," on the reception of the Roman date for the nativity by the Eastern churches.

will often zero in on this period of the fourth and fifth centuries as the one that gave the basic form to the church's calendar, and Augustine will, as ever, provide essential testimony. His philosophy of time appears in his autobiographical paean to God, the *Confessions*, the work for which Augustine is most known. There the creative and ever-contentious North African theologian mused on his experience, trying to understand how past, present, and future relate to one another in Christian experience. The candor of his arguments and perplexities when addressing God directly is the main reason the work is still popular today.

Among the many theological puzzles he takes up is the enigma of the experience of time in human life:

> What, then, is time? If no one asks me, I know what it is; but if someone asks for an explanation, I do not know. But I can confidently say that I know that if nothing happened, there would be no past time. And if nothing were going to happen, there would be no future time. And if there were nothing now, there would be no present time.[27]

His statement is of the obvious, perhaps, but he expressed the difficulty any person encounters in thinking about the nature and role of time in the life of humanity as a whole. Time is a gift of God to the world and to humanity. As he explained how time is experienced as past, present, and future, he turned to concrete examples from his experience of time, and each is revelatory about Christian understanding of this elusive phenomenon.

The first example St. Augustine drew upon was from nature, an experience perceived by all human beings and still readily accessible and appreciable centuries later:

> If I am waiting for dawn, I anticipate the rising sun. I see what is already present, but I look forward to the future. It is not that the sun itself is in the future, for it already exists, but its rising has not yet happened. Yet I would not be able to look forward to its rising unless my soul could somehow picture it, in the same way that I could not speak of it now were I not able to look forward to it. Yet the dawn — which I see in the sky — is not the rising sun, even though dawn precedes that rising.
>
> My image of the rising sun is not the same thing as its rising, even though it is from those two — the dawn and my image of

---

27. Augustine, *Confessions*, 11.14; trans. Connell.

the rising sun, both of which exist in the present — that I am
able to speak of the rising of the sun before it takes place. Therefore, future events have not yet taken place, and so, if they have
not taken place, they do not exist. And if they do not exist, they
are not able to be seen by anyone. They can, however, be anticipated from what already exists now, because they exist and can
be seen.[28]

Augustine, as ever, is keen and enthusiastic as he chooses the rising
sun as the example for catechesis, for it is a universal phenomenon,
seen with the eye and felt on the skin, for each person and for the
whole of the human race. In the end Augustine did not answer his
own inscrutable query about the relationship of the present to the past
and the future, but he posed the question with poignancy, urgency, and
accessibility — the qualities that keep his work perennially engaging.
His account confirms that the natural world is a fundamental marker
of the passage of time independent of religious orientation.

For Augustine creation and the life of the church, both gifts of God,
were reliable markers of time. The foundational place of worship, of
daily prayer, in the Christian conception and imagination of time is
firm for him, as his second example clarifies:

Let's say I am about to recite a psalm I know. Before I begin, my
anticipation thinks of the psalm as a whole. But when I have
begun, the amount that I have already recited has passed into
my memory, and the measure of what I have done has passed
into memory because I have already spoken it. What I have not
yet said exists in anticipation. My attention, however, remains
in the present, and in this process what was in the future passes
into the past.

As what has happened already increases, the part I remember
is extended as the part I anticipate is abbreviated. Eventually the
whole anticipation is gone, when the whole action has ended and
passed into my memory. What is true of the whole psalm is also
true of each part, of each syllable even. This process of time is
true still of an even longer act, an act of which, perhaps, the
recitation of the psalm would be only a fraction. As is true of the
psalm recitation, so of the whole of a person's life, of which each
act is just a fraction. And so is this true of the whole of human
existence, of which each human life is just a part.[29]

---

28. Ibid., 11.18; trans. Connell.
29. Ibid., 11.28; trans. Connell.

Juxtaposed to the universality of the rising sun, the psalm recitation is an experience circumscribed, for the most part, to the daily prayer of Jews and Christians. Psalm-singing punctuated the life of Augustine and his church in Africa, so the juxtaposition of waiting through the psalm's length to waiting for the rising sun reveals how deep the experience of worship and prayer was for believers, after nature itself. Along with the sun and moon, liturgy enabled Christians to appreciate time in Augustine's Hippo, near the Mediterranean Sea at the north of the African continent.

Augustine's works are so engaging, sixteen centuries after he wrote, because his rhetoric is accessible and theologically profound, candidly personal and revelatory about the quandaries of human life in general and the role of Christian faith in human life in the tumultuous tentativeness of existence. In the example of the psalm recitation, readers can imagine the place in a community where Augustine might have been as he sang or recited the psalm, and one can sense his mental and perhaps emotional perplexities in coming to grips with the elapsing of time as it orients each person.

Augustine looked to nature and worship as two basic ingredients in his investigation. As some ingredients in the liturgical year originally found their places in the calendar according to the planting, growing, and harvesting of food — thus according to the varying lengths of the day in the year, by seasons of natural warmth and cold, and by the flooding of rivers and seas — so Augustine's turning to the rising sun in his consideration of the human experience of time is accurate because the church year itself was formed on this foundation, and the prayers and impulse of the liturgy reflect the natural world from which they sprang.

Yet, still, the natural world is not the only basic ingredient in Christian formation and growth over time. The community at prayer also shapes the baptized after they are plunged into the death- and life-yielding waters. Though the church is now at a considerable remove from the awe-inspiring rites by which Augustine was brought into the church, its days are no less filled with awe-inspiring experiences of the sacraments. When gathering to pray and process and bathe and eat and drink with baptized others who have shared the story the assembled know so well, time changes as the body changes, as believers rest more peacefully and trustfully knowing that God is indeed God, greater than any individual alone can measure or imagine.

This book's title is derived from the Latin of St. Augustine: *Hodiernus tuus aeternitas (Confessions* 11.13); because Augustine addressed the book to God, a literal translation would be, "Your today is eternity," or, perhaps, in the church, "God's eternity today." But in *this* time God's people find eternity, God's time. In this expression "eternity" is distinguished from "afterlife," for the former, in Augustine's philosophy, is accessible to human experience in the present, not something toward which human life is merely pointed but without access now. Eternity, by God's gift, is indeed today.

The Three Days

The same work that gives the church this theology of time, the *Confessions*, also chronicles Augustine's progress in faith toward baptism. During his catechumenate and formation in the faith, he lived in Milan and was baptized there at the Easter Vigil in the year 387 by Bishop Ambrose (ca. 339–397). Augustine witnessed Ambrose's virulent opposition to the Arians, and his experience in this anti-Arian church in northern Italy helped form his high theology of the relationship of God the Father and the Son.

The emergence of the Three Days of Easter in the late fourth century was the temporal reckoning necessary to distinguish the mutable human nature of the Son from his immutable divine nature.[30] In the new configuration Easter no longer embraced the death of Jesus, as it had for centuries, but now *remembered* the resurrection rather than *celebrated* it. As initiation was moved away from Easter over time, the paschal mystery was understood as more sacred *in the past*. The division of the one paschal event into the Three Days theologically held the mutable, dead corpse of the Savior's human nature apart from God the Father, and a consequence of this was the high conceptualization of consubstantiality that thereafter put the Son at a distance from humanity.

The change from predominantly adult baptisms to primarily infant baptisms during the early Middle Ages is attributed to Augustine's introduction of a theology of original sin. While this is so, there is another theological reason for the loss: Once the humanity and death of the Son were removed from the Easter Vigil, it was only a short step to excising the humanity of humanity (in the elect to be baptized) from the Great Vigil.

Another impression about the liturgical year of Augustine's age was the emerging cult of the saints, still another consequence of the high theology and Christology after the ecumenical councils. Once Jesus

---

30. On the theological foundation of the Three Days, see Volume 2, Chapter 3, "The Three Days."

was seen as "one in being with the Father," he was no longer as accessible to the lives and beliefs of most believers as he had been in their imaginations during the first three Christian centuries. As the church's Christology grew higher and more exalted, believers sought more intimate "friends of God" to whom they could relate, and the cult of the saints would facilitate these intimate friendships between believers and their familiar matrons and patrons in heaven.[31]

The fervor for the cult of the saints grew from the definition of God the Father and God the Son as equal in being and coeternal, and the familiarity of the lives of the saints gave believers a new society in which to ground their faith once Jesus Christ was set at a distance from the lives of believers. The relationship between baptism and Easter disintegrated; as baptisms happened throughout the year, the names of the saints grew in importance, particularly when the birth or baptism of a child was on or proximate to the feast day of a saint. The annual cycle of the feast days of the saints overlaps the temporal cycle of the liturgical year, with its Advent, Christmas and the Christmas season; Lent, Easter, and the Easter season. As the catechumenate, baptism, and mystagogy were dislodged from the temporal cycle of the year, the cycle of saints' feasts rose in their stead. The life of Augustine reflects the time when the catechumenate was vibrant and flourishing, but also the age in which the consequences of the theological decisions of the ecumenical councils began to echo in how time was kept by the church. The importance of the feast days of the saints continued for centuries without any curbs, at least until the sixteenth-century Reformation.

Bede

In the early centuries of the Middle Ages, the societies in which the Christian good news was proclaimed and received changed significantly. In the first four Christian centuries the faith attracted adherents in places much like the place of its birth: urban, Mediterranean places with a large measure of social turbulence and fluidity. In the seventh through ninth centuries, this gradually changed as missionaries began to preach the faith and gain converts in the rural regions of today's northern Europe.[32] A challenge to those bringing the faith to the northern areas of the continent was in making the narratives, rites, and feasts of an urban faith attractive to people not living in cities.

31. See Peter Brown, *The Cult of the Saints: Its Rise and Function in Latin Christianity* (Chicago: University of Chicago Press, 1981): 50–68.

32. See James C. Russell, *The Germanization of Early Medieval Christianity: A Socio-historical Approach to Religious Transformation* (New York: Oxford, 1994).

One of the great conflicts as the faith was received in remote places was in establishing and maintaining the date of Easter because it was determined by the complex formula established at the Council of Nicea. The Northumbrian monk who accepted the challenge of studying many of the earlier authorities who had written on the date of Easter was the Venerable Bede (ca. 673–735).

In a time when instant communication is omnipresent, it is difficult to imagine a world in which information circulated slowly, yet believers in Ireland and Britain during the early Middle Ages ever worried that they were not celebrating Easter on the correct day because the texts used for calculating the date disagreed with one another or had different degrees of authority from place to place. Moreover, there were traditional disputes about the reckoning of Easter between churches of the East (in Egypt in particular), and churches of the West (especially Rome). Aware that the date for Britain's Easter had differed from Rome's in some years, Bede undertook the work of studying and systematizing the calendar so that the Celtic church could confidently celebrate Easter on the same day as the church of Rome.

Bede's masterwork is *The Reckoning of Time*, which in Latin is *De temporum ratione*. It was not Bede's first attempt to explain the rationale behind the Christian system of dating, as he confessed in his Preface:

> Some time ago I wrote two short books in a summary style which were, I judged, necessary for my students; these concerned the nature of things, and the reckoning of time. When I undertook to present and explain them to some of my brethren, they said that they were much more concise than they would have wished, especially the book on time, which was, it seems, rather more in demand because of the calculation of Easter. So they persuaded me to discuss certain matters concerning the nature, course, and end of time at greater length. I yielded to their enthusiasm, and after surveying the writings of the venerable Fathers, I wrote a longer book on time. I was enabled to do so by the largesse of Him who, abiding eternal, established the seasons when it pleased Him, and who knows the limits of the ages; indeed, when He sees fit, He Himself shall decree an end to the unstable cycles of time.[33]

---

33. *Bede: The Reckoning of Time*, trans., intro., notes, and commentary by Faith Wallis (Liverpool: Liverpool University Press, 1999): 3. The introduction and commentary by Wallis are strong and engaging, particularly in her explanation of that ancient science of *computus*, that is, the calculating necessary to determine the date of Easter.

Between the preface and the end of the work is a long treatise of dizzy-ing complexity, surely simpler — as he himself describes it — than what had been put forth by his forebears in the system of calculations; but the complexity helps one understand the gravity of this science of time, a science called *computus*, in the early Middle Ages.

Although Bede's voice throughout the work is one of authority, he finished the work, as he had begun it, in deference to the Creator:

> And so our little book concerning the fleeting and wave-tossed course of time comes to a fitting end in eternal stability and sta-ble eternity. And should those who read it deem it worthy, I ask that they commend me in their prayers to the Lord, and that they behave with pious zeal towards God and their neighbor, to the best of their ability, so that after temporal exertions in heav-enly deeds, we may all deserve to receive the palm of heavenly reward.[34]

As the emperor Constantine had called upon the bishops of the early fourth century for a common date for Easter, so did Bede and those preceding him seek unity in calculations and date, the very impetus for his work. But as in Constantine's fourth century, so in Bede's eighth, there was still no common date for Easter.

Another of Bede's contributions to the church was his advocacy for counting years from the conception of Jesus. He did not introduce the matter, for it had been proposed in the sixth century by Abbot Diony-sius Exiguus, Abbot "Little Dennis" (of the late fifth and early sixth centuries), who proposed that the years be counted *ab incarnatione*, from Jesus' taking on flesh, when he was conceived in the womb of his mother. Once Bede became an advocate for Dionysius's temporal in-vention, it was adopted first by the Anglo-Saxons, and over the course of the Middle Ages the reception spread, evident in papal records of the tenth century, but not universal in Europe until the age of the printing press, that is, in the fifteenth century.[35]

Advent

ADVENT

Although Bede's work was more on the computation of time than on the liturgical year, his life is coincident with the period in which Advent was reckoned as four weeks in the Roman tradition. Earlier

---

34. Ibid.: 249.
35. Uta C. Merzbach, "Calendars and Reckoning of Time," *Dictionary of the Middle Ages*, volume 3 (New York: Scribner's, 1983): 17–30.

than Bede, there had been a variety of spans for Advent,[36] but by his time the church had come to standardize the four Sundays of the pre-Christmas season. There were still some places that observed both the four weeks and another span extending back from Christmas to the feast of St. Martin of Tours (November 11), but the latter was never a universal practice as the former eventually eclipsed it. The time between Augustine and Bede marked a period in which the church of Rome moved from being one of a number of ecclesial centers in the early period — with places like Constantinople, Jerusalem, Alexandria, and Milan — to being a church that rose in ecclesial influence so that it was the overseer of the overseers, the one *papa* from whom others would seek advice and direction. Acceptance of Rome's authority — supported, of course, by Augustine's long work *The City of God* — led to its calendar gaining more authority and reception in the churches of the Latin tradition and, to a large extent, even in the Greek and other Eastern traditions. Advent, like Christmas, was just one of the many elements of the calendar in which Rome's judgment would guide the time-keeping decisions other churches.

Thomas Aquinas

Although ancient Greek philosophical thought had had some influence in theology during late antiquity, for centuries in the early Middle Ages the church had not drawn from ancient Greek philosophy for its theology. In the twelfth century philosophical theology was reborn and its perennial advocate and "angelic doctor" was Thomas Aquinas (ca. 1225–1274). In his capstone and most influential work, the *Summa Theologica*, Thomas drew from the Bible, the fathers of the early church, and ancient Greek philosophy — Aristotle especially — to bring Latin theology to its medieval acme. Although he wrote with great consequence about the seven sacraments, and it is supposed that he penned the eucharistic hymns *Pange lingua*, *O Salutaris*, and *Panis angelicus* for the feast of Corpus Christi, little of his work bore directly on the liturgical year. However, his philosophy taught directly about God and time. In the First Part of his three-part *Summa*, he took up the issues of the immutability and the eternity of God.

In the question-and-answer format of the whole of the *Summa*, Thomas asserted without hesitation that "God is altogether immutable" and that "it is impossible for God to change." He takes up some

---

36. On the various spans observed as the pre-Christmas season in different places, see Volume 1, Chapter 2, "Advent."

of the scripture verses in which God is described as moving and changing, but he says that these verses speak merely metaphorically, not of
the essence of God, which is forever unchanging.[37] In this Aquinas repeats what the fathers of the church in the fourth century argued about
the two natures of Christ, the divine and human, as they relegated
anything admitting of temporality, emotion, and change to his human
nature, and kept the divine nature — as Aquinas kept the nature of
God — as unchanging and all-powerful.

Also bearing on the relation of God and time is the very next question of the *Summa*, on whether God is eternal. Thomas posits it
as a corollary to the previous question, for "the idea of eternity follows immutability. . . . As God is supremely immutable, it supremely
belongs to Him to be eternal."[38]

The question to be raised about this philosophical theology is how
any human being would know or not know of God's mutability or
immutability, eternity or temporality. Although pre-Christian philosophy presented the deity in such speculative terms, the Bible, the
canon of Christian faith, presents God as engaged in the world and
the lives of those who inhabit it — a quite different presentation than
the testimony from the pagan philosophers at the foundation of late
medieval systematic thought. Aquinas himself demonstrates that the
testimony of the Bible could be used to prove either God's mutability or immutability. So too with God's eternity, Thomas writes that
the Bible speaks of God's works in the past, present, and future, yet
he nonetheless ceded to immutability and eternity in God based on
the non-Christian Greek philosophies on which his theology rested.
As started in the fourth- and fifth-century conciliar theology that
squelched heresies by identifying the Son's divine nature as "one in
being with the Father," so the Thomistic divine attributes continued
to move God away from humanity, to separate the life of God from the
life of human beings generally. If, like God, the Son is eternal, then he
is removed from the fragile and vulnerable life of humanity. And if,
also like God, the Son is immutable, then he is far removed from the
temporality and fragility of human experience, in which all people, like
Jesus of Nazareth himself, are born and die, have beginnings and ends.

Human beings live in time and place, and to predicate immutability of God based on pre-Christian philosophical works distanced God
from the quotidian, time-bound lives of all people, believers or not.

---

37. *Summa Theologica* I, q. 9, a. 1.
38. Ibid.: q. 10, a. 2.

That God would be distant from human lives filled with change, movement, and emotion set God far away from human life. As mentioned above, in the section on the Three Days, the growth of the sanctoral cycle is a fruit of humanity's desire for a bond with the holy, and the cycle's grandeur and complexity in the late Middle Ages reflect a high Christology and speculative theology that set God and Christ apart from human experience. Once God is at a distance, people who are born, change, suffer, and die direct their prayers and aspirations to other believers whose lives reflect that they too were born, changed, suffered, and died, that is, the saints.

The Sanctoral Cycle

By the thirteenth century of Thomas Aquinas, nearly all baptisms into the church were of infants and these baptisms were no longer coordinated with the annual cycle of Easter and its seasons. The process of the catechumenate and of formation for baptism with adults had virtually disappeared. So as the systematic theology of the later Middle Ages reigned in the *schola* (or classroom) and among the educated of the church, the efficacy of the sacraments on the life and formation of the baptized was less apparent to church-goers because baptisms were removed from the local community of faith. Baptism *quam primum*, "as soon as possible"—for fear of the early death (and perdition) of an unbaptized infant—was rarely celebrated within the Sunday assembly, and so few could consciously distinguish in their own lives or the lives of others what effect initiation into the church wrought in human existence.

Regarding the liturgical year, the cult of the saints was intricate and complex in the centuries between Aquinas and the Reformation. To the extent that the sanctoral cycle was crowded, the church lost its appreciation of the formative character of the Forty Days of Lent, the baptismal character of the Three Days of Easter, and the mystagogical character of the Fifty Days of the Easter season.[39]

Nicholas Oresme

Like the thirteenth-century Italian theologian Thomas Aquinas, the fourteenth-century French mathematician Nicholas Oresme (ca. 1320–1382) — among the earliest philosophers of the emerging scientific age — mediated matters of ancient Greek philosophy to Christian theology in the later Middle Ages. His work was not only in speculative

---

39. See Volume 2, Chapters 2–4: "Lent," "The Three Days," and "The Easter Season."

philosophy and mathematics but in practical linguistics, for he translated the Greek of Aristotle into Latin, writing a commentary on the
philosophy he rendered into a new tongue.

Oresme's work gives us a historical link between scholastic theology's mining of ancient philosophy and the new invention for
time-keeping in this period, the "clock," or *horologium,* as it was called
in Latin. Nicholas Oresme contributed an elaboration on Aristotle's
cosmology, his "view of the world," by setting Aristotle in the cultural context of the fourteenth century. As he translated, in words and
thoughts, this ancient Greek philosophy, he fashioned God's perfec-
tion, orderliness, and dependability, and posited the measured, orderly
machinations of the newly invented clock as an apt image for God.

In the third part of his "Oration of Arithmetic," Nicholas queried,

> If an irrational balance [in the world] is disagreeable and displeas-
> ing to us, how could we suppose that moving intelligences, who
> lead the highest kind of life, act with unpleasant and sadden-
> ing disparity and are filled with the greatest joy in the animation
> and applause of the orbs? For if someone were to make a clock,
> would he not make all the motions and wheels as coordinated
> as possible? How much more, then, should we expect this of the
> Architect who, as they say, made all things according to their
> number, weight, and size?[40]

Like Thomas, using the question-and-answer format of the age, Nicholas speculated on the conditions necessary for one heavenly body
moving uniformly in circular motion to meet another, and he won-
dered if they might ever meet, and, if so, how often. Nicholas had
studied theology in Paris, where one of the most famous public clocks
of the fourteenth century had been built.

Early in the fourteenth century, public clocks began to appear in
Italy, some with a twenty-four-hour face, some with dials for marking
cycles of the sun and moon (as had the clock in Padua at the Palace
of Capitano). Regarding the relations of time-keeping and theology,
one must make the link between the objective measure of time with

---

40. Latin text from *Nicole Oresme and the Kinematics of Circular Motion: Tractatus de
commensurabilitate vel incommensurabilitate motuum celi,* ed., intro., trans., and commentary Edward Grant (Madison: University of Wisconsin Press, 1971): 292–295. *Et si
irrationalis proportio nostro disconvenit et displicet ingenio quomodo ponemus intelligentias
motrices vitam ducentes optimam tam inamena et tristabili disparitate movere que tamen
in agitatione et plausu orbium summo gaudio delectantur? Nam et si quis faceret horologius
materiale nonne efficeret omnes motus rotasque commensurabiles iuxta posse? Quanto
magis hoc opinandum est de architectore illo qui omnia fecisse dicitur numero, pondere, et
mensura?*

an instrument like the clock and the subjective experience of time in the lives of people and societies. Clocks are, now as then, predictable and dependable, but (especially in this "digital" age) they are not the most animated or engaged participants in the world and the lives of its inhabitants. The regularity and predictability of God as clock is an image disengaged from the world of the spontaneity, disorder, chaos, expanses and strictures, highs and lows of humanity.

The clock was an apt depiction of the straitened God of Scholasticism, for the high theology of a God distant from humanity, the "unmoved mover" and "uncaused caused" of Aristotle's philosophy, emerged in the Scholastic Age of Thomas Aquinas and Nicholas Oresme. These two men are laudably remembered for having retrieved ancient Greek philosophy as the new thought for the new age, yet the high theology and its distant God begotten in their new sources reverberated in changes in the liturgical year that marked God's distance from humanity.

Part Three:
Time in the Reformation
and the French Revolution

Martin Luther

Saints

At the dawn of the Reformation — which began when Martin Luther legendarily posted his "95 Theses against Indulgences" on the door of the Castle Church at Wittenburg, on October 31, 1517 — the cult of the saints was not an issue that bore directly on the issue of indulgences, but the saints were part of an intricate method for money-making in church in the later Middle Ages and in the early sixteenth century. Luther's main theological foundation was that of salvation by grace through faith, set against sixteenth-century Roman Catholicism's salvation by works. Indulgences were an element of his indictment of the teaching of the Roman church's tradition, but not far behind the works of indulgences were some of the works involved in piety toward the saints. For there were various devotions connected with the saints and their relics, in which a certain type and number of prayers were to be prayed at certain times in the calendar to win the favor of a particular saint, whose intercession before the throne of God, by medieval piety and practice, was more efficacious than one's own prayer. In other words, devotions to dead saints — in Luther's catechesis — put the living members of the church at a remove from their own praise, thanksgiving, and intercession before God.

In Luther's reformed theology, the baptized *are* the saints of God, for through the rite of baptism they are admitted to the communion of the saints, and this admission brings them into contact with the life of God, earned not by a holy life but by God's grace, for Luther wrote expansively of the sinfulness of all humanity apart from God; rather, believers were holy saints by God's election and ritual access to this sanctity was baptism.

In his words, as he preached in a long series of sermons on the Gospel of John:

> With good reason we may glory and confidently say: "We are holy. We are members of a holy fraternity in Wittenberg, in Rome, in Jerusalem, and wherever holy Baptism and the Gospel are. And we do not regard one another otherwise than as saints of God. Even though we are still sinners and many failings always remain in our flesh and blood, He covers up our sins and impurities. Thus we are accounted entirely pure and holy before God, as long as we cling to Christ and His Baptism and rely on His blood."[41]

The combination of baptism and attention to God's words were sufficient in making believers "members of a holy fraternity," the living society of the "saints of God." By 1517 this profound understanding of the social effects of baptism had languished for a long time in Christianity, particularly after baptism became a rite celebrated apart from the community of the church. Baptism was not the only sacrament through which one participated in the fellowship of the saints:

> To receive this sacrament in bread and wine, then, is nothing else than to receive a sure sign of this fellowship and incorporation with Christ and all saints.[42]

As baptism was the unrepeatable admission to the society of the saints, so the celebration of the Lord's Supper was the regular, repeated sign of a living saint's incorporation into the church, in which God's life and love are realized.

For believers who looked either to dead saints or to priests or religious living in communities as primary exemplars of holiness, Luther

---

41. Martin Luther, "Sermons on the Gospel of St. John, Chapters 14–16," in *Luther's Works*, volume 24, ed. Jaroslav Pelikan (St. Louis: Concordia, 1961): 171.

42. Martin Luther, "A Treatise on the New Testament, that is, the Holy Mass (1520)," *Luther's Works*, volume 35, ed. Helmut T. Lehmann (St. Louis: Concordia, 1960): 51.

reminded the baptized that these Christians were no more holy than themselves:

> For surely you know, thank God, who God's saints are; that [by the word "saints"] the Scriptures do not mean the saints in heaven above, as the pope creates saints, whom one should invoke, whose days one should observe with fasting, and whom one should choose as mediators. Nor does it mean those who have sanctified themselves, like the Carthusians, the barefooted friars, and other monks or pilgrims and such like devils who want to make themselves holy through their works. It means rather those whom God has sanctified, without any of their works or cooperation whatsoever, by reason of the fact that they are baptized in Christ's name, sprinkled and washed clean with his blood, and endowed and adorned with his dear Word and gifts of the Holy Spirit.[43]

It is striking that, among the many revolutionary and dormant theological foundations of Christianity reignited by Luther's reform, this pastoral sensitivity to who are the saints and what this means in the lives of believers is extraordinary. He confessed his own devotion to the Blessed Virgin Mary and her mother, St. Ann, and he wrote of the pain it caused him to relinquish his devotions to them. Nevertheless, giving up devotion to even favorite saints was required as a way of appreciating the access to God that the Word of God reveals in baptism and the Lord's Supper.

Luther — intent on reminding the church of the fellowship of the saints that is the gain of the sacrament of baptism — saw, as above, devotions to the saints predicated on putting oneself at a distance from God. Although Luther's theology of baptism was strong, he was still an advocate for infant baptism, and he did not seek to reorient baptism to Easter, the Forty Days of Lent, or the Fifty Days of the Easter Season. There were more pressing problems regarding Easter that, in his age, weighed on the church more than its lost link with the sacrament of Baptism.

The Date of Easter

The problem with the date of Easter in the sixteenth century was that, over the centuries since the solar calendar had been introduced in antiquity, the calendar's reckoning had fallen little by little behind the

---

43. Martin Luther, "Two Funeral Sermons; Second Sermon at the Funeral of the Elector, Duke John of Saxony, I Thess. 4:13–18 (August 22, 1532)," in *Luther's Works*, volume 51, ed. Helmut T. Lehmann (Philadelphia: Fortress, 1959): 247–248.

natural cycles of the sun and moon. This disjuncture resulted in a cal-endrical lag — part of what had prompted Bede's eighth-century work on "The Reckoning of Time" — that was not yet fixed in the sixteenth century. As Luther himself was writing a commentary "On the Coun-cils and the Church," in 1539, he commented on the Council of Nicea and the emperor Constantine's wish regarding the date of Easter as it had been configured at that first ecumenical council in the year 325:

> One ember from these wooden articles [of Nicea] has kept glow-ing, namely, the one about the date of Easter. We do not observe this article quite correctly either — as the mathematicians and as-tronomers point out to us — because the equinox in our time is far different than in that time, and our Easter is often celebrated too late in the year.... I suppose [as did Constantine] that the present again calls for a reform and correction of the calendar in order to assign Easter its proper place. But no one should under-take that except the exalted majesties, emperors and kings, who would have to unanimously and simultaneously issue an order to all the world saying when Easter is henceforth to be celebrated. Otherwise, if one country were to start without the others, and worldly events, such as markets, fairs, and other business, were governed by the present date, the people of the country would ap-pear at the markets of another country at the wrong time, which would result in wild disorder and confusion in everything.
>
> It would be very nice, and easy to do, if the high majesties would want to do it, since all the preparatory work has been done by the astronomers and all that is needed is a decree or command. In the meantime we hold to the flickering ember from the Nicene council that Easter is to be kept on a Sunday; meanwhile the date may wobble back and forth, for they are called "movable feasts"; I call them "wobbling" festivals since the day of Easter, with its associated festivals, changes every year, coming early in one year, late in another, and not on a certain day like the other festivals.[44]

Luther was wise in recognizing presciently that the mandate would have to be issued from some "exalted majesties, emperors and kings," for on the religiously heated continent that was sixteenth-century Eu-rope, division over the calendar would surely have followed if he or any religious authority had dictated the change.

---

44. Martin Luther, "On the Councils and the Church," as in *Luther's Works*, volume 41, ed. Eric W. Gritsch (Philadelphia: Fortress, 1966): 61–62.

His warning was not only in lieu of a papal initiative because he recognized that, even among his fellow reformers, dissent and division would also have followed any prescription about the calendar coming from the church, and such division would wreak havoc on time-keeping not only in the church but in civil society and business:

> I am entering into this lengthy and needless chatter solely for the purpose of expressing my opinion, in case several sects in the course of time dare arbitrarily to move the Easter festival to another date than that which we now observe. And I believe if the Anabaptists had been sufficiently versed in astronomy to understand these things, they would have rushed in headlong, and (as is characteristic of the sect) introduced something entirely new and observed Easter on a different day than the whole world. But since they were unlearned in the sciences, the devil was unable to employ them as that kind of instrument or tool. Therefore, I advise that one let Easter come as it now comes, and keep it as it is kept now, and let the old garment be patched and torn (as was said); and let Easter wobble back and forth until the Last Day, or until the monarchs, in view of these facts, unanimously and simultaneously change it.[45]

One might suppose that in northern Europe Luther was more aware of the divisions and divisiveness of the post-Reformation religious climate than the pope or prelates of the Roman Catholic church, at the southern, and predominantly Roman Catholic, end of the continent would have been. But Luther's indication that the change be initiated by a non-church authority was not heeded, and the "result" of "wild disorder and confusion in everything" split the continent for centuries in its modes of keeping time and marking dates.

Pope Gregory XIII

The calendar's lag behind the sun and the moon had been apparent to astronomers for a long time, and in the thirteenth century Roger Bacon (ca. 1214–1294) wrote about the gap and suggested to Pope Clement IV (pope from 1265 to 1268) that he remedy the problem by promulgating a new calendar. In this age, centuries before the Reformation that would make such a move a graver problem, the pope did not heed Bacon's suggestion.

One of the works in Roman Catholic liturgical reform after the Council of Trent (1545–1563) was the reform of the breviary, and in

---

45. Ibid.: 66.

that work the church realized again its centuries-old concern with the date of Easter and with how the calendar lagged behind the skies to the embarrassment of many educated people.[46] The reason for the pope's concern, as Gregory XIII expressed it in his bull *Inter gravissimas,* was that the vernal equinox "has deviated by about ten days since the time of the Council of Nicea,"[47] the meeting of bishops in the year 325, the council about which Luther was commenting over four decades earlier when he noted the need for a change in the date.[48]

Pope Gregory's instruction and corrective for moving the calendar ten days ahead reflect the high place of devotion to the saints in late medieval, now counter-reformation piety. The main concern of the pope regarding any changes in the calendar was the juggling required in the calendar of the saints, so it was necessary as he sought to adjust the calendar that he reassign the feasts of the saints that were usually celebrated and would therefore be missed during the skipped ten days. Thus most of his bull was spent according temporary assignations for the saints whose feasts were elided over the ten days. Here was the complicated formula of his prescription:

So that the spring equinox, fixed on March 21 by the fathers at the Council of Nicea, be returned to its place, we instruct and command that ten days be removed from the month of October of the year 1582, which include from the third day before Nones [October 5], to the day before the Ides [October 14]. The day following Nones [October 4], when the feast of Saint Francis [of Assisi] is usually celebrated, will be the Ides of October [October 15]. On that day the feast of Saints Denis, Rusticus, and Eleutherius will be celebrated,[49] and also the commemoration of Saint Mark, pope and confessor, and the martyred Saints Sergius, Bacchus, Marcellus and Apuleius.[50] The following day, the seventeenth kalends of November [October 16], the feast of Saint Callistus, pope and martyr, will be celebrated.[51] On the sixteenth kalends of November [October 17], the office and the mass for the Eighteenth Sunday after Pentecost will be celebrated, and the

---

46. *Inter gravissimas,* 2.

47. Ibid., 6; trans. Connell.

48. When the "Gregorian calendar" is mentioned, many people often think of the famous Pope Gregory the Great, the first pope with this name. But the "Gregory" of the reform of the calendar is this sixteenth-century Pope Gregory, that is, XIII.

49. Their day was ordinarily October 9.

50. All of these — Mark, Sergius, Bacchus, Marcellus, and Apuleis — were ordinary on October 7.

51. This day was usually October 14.

Sunday letter will change from "G" to "C."[52] Finally, the fifteenth kalends of November [October 18] will be the feast of Saint Luke, the evangelist,[53] after which the remaining feast days will follow as usual in the calendar.[54]

Gregory ordered that all printers submit to his authority and print no calendar other than that of the "*S.R.E.*," as it was written, that of *Sacra Romana Ecclesia*, or "Holy Roman Church." If the printers did not obey, they could expect "the loss of contracts and a fine of one hundred gold ducats payable to the apostolic see."[55]

He indicated further that "regarding any others, wherever they may be, we give the same prohibition under the penalty of excommunication or other pains at our discretion."[56] Further, "no one is permitted to contradict this page of our precepts, commands, statutes, desire, effort, prohibition, suppression, abolition, exhortation and request or dare opposition.[57] If anyone does tamper with this, he should know that he provokes the anger of Almighty God and his blessed apostles Peter and Paul."[58] The papal bull was dated February 24, 1581, the tenth year of the pontificate of Gregory XIII.

Even though the problem with the calendar had been known for centuries, since the split of the church at the Reformation, the solution, as Luther had recognized, should have come from outside the church. Nevertheless, Gregory promulgated the bull, and thereafter the continent was divided in its dating as it was divided in its churches. The areas that changed the calendar according to Gregory's decree were Spain, Portugal, and the Italian states, though even in these regions the reform of the calendar required civil legislation. In France there were objections, but at the end of the year, from December 10 to 19, 1582, France skipped the dates that made up the gap. The last

---

52. These letters "C" and "G" refer to the A through G assignments for seven-day cycle of the Christian week. The course of A through G would continue through the days of the year, and from one year to the next Sunday would take the appropriate letter in the sequence through that full calendar year. So, in relation to the rhetoric of Pope Gregory XIII's bull, in that year 1582, from the previous January to the October of the days skipped, Sunday had been on day "C" as it usually remained one letter for the whole of the calendar year. But with the skipped days in October the "dominical" day, that is, Sunday, was shifted from "C" to "G," that is, a whole "week," A to G, plus three more days, "A," "B," and finally "C," which remained the dominical letter until December 31, 1582.

53. The usual day for Saint Luke.

54. *Inter gravissimas*, 7; trans. Connell.

55. *Inter gravissimas*, 13; trans. Connell.

56. Ibid.

57. In Latin, each of the words on the list refers to the same word in earlier parts of the bull.

58. Ibid., 17; trans. Connell.

Roman Catholic region to accept the reform of the calendar was Transylvania, which skipped from December 15 to 24 in the year 1590. In religiously divided lands, like Luther's Germany itself, two dates were maintained for each day, one according to the Catholic system (the "Gregorian calendar") and the other according to the Protestant reckoning (the "Julian calendar," after the ancient Roman emperor Julius Caesar). Most Protestants knew that their date was incorrect, but their church's antipathy to Rome was stronger than the need to correct the lagging Julian calendar.

During the seventeenth century, a number of predominantly Protestant regions accepted the Gregorian dating, but the Lutheran states were persuaded to do so only when in the year 1700 they advanced from February 19 to 29. Denmark and Protestant areas of Switzerland followed the German Lutheran change. A half-century later Great Britain skipped eleven days, from September 3 to 13, 1752. In many regions of the Orthodox churches of the East, ever resistant to Roman hegemony, the reform of the calendar did not happen until the second half of the twentieth century, with the Bulgarian Orthodox church finally accepting the Gregorian reform and skipped fourteen days, from December 7 to 20 in the year 1968.[59]

As in the first century, with the Sabbath-Sunday division, and again in the fourth century with the division between December 25 and January 6 as the day for celebrating the nativity, so here with the dual dates of the calendar, Julian or Gregorian. Time-keeping reflects social and ecclesial allegiances more than accurate or scientific time-measurement.

The French Revolution

The interaction between theology and time-keeping influenced the liturgical week and liturgical year not only in periods of faith but also in periods of agnosticism and atheism, and in periods when governments mistrusted the church. During and after the French Revolution (from 1789 to 1806), for example, changes in the maintenance of time were introduced to distance the government and the populace from the influence of the church after centuries of too comfortable a relationship between the French royalty and church hierarchy, to the detriment and fear of all others.

Until the end of the eighteenth century, the church had been the main keeper and measurer of hours and years. About three years after

---

59. Bonnie Blackburn and Leofranc Holford-Strevens, *The Oxford Companion to the Year* (Oxford: Oxford University Press, 1999): 683–688.

the Revolution itself, in an effort to eclipse the influence of faith on the lives of French citizens, the Committee of Public Instruction offered a prize to the person who would propose the best reform of the calendar. Proposals were presented to the National Convention in September 1793, and on October 5 the calendar of the winner was put into effect. The dawn of the era of the Republic was retroactively dated as September 22, 1792, which coincided with the autumnal equinox, an auspicious occasion politically and astronomically. Thenceforth, years would begin at midnight on the day of the autumnal equinox, as the equinox was reckoned from the official Paris Observatory.

The year itself was less variable than in the former calendar, in which the number of days in each month varied without a formula (as today). In the new calendar of the Republic, each year would have twelve months of 30 days, with those 360 days of the year followed by five *jours complémentaires*, "complementary days," adding up to the 365-day year. Leap years would have six *jours complémentaires*, with the first of the leaps years occurring in the Republic's "third year," or *année III*.

Each thirty-day "month" was divided into three parts, each part with ten days, or three "decades," as they were called, replacing the seven-day "week" of pre-Revolutionary time. In turn each day was divided decimally, that is, into ten hours, each hour into 100 minutes, and each minute into 100 seconds. As a product of the hyper-rationalist impulse against the less orderly calendar the church had kept, each day had 1,000 minutes and 100,000 seconds, displacing (or suspending for a time) the 1,400 minutes and 86,400 seconds of the old calendar. Clock- and watch-makers were instructed to begin the manufacturing of the new decimal clocks and watches immediately.[60] Within three weeks after the start of the new calendar, names were drawn up for the months and days:

> Wheezy (*Vendémiaire*)
> Foggy (*Brumaire*)
> Frosty (*Frimaire*)
> Snowy (*Nivose*)
> Rainy (*Pluviose*)
> Windy (*Ventose*)
> Bloomy (*Germinal*)
> Flowery (*Floréal*)
> Meadowy or Wheaty (*Messidor*)

---

60. Ibid.: 742–745.

Hot (*Thermidor*)
Fruity (*Fructidor*)[61]

The ten-day weeks were named simply numerically, with the suffix, -di, from the Latin *dies* for "day":

Day One (*Primedi*)
Day Two (*Duodi*)
Day Three (*Tridi*)
Day Four (*Quartidi*)
Day Five (*Quintidi*)
Day Six (*Sextidi*)
Day Seven (*Septidi*)
Day Eight (*Octidi*)
Day Nine (*Nonidi*)
Day Ten (*Decadi*)

The five extra days of the year — intercalary days, that is, days "inserted" to keep the calendar and the seasons in synch — were the Feast of Virtue, the Feast of Wit (or Ingenuity), the Feast of Work, the Feast of Ideas, and the Feast of Recompense. The sixth extra day of leap years would be the Feast of the Revolution.

The reformed calendar was introduced not from scratch, but from an ancient Egyptian reckoning, in which the days were dedicated to individuals who had contributed significantly to humanity and the world.[62] Perhaps as a sign of the fate of his inventive calendar, the man who came up with the 360 names for each of the days of the year, Fabre d'Eglantine, was tried during the Reign of Terror on a trumped-up charge and decapitated in April, 1794.

The new configuration of the hour caused disorientation, for business and trading with other parts of Europe, which maintained the Gregorian calendar, became difficult. The Republic's calendar died gradually; in 1799, in an agreement with Pope Pius VI, Napoleon repealed the calendar's imposition on Rome. After he became emperor, Napoleon restored the Catholic faith to France, and in line with this in September 1805, he officially restored the Gregorian calendar and redesignated Sunday as a day of rest on January 1, 1806.

Historians find it difficult to ascertain what people had found most objectionable about the new calendar and its ten-day weeks as imposed

---

61. Most of these are my English renderings of the French terms, but Wheezy and Wheaty are taken from a British caricature of the French months.

62. E. C. Richards, *Mapping Time: The Calendar and Its History* (Oxford: Oxford University Press, 1998): 257–264. There are various accounts of the calendar of the Republic, and Richards' description of its emergence is perhaps the clearest.

by the Consistory after the Revolution. The reasons why the calendar failed were numerous, but the main one was simply that workers objected to a ten-day work week; people objected to working on Sunday (or on the day that had been Sunday). Some suppose that people more missed certain aspects of the old reckoning — such as saints' days or other Christian designations such as Christmas, Easter, or Pentecost — than they actually disliked the Consistory's time-reckoning.[63]

Part Four:
Time in the United States

Time in the Colonies

For nearly three centuries after the Pilgrims ventured westward over the Atlantic Ocean from Britain near the beginning of the seventeenth century, people measured time from the seasons of nature — from the sowing and reaping of crops, from the daily and annual cycles of the sun and the monthly cycles of the moon — more than they did from public clocks. Time-measurement in the colonies was not much different from that in the late Middle Ages, with days measured by the rising and setting of the sun, and their lengths short or long according to the time of year.[64] Nicholas Oresme's fourteenth-century image of

---

63. Another politically charged reconfiguration of the week was introduced after the Russian Revolution of 1917. Russia had still been using the pre-Gregorian Julian calendar at the time of the Revolution, so the first mandated change was the use of the Gregorian calendar. Like France over a century earlier, Russia attempted the ten-day week without success. Only in May 1929 did the Fifth Congress of the Soviet Union come up with a proposal introducing a five-day week, which was to begin on September 24 of that year. The Russian five-day week was intended to increase productivity in the workforce, for each worker would have off one of each five days. Workers were given colored slips of paper to designate which of the five days would be their free day — yellow, orange, red, purple, and green — and the days were named by the same colors. The hope was that the same percentage of the workforce (80 percent) would be at work everyday and that the religious character of Sunday would diminish over time.

The fundamental problem was not that the population longed to return to the former calendar but that the system had ignored that members of families, friends, even spouses would want to have the same day off, yet had been given different colors. The first accommodation to popular disapproval was on March 16, 1930, when workers were invited to submit requests to synchronize their days off. Two practical problems thwarted the original design of worker participation, namely, that there could be no workers' meetings (deemed necessary by Marxist economic theory) and there was no continuity in production, for no one was at work all the time to supervise or take responsibility for the smooth functioning of the workplace and its production. In the end, the staggered work week was dropped on November 23, 1931, and replaced by a six-day work week, with every sixth day a day of rest for all. The rural populations continued the seven-day week clandestinely, causing administrative mayhem, so that a seven-day week and Sunday rest were reinstated on June 26, 1940.

64. Michael O'Malley, *Keeping Watch: A History of American Time* (Washington: Smithsonian Institution Press, 1990): 14; cited also in Marion B. Stowell, *Early American Almanacs: The Colonial Weekday Bible* (New York: B. Franklin, 1977).

God as a "clock," *horologium*, was qualified in the United States in the eighteenth century only because it was predicated no longer on the clock but on the watch, as in the following poem from a work of 1769 called *Abraham Weatherwise's Almanac:*

On a Watch

Could but our Tempers move like this Machine,
Not urged by Passion, nor delay'd by Spleen;
But true to Nature's regulating pow'r,
By virtuous Acts distinguish'd every Hour;
Then Health and Joy would follow as they ought,
The Laws of Motion, and the Laws of Thought:
Sweet Health, to pass the Laws of Moments o'er,
And everlasting Joy, when Time shall be no more.

Although there were some public clocks installed in the colonies before the Revolutionary War, there was in reality no substantial watch industry before the Civil War.[65]

An American instrument of measuring time was the "orrery," the measurer of "hours," designed by the City of Philadelphia's David Rittenhouse in 1767, and, as had many late medieval instruments, Rittenhouse's instrument depicted the movements of the moon, stars, and planets to complement numbers marking the hours, thereby bridging the usual divide between those who felt that time was God's, marked by nature, and those who measured time by clocks and numbers, which some Puritans felt was a merely human invention.[66] After the French and American Revolutions, churches were no longer deputed as the keepers of time, and each city magistrate was admonished to be the keeper of one main clock for the region. Eventually post offices, because of their need to coordinate daily pick-ups and deliveries, became the time-keepers.[67]

Time and Faith in the Nineteenth Century

Catharine Esther Beecher — eldest child of Presbyterian minister Lyman Beecher and sister of Harriet Beecher Stowe, author of *Uncle-Tom's Cabin* — wrote *A Treatise on Domestic Economy*, first published in 1841, in which she strongly encouraged women to be keepers of time

---

65. O'Malley: 23.

66. Carlene E. Stephens, *On Time: How America Has Learned to Live by the Clock* (Boston: Little, Brown, 2002): 35.

67. Gerhard Dohrn-van Rossum, *History of the Hour: Clocks and Modern Temporal Orders,* trans. Thomas Dunlap (Chicago: University of Chicago, 1996): 346; see also O'Malley: 24.

in their homes, relaying to women the Protestant work-ethic in the domestic sphere. Hard work and thrift with time were held up as the Godly habits of industry and regularity for the family and the home:

> A woman is under obligation to so arrange the hours and pursuits of her family as to promote systematic and habitual industry; and if, by late breakfasts, irregular hours of meals, and other hindrances of this kind, she interferes with, or refrains from promoting regular industry in others, she is accountable to God for all the waste of time consequent on her negligence.

At the core of Beecher's ethic of the home was her poignant assertion, in the chapter "On Economy of Time and Expenses," that "Christianity teaches that for all the time afforded to us, we must give account to God; and that we have no right to waste a single hour."[68]

The reverence for the economy and sanctity of time in the United States burst into the culture just before the mid-nineteenth century, as the century-long omnipresence in children's readers of Henry Wadsworth Longfellow's "The Old Clock on the Stairs" demonstrated:

> Halfway up the stairs it stands,
> And points and beckons with its hands
> From its case of massive oak,
> Like a monk, who, under his cloak,
> Crosses himself, and sighs, alas!
> With sorrowful voice to all who pass, —
>> "Forever — never!
>> "Never — forever!"
>
> Through days of sorrow and of mirth,
> Through days of death and days of birth,
> Through every swift vicissitude
> Of changeful time, unchanged it has stood,
> And as if, like God, it all things saw,
> It calmly repeats those words of awe, —
>> "Forever — never!
>> "Never — forever!"
>
> Never here, forever there,
> Where all parting, pain, and care,
> And death, and time shall disappear, —
> Forever there, but never here!

---

68. O'Malley: 50.

The horologe of Eternity
Sayeth this incessantly, —
"Forever — never!
"Never — forever!"

One sees in the native-born Longfellow's verses the surprising image of the Catholic monk making the sign of the cross, for it seems out of place coming from the overwhelmingly Protestant culture of the United States before the Civil War; yet the monk is juxtaposed to the clock, and the visage of the clock is like that of God, pronouncing on eternity and perdition.[69] The verse harks back to the religious communities that in many towns in late medieval Europe were the time-keepers according to their schedule of daily prayer. As then, when people did not distinguish between God's time and their town's time, so in the United States of Longfellow's age, people resisted when business or government tried to coordinate time for improving communications and transportation. As debates over time zones would reveal later, people did not see the clock as an *instrument* of time; for most people, the clock *was* time, much as in Longfellow's poem. In human imaginations the clock reflected God's time for humanity rather than being humanity's medium for keeping and coordinating society.

Not all authors of the age praised the introduction of clocks and watches into the culture as media of time-keeping. Edgar Allan Poe's story "The Devil in the Belfry,"[70] published six years before Longfellow's poem, supplied a satire about a town whose population was stultified by its dependence on its great clock. Poe (1809–1849) called the town "Vondervotteimittiss," mimicking the quotidian query, "Wonder what time it is?" that Poe was probably unhappily hearing ever more frequently in his days. The story was Poe's attack on clock time, as its invasion into the U.S. culture drew people away from nature as their time-keeping instrument. Poe described the scene in Vondervotteimittiss.

The town has a great clock with seven faces, and "the hours have been regularly struck by the big bell. And, indeed, the case was just the same with all the other clocks and watches in the borough. Never was such a place for keeping the true time. When the large clapper thought proper to say 'Twelve o'clock!' all its obedient followers opened their

---

69. Henry Wadsworth Longfellow, *Best Loved Poems* (Chicago: Peoples Book Club, 1949): 27–29. These three are the second, fourth, and ninth of the nine-stanza poem.

70. Edgar Allan Poe, "The Devil in the Belfry," *Collected Works of Edgar Allan Poe, Tales and Sketches 1831–1842*, ed. Thomas Ollive Mabbott (Cambridge: Harvard University Press, 1978): 365–375.

throats simultaneously, and responded like an echo. In short, the good burghers were fond of the sauer-kraut, but then they were proud of their clocks."[71]

The population is set in disarray by the arrival one day, at three minutes before noon, of "a very diminutive foreign-looking young man," who "pigeon-winged himself right up to the belfry of the House of the Town-Council, where the wonder-stricken belfry-man sat smoking in a state of dignity and dismay." The stranger assaulted the keeper of the bell, and, upsetting the town's routine, rang the bell more than the town's anticipated twelve tolls. The foreigner's actions set the town into a rage, which Poe described in animated details, as he concluded the narrative with this summary: "Affairs being thus miserably situated, I left the place in disgust, and now appeal for aid to all lovers of correct time and fine kraut. Let us proceed in a body to the borough, and restore the ancient order of things in Vondervotteimittiss by ejecting that little fellow from the steeple." Poe was clearly not keen on the new culture of "lovers of correct time and fine kraut," but they were many in mid-nineteenth-century America.

Personalized Time-Keeping

One addition to nineteenth-century commerce and gift-exchange was wrought by American success in the industry of watch-making. In the single year 1876, the year of the celebration of the centennial of the nation's independence from England, American mass-production innovations and techniques allowed the two largest watch-manufacturing companies, Waltham and Elgin, to produce more than 200,000 watches.[72]

Watches, perhaps because they were originally tagged as "bracelet-watches" in the United States, were originally decorative jewelry items for women only. Men, particularly the educated and wealthy, had traditionally kept pocket-watches, and as the social behaviors and routines of reading time proved important to them, they resisted the female device of the wristwatch. Its convenience, however, eventually prompted men to give up the regular patterned routine of consulting their pocket-watches, and the production of wristwatches came to be an industry for the whole American population, for women first, and later for men, women, and children.

---

71. Ibid.: 370.
72. O'Malley: 103.

Railroads and the Battle for Keeping Local Time

A consequential crisis in time-keeping in the United States was the gradual coordination of the intricate system of railroads in the new country, and in the 1850s trains became more regular and dependable in their running. In Massachusetts in 1854, Henry David Thoreau observed the daily trains on the Fitchburg line from his solitary spot on Walden Pond:

> The startings and arrivals of the cars are now the epochs in the village day. They go and come with such regularity and precision, and their whistle can be heard so far, that farmers set their clocks by them, and thus one well-conducted institution regulates a whole country. Have not men improved somewhat in punctuality since the railroad was invented? Do they not talk faster in the depot than they did in the stage-office?[73]

The third quarter of the nineteenth century occasioned a tussle between farm-dwellers, who kept time by the sun, and city-dwellers, who increasingly kept time by the clock. The railroad linked these two "worlds" of the States, though on the horizon was the mass emigration from Europe, when refugees to the United States flooded into the cities, generally giving the culture more urbanity than it had had before the middle of the nineteenth century.

Between 1840 and 1860, the number of miles of train tracks in the United States increased ten times, yet each railroad company ran its lines according to the local clock. In the middle of the nineteenth century, there were about eighty different timetables, an impeding obstacle for passengers who needed to transfer from one line to another. Over the next few decades, individual regions tried to coordinate their timetables, but it was always precarious for travelers taking trips over long distances, from one region to another, transferring from a train of one company to a train of another, each with its own time.[74]

The railroads had worked hard to get clocks in the country set at or close to the same time. Earlier, on August 12, 1853, two trains crashed outside Pawtucket, Rhode Island, and fourteen people were killed, the result of two conductors having different times on their watches as they approached a blind curve. The accident highlighted the need for a better coordination of time in the country, and brought a call for a time standard from the railroads. Beginning in 1869, four North American societies — the American Metrological Society, the

---

73. From Stephens, *On Time:* 103.
74. Ibid.: 99–103.

American Association for the Advancement of Science, the American Society of Civil Engineers, and the Canadian Institute — formed a committee toward consensus on the issue of standard time.

William Frederick Allen, a publisher of railroad timetables, organized coordination of the nation's six hundred railroads and encouraged the abandonment of the regional times that they ran by. He proposed time zones as a way to coordinate time-keeping, and the country would coordinate its time-keeping and begin using four time-zones across the continent on Sunday, November 18, 1883. Though it was a much-publicized event, the "day of two noons" — as it was called, because many towns had to reset their clock at the appointed time, and for at least half this meant that they indeed had had two noons — went off smoothly and with little protest, at least for a few years. The railroads were the nation's biggest and most powerful business, so the change set deeply into the country and its commerce, and eventually touched the whole of life in the United States.[75] The front-page of the *Washington Post* for that day called the new system of time-keeping "scarcely second to the reformation of the calendar by Julius Caesar, and later by Pope Gregory XIII."[76]

There had never been a creedal tenet in which God was professed as the source of time, but that had been the assumption in the faith and imaginations of most people. When railroads became the impetus and astronomers the source for synchronizing time, a fundament of human existence shifted and left the population unsettled. As, in 1583, some thought that the pope had shortened their lives by ten days, so in 1883 people thought that the railways had stolen minutes. (The number of minutes varied from locality to locality according to how much the local clock varied from the national "standard" time.)

A year after the nation's imposition of standard time, at the International Meridian Conference in Washington, DC, in 1884, scientists advocated for standard time throughout the world. In spite of that earlier wave toward synchronicity, some places resisted the change for years, particularly in places close to a time zone's dividing line. Pittsburgh, for example, rejected standard time until 1887, and in its paper, the *Pittsburgh Dispatch*, one malcontented reader wrote: "God Almighty fixed the time for this section just as much as he did for Philadelphia or New York."[77] On the other side of its time-line was Cincinnati, whose railway published time schedules until 1890 under

---

75. Ibid.: 109–111.
76. O'Malley: 124.
77. December 28, 1886, page 4, as cited in ibid (see note 63): 135.

the heading, *"This is Cincinnati Time,* Twenty-two minutes faster than railroad time."[78] People wanted time to be buoyed up by a source less commercial than the transportation system.

Resistance to Standard Time

Because the imposition of standard time left many people uneasy, resistance to it came from the clergy, who declared that the railroads should not have usurped God's prerogative. Time should not have been tampered with by humans, they said, and by the assessment of one minister, the Reverend William B. White of Boston, standard time was "not exactly an invention of the devil, but a fraud, an immoral thing, an attempt to play Joshua's part, which should not be allowed to succeed, and a monopolistic work adverse to the working man's interests."[79]

An admiral of the U.S. Naval Observatory, John Rogers, wrote to William Allen (of the railroads) that "The sun regulates all life upon the earth, vegetable and animal. To take Greenwich time, or Paris time, or Washington time, scarcely serves man's necessities. By local time he must live." The mayor of Bangor, Maine, Frederick A. Cummings, vetoed standard time for his city twice, arguing that "neither railroad laws nor municipal regulations have the power to change from the immutable laws of God."[80]

The resistance was not short-lived. For more than two decades after the introduction of standard time, waves of resisters brought the issue to trial in the Supreme Courts of various states at least fifteen times: In the Supreme Courts of Nebraska (1890) and Kentucky (1905), and in the United States Court of Appeals (1907). The courts ruled time and again that standard time was the national rule, but that local time could still be maintained as an alternative if the local populace elected it to be so. Standard time was also tried in Minnesota (1898), North Dakota (1905), Utah (1911), New York and California (1917). Though standard time was upheld each time, the willingness to test standard time points to the heightened resistance to humanity's tinkering with time, also highlighting that people thought of clocks and the twenty-four-hour day as eternal and God-given, rather than as the medieval and modern human inventions of social organization that they were and are.[81]

---

78. Ibid., 137.
79. As in William Frederick Allen, *Short History of Standard Time and Its Adoption in North America* (Philadelphia: Stephen Green, 1904): 10–11.
80. Stephens: 119.
81. O'Malley: 139.

The theology of time was a debated topic regarding evolution in the Scopes Trial in 1925. Clarence Darrow, the defender of the school-teacher who had been teaching evolution, grilled William Jennings Bryan, handing him a Bible to prompt him to calculate the age of the world and to ask him whether he believed that Joshua had made the sun stand still (Joshua 10:12–14) and that Eve had been created from a rib of Adam (Genesis 2:21). The link between evolution and liturgical time in theology was and is not a direct one in American courts or American religious life, but each bears uniquely on the issues of the origin of time, in God or in humanity, and of authority in chronometry, how time will be measured.

Regarding the liturgical year, particularly regarding Christmas,[82] the resistance to tinkering with time also came to bear on the American market's profit-driven change of the significance of the Christian holy day to a more domestic, gift-buying occasion rather than, as in the past, a span focused on social justice and renewal, when wrongs were righted and the poor could count on improving their state, if only temporarily. In New York City in particular, department stores began to promote the day as the occasion for buying gifts for family members and friends. Even though this was a new spin on the ancient feast, it was clearly well received, revealing that the market was more influential in the meaning and even the "theology" of the liturgical year than the church, for the liturgy of Christmas stayed relatively constant even as the cultural context in which the feast was celebrated changed dramatically to increase sales.

Unlike the birth of Protestantism in Europe in the sixteenth century, where a Catholic culture was challenged by the emergence of the reformers' new conception of faith, church, authority, and the Bible, Christianity in the United States was a Protestant culture challenged by waves of Catholics emigrating from Europe in poverty between 1820 and 1920. The Catholic immigrants overwhelmed faith traditions of the formerly unrivaled Protestant revivalist culture. The chapters of this book on Sunday, Christmas, Candlemas, and Ordinary Time, in particular, will reveal how the Protestant foundation of culture in the United States has given the Catholic conception of time new opportunities and challenges.[83]

---

82. See Volume 1, Chapter 3, "Christmas."
83. See Volume 2, Chapter 1, "Sunday"; Volume 1, Chapter 3, "Christmas"; Volume 1, Chapter 5, "Candlemas"; and Volume 2, Chapter 5, "Ordinary Time."

Daylight Saving Time

A final ingredient in keeping time in the United States was the advocacy for Daylight Saving Time, promoted by President Woodrow Wilson, and approved by Congress on March 19, 1918, as an effort to assist the country's participation in World War I. But, as after standard time was approved in 1883, so with Daylight Saving Time, protests resulted, mainly from farmers, after the end of the war. Congress, which had earlier approved of the change, repealed the new time-keeping measure, only to find that President Wilson vetoed their repeal twice. But Congress eventually overrode the executive vetoes and Daylight Saving Time ended at the end of October 1919, a year and a half after it had been implemented.

Again piggy-backing on a war initiative, Daylight Saving Time was reintroduced by President Franklin Roosevelt on February 9, 1942, at the start of World War II as a medium for conserving electricity, but again it was stopped, on September 30, 1945, when the war ended. Some states did not return to the old time, but many did, and it was not until the Uniform Time Act of 1966 that Daylight Saving Time became a lasting feature of American time-keeping. Even with that, parts of the states of Arizona and Indiana still do not change their clocks, resisting the change as against "God's laws of nature." The same rhetoric that the resisters to standard time used was introduced again, as when Kentucky congressmen, representing their citizens, condemned Daylight Saving Time as an invention by "modern Joshuas," those who thought they could stand in God's stead and change time as Joshua had commanded the sun to stand still. Unlike the nineteenth-century religious rhetoric against standard time, however, the resistance to Daylight Saving Time had extra strength with apocalyptic religious groups like the Mormons, Seventh-Day Adventists, and those who wanted businesses closed on Sundays, the American "Sabbath."[84]

Through these vicissitudes of time-keeping in U.S. history, the battles over religious matters have, as ever, been colored by issues of contention in the culture. With standard time, the cultural divide was between the nation's earlier rural roots, after its independence from England, and the growing urban culture, with the farmers resistant to tinkering with time and the urbanites seeking to move toward uniformity throughout the land and maximize the number of daylight hours.

---

84. See Volume 2, Chapter 1, "Sunday," for more on Sabbath rest and the American tradition of Blue Laws.

With Daylight Saving Time, one of the influential divides was between Biblical literalists and more educated citizens, with the former seeking to measure science by faith and the latter inclined to measure the tenets of faith by the canons of science. The religious sought to protect sacred time from cultural marauders by not moving their clocks ahead in the spring and back in the fall, thereby staying with "time as God meant it to be" from the creation of the world. The American culture is still as vibrantly divided on such matters today as it was when standard time and Daylight Saving Time were being debated in Congress and courthouses. There are, nevertheless, nascent indications that people see how the measurement of time reflects personal, social, cultural, and religious values.

Rent

The song "Seasons of Love" from the movie-musical *Rent* (2005),[85] reflects on the interaction of modes of time-keeping and human values. After quantifying a year's length — "525,600 minutes," that is, the number of minutes in a year — the song asks, "How do you measure, measure a year?" The computer age has certainly brought the science of time-measurement to a precision that, at the ordinary level, was unimaginable a half-century ago. Watches are inexpensive and omnipresent, and the time display of computer networks keeps time synchronically in view on the screens of all who log into them.

Though this is a culture that hastens to the passage of time, with people doing a few things at the same time all day everyday, the United States is also a culture in which the inevitability of death is ignored. Though time-keeping might incline people to be more aware that each human life is just a fraction of time, the frantic and market-driven environment distracts most people from squarely facing their inevitable ends.

Like the life of each believer, the life of the church itself is just a fraction of time, a fraction that brings humanity together as "all in all." There are many ways we mark the fractions of time, and the lyrics of "Seasons of Love" highlight some ways time was measured at the end of the twentieth century:

> Five hundred twenty-five thousand six hundred minutes,
> Five hundred twenty-five thousand moments so dear,
> Five hundred twenty-five thousand six hundred minutes,
> How do you measure, measure a year?

---

85. *Rent*, by Revolution Studio and Columbia Pictures (2005), directed by Chris Columbus, written by Chris Columbus and Stephen Chbosky, music by Jonathan Larson.

Set at the turn of the new year, the play considered the changes in the lives of the characters and asked what might be the occupations by which we measure out each fraction of a life:

> How do you measure, measure a year?
> In daylights? In sunsets? In midnights? In cups of coffee?
> In inches? In miles? In laughter? In strife? . . .
> In diapers? Report cards? In spoke wheels? In speeding tickets?
> In contracts? Dollars? In funerals? In births?
> How do you measure a year in the life?

As the song captures these aspects of life in the United States, so about human life in general: All human beings orient themselves fundamentally in the world by marking significant seasons, days, and times. Such times are determined according to the familial, social, and religious communities to which people belong and according to the experiences and values drawn from lives lived and values inculcated by overlapping or disparate influences. Though measured time-spans vary in length — centuries, years, seasons, weeks, days, hours, minutes, and fractions of minutes — calendars organize points in the continuum by which people establish meaning, community, and identity and celebrate these when found. This is as true of the civil calendar as of the liturgical calendar of Christians.

Conclusion:
Pope Benedict XVI and Liturgical Time

A theological foundation of this book on the liturgical year is that the church of the present age is not underprivileged because it does not exist in first-century Palestine or at the end of the world, but in the twenty-first century, a time between the incarnation in Jesus of Nazareth and the apocalypse. Shortly after the Second Vatican Council, a theme of theological books was that the present age lives in an eschatological time of "already but not yet," that is, between the time when God was already in its midst (in Jesus) and the time when the fullness of revelation would come at the end of the world. This is a thwarted theology of time, for the incarnation of Jesus Christ continues unabated in the life of the church and its members gathered at prayer according to the celebrations of the liturgical year.

Pope Benedict XVI (born in 1927), as Cardinal Joseph Ratzinger before his election to the papacy, commented on the verse from the

Letter to the Hebrews, "Jesus Christ is the same yesterday and today and forever" (13:8):

> This was the profession of those who had known Jesus on earth and had seen the Risen One. This means that we can see Jesus Christ correctly today only if we understand him in the union with the Christ of "yesterday" and see in the Christ of yesterday and today the eternal Christ. The three dimensions of time as well as going beyond time into that which is simultaneously its origin and future are always a part of the encounter with Christ. If we are looking for the real Jesus, we must be prepared for this suspenseful tension. We usually encounter him in the present first: in the way he reveals himself now, in how people see and understand him, in how people live focused on him or against him, and in the way his words and deeds affect people today. But if this is not to remain simply second-hand knowledge, but is to become real knowledge, then we must go back and ask: Where does all this come from? Who was Jesus really at the time he lived as a man among other men and women?[86]

This "suspenseful tension" is an animating condition that keeps the church alive in the surety of Christ's presence where two or three (or more) are gathered and always reforming to better reflect God's life in the world. Though the church exists "in a world of fragile peace and broken promises,"[87] God touches the hearts of all no less than in the past and no less than in the future. The liturgical year is the church's temporal medium for assembling its people to celebrate as the communion of saints at prayer. The media are the culture and time-keeping instruments of the age, but the result is ever the same, recognizing the gift of God's love incarnate in Jesus Christ, and, from that, of "measuring your life in love."

Informing the church of its mission by its calendar, the church heeds what the pope taught, namely, that we encounter the real Jesus now. Cited by Pope Benedict XVI, the author of the Letter to the Hebrews taught that "Jesus Christ is the same yesterday and today and forever" (13:8); saint Emily Dickinson that "Forever — is composed of Nows"; and St. Augustine — as he wrote in Latin in North Africa sixteen centuries ago — that "Eternity is Today."

---

86. Joseph Cardinal Ratzinger, *A New Song for the Lord: Faith in Christ and Liturgy Today*, trans. Martha M. Matesich (New York: Crossroad, 1997): 10.

87. Eighth Sunday in Ordinary Time, Alternative Opening Prayer, in *Sacramentary* (New York: Catholic Book, 1985): 290.

Chapter 2

ADVENT

Though many church observances during the season of preparation for the feast of the nativity have an orientation toward reviving or restaging the past as believers imagine the scene was in first-century Bethlehem, the tradition of the season was not so at its origins or through its medieval development. The sermons of St. Bernard of Clairvaux (1090–1153), a theologian who early on contributed to the church's theology of Advent, make this abundantly clear.

Bernard was born to noble parents, but left his family in his early twenties to join the recently founded monastery at Cîteaux, which became one of the main hubs of the Cistercian monastic order, communities known more colloquially as "Trappists." Bernard helped the young community secure its stability in the early and tumultuous days of its existence. In addition to his role in the order and his monastery, Bernard wrote prolifically; the church has almost one hundred of his sermons, among them a series of sermons that reveals a remarkable theology of Advent. A compelling quality of his preaching was the fundamental theological point that Advent has a three-fold character, though in different sermons the taxonomy of the triplicity is different.

In some sermons the three-fold character of the season, according to Bernard, is differentiated not by the modes of Christ's coming but by the orders of time — past, present, and future. In his fifth sermon of Advent, for example, Bernard took up the theme of the three comings with a different interpretation of the three. In the first advent, Christ *took* on our "flesh and infirmity"; in the second advent, Christ *takes* on "spirit and power"; and in the third, he *will take* on "glory and majesty." The three orders include the one in the past, in Jesus of Nazareth; the one in the future, at the end of time, which has ever been at the forefront of the theology of Advent; and the middle coming, which is in the present time. This coming gives humanity "rest and comfort," yet, as in his third Advent sermon, the present coming is mysterious and difficult to recognize.

Bernard's rhetoric in the sixth Advent sermon clarifies these further, as he taught of the first coming that "the Lord of power and the

King of glory... came down to shape our bodies anew and to bring his brightness to the [human] body."[1] As before, Bernard moved from his interpretation of the first coming to the third, teaching that "so great will that glory be that its exaltation is beyond words, when the maker of the universe will justify the souls that before his coming were lowly and hidden. For to glorify you, O miserable flesh, he will come lofty and visible, not in sickness, but in his own glory and majesty!"[2] The sermon continues by describing the "day of that coming" as one "when he will come down with the fullness of the stars, with angels preceding him, and with the harmony of trumpets blaring to stir up from the dust those who are without a body and harkening to those caught up in the air with Christ?"[3] Though the taxonomies of his theology of Advent changed through the experience of God, church, community, and, perhaps, his own appreciation of the Advent season, Bernard's conviction that there is a triplicity in Advent was constant, with the second coming, the one in the present, of Christ today, being mysterious and hidden.

The liturgical tradition of Advent through the ages, from a time before St. Bernard and still today, has not been shy in acknowledging the awesome power of the Lord's coming today. These appear, for example, in Advent hymns: "The might and power of your glory and the reverence that the mention of your name inspires are so great that both heaven and the lower world tremble and bow down";[4] in verses of daily prayer: "Drop down dew from above, you heavens, and let the cloud rain down the just one," and its responses: "Let the earth be opened and sprout forth the Savior";[5] and in the season's opening prayers: "We ask you, Lord, stir up your power and come! We trust in your holiness, so hurry up and free us from all harm!"[6]

---

1. *Dominus virtutum et rex gloriae, ipse descendet ad reformanda corpora nostra, et configuranda corpori claritatis suae* [Sermo VI, *De triplici adventu, et carnis resurrectione*, as in PL 83:54]; trans. Connell.

2. *Quanta erit illa gloria, quam ineffabilis exsultatio, quando Creator universitatis, qui pro animabus justificandis humilis ante venerat et occultus, pro te glorificanda, o misera caro, sublimis veniet et manifestus, non jam in infirmitate, sed in gloria et majestate sua!* [Sermo VI, *De triplici adventu, et carnis resurrectione*, as in PL 83:54]; trans. Connell.

3. *Quis cogitabit diem adventus illius, quando descendet cum plenitudine luminis, praecurrentibus angelis, et tubae concentu excitantibus de pulvere corpus inops, et rapientibus illud obviam Christo in aera?* [Sermo VI, *De triplici adventu, et carnis resurrectione*, as in PL 83:54]; trans. Connell.

4. *Cujus potestas gloriae, / Nomenque cum primum sonat, / Et caelites et inferi / Tremente curvantur genu.* As from *Breviarium Romanum*, winter volume (Boston: Benziger, 1941): 389; trans. Connell.

5. *Rorate, caeli, desuper, et nubes pluant iustum,* and its response: *Aperiatur terra, et germinet Salvatorem*, Ibid.

6. *Excita, quaesumus, Domine, potentiam tuam, et veni: ut hi, qui in tua pietate confidunt, ab omni citius adversitate liberentur.* Ibid.: 441.

For his part Bernard did not ignore the verity of Christ's coming today, but he explains why Christians at times have a hard time recognizing the coming of Christ, "for we quickly give in to temptation, we are weak in the face of con artists, and fragile before the obstinent."[7] We waste time "in the shadow of death, in ailments of the body, in the place of temptation," and if Christians are "to turn away from the malaise of the human condition, they must match the triple 'coming' of Christ with a triple 'effort' to remedy their wretched human states."[8] In Bernard's twelfth century and in our twenty-first, Advent is the time during which people indeed recognize and experience the incarnate coming of God in the Son who wrought redemption and heaven on earth.

Bernard's theology is sober about the human condition and the impediments it occasions for people of faith, but he is also bright-eyed in assessing the remedy for human misery, for Christ "comes into the world, so that — living in people, with people, for people — he might shine on our darkness, lighten our loads, and destroy all dangers."[9] This is yet another reckoning of the three-fold character of Christ's coming, which shows the burden of sin on humanity eased not by human effort but by Christ's advent, whether one reckons it singly, as Christ's one "triple coming," or plurally, as his "three comings," for Bernard used both phrases in his theology of the span.

In the end the church's prayers of the season reveal that Advent's orientation toward the future, toward the manifestation of God's reign in the final days, is not blithely separated from the life of God in human life today. Indeed, for people near death, the last days are indeed now, and proximity to the very sick and almost dead reveals the compression of past, present, and future and the fruitlessness of staking a claim on that elusive future. As time runs out — for individuals or for the world itself — today is the last day. So, too, note the present tense of Jesus' proclamation, "Yours *is* the kingdom of God" (Luke 6:20), and "The kingdom of God *is* in the midst of you" (Luke 17:21).

---

7. *Nam et faciles sumus ad seducendum, et debiles ad operandum, et fragiles ad resistendum* [Sermo VII, *De triplici utilitate Adventus Domini,* as in PL 83:55]; trans. Connell.

8. *Nimirium generalis est humano generi miseria triplex; et quotquot degimus in regione umbrae mortis, in infirmitate corporis, in loco tentationis, si diligenter advertimus, triplici hoc incommodo miserabiliter laboramus* [Servo VII, *De triplici utilitate Adventus Domini,* as in PL 83:56]; trans. Connell.

9. *Qui ad hoc ipsum venit in mundum, ut habitans in hominibus, cum hominibus, pro hominibus, et tenebras nostras illuminaret, et labores levaret, et pericula propulsaret* [Servo VII, *De triplici utilitate Adventus Domini,* as in PL 83:56]; trans. Connell.

In human experience and in Christian interpretation of that experience, these present days and those last days are not readily spliced apart, as poet Mary Oliver captures in her work:[10]

LAST DAYS

Things are
    changing; things are starting to
    spin, snap, fly off into
        the blue sleeve of the long
        afternoon. *Oh* and *ooh*
come whistling out of the perished mouth
    of the grass, as things
turn soft, boil back
        into substance and hue. As everything,
            forgetting its own enchantment, whispers:
                I too love oblivion why not it is full
                of second chances. *Now,*
hiss the bright curls of the leaves. *Now!*
    booms the muscle of the wind.

Heaven and earth indeed "sprout forth" the Savior of the world, as Advent teaches that God's embrace was manifest in the salvation occasioned by the Son, and the church remembers, proclaims, and anticipates that occasion in the season of Advent. Finding and discerning that incarnate word in humanity, as Bernard often reminded those he exhorted, is no easy feat, for it is found in humanity as the body of Christ by the gift of the Holy Spirit. Earnest believers may be more inclined to search for God apart from incarnate humanity, as a Trappist monk eight centuries after Bernard reminded the church in his spiritual writings, but the tradition reveals that such a displacement thwarts the gift of God celebrated in Advent:

> Great though books may be, friends though they be to us, they are no substitute for persons, they are only means of contact with great persons, with men who had more than their own share of humanity, men who were persons for the whole of the world and not for themselves alone.
>
>   Ideas and words are not the food of the intelligence, but truth. And not the abstract truth that feeds the mind alone. The Truth that a spiritual person seeks is the whole Truth, reality, existence and essence together, something that can be embraced and loved,

---

10. Mary Oliver, from *Twelve Moons* (Boston: Little, Brown, 1979): 52.

something that can sustain the homage and the service of our actions: more than a thing: persons, or a Person. Him above all Whose essence is to exist. God.

Christ, the Incarnate Word, is the Book of Life in whom we read God.[11]

That unique incarnate Word is, by God's grace, given through the Holy Spirit, the saving gift to humanity. Advent is the time when the pathetic remnant of humanity gathered in the church for worship celebrates the surprising accessibility of God in the life of the world. The battered remnant does this as humanity's representative before the throne of God.

Part One:
The History of Advent

Northern Italy

Although the origins of the season of Advent are usually located by scholars at the beginning of the Middle Ages, a few centuries after the introduction and reception of the Roman date of the nativity of Jesus (December 25), there was one region of the church where a season of preparation for Christmas was observed as early as the late fourth and early fifth centuries. Though the region did not have one of the major figures of the early church — no Augustine or Gregory the Great, no Chrysostom or Gregory of Nyssa — Northern Italy had in numbers what it might not have had in church celebrity.

Among the groups of bishops whose writings are extant in the historical record was St. Ambrose of Milan (died 397). He was not the earliest of the witnesses in the region, but he is its best known. His testimony occurred in the last quarter of the fourth century, and the sermons and writings of five or six of his episcopal peers have survived. In their work is found the earliest testimony regarding a season of preparation of Christmas, the season that would become Advent. The testimony for Advent in the Northern Italian churches is presented in the chronological order of the witnesses: Bishop Filastrius of Brescia, lists of Gospel readings from the church of Aquileia, and a series of sermons from two loquacious bishops, Maximus of Turin and Peter Chrysologus of Ravenna.

---

11. Thomas Merton, *Thoughts in Solitude* (New York: Farrar, Straus & Cudahy, 1958): 63–64.

Brescia

The first evidence for the season of anticipation of the newly dated Roman feast of Christmas comes from a catalogue of heresies and heretics from the hand of Bishop Filastrius of Brescia, who died at about the same time as Ambrose, near 397. In the catalogue, Filastrius wrote of the four annual fasts: "Through the year four fasts are celebrated by the Church: the first at his birth, then at Easter, the third at the Ascension, the fourth at Pentecost."[12] This is the earliest reference for what might be considered an Advent span, though one discerns little of its observance save for its existence and ascetic character. Because the celebration of the birth on December 25 had only recently been received by the church of Brescia, one cannot be sure if the same kind of preparatory fast had earlier anticipated the observance of the birth of Jesus when it was celebrated on January 6 in non-Roman churches or if the fast was introduced only after the date had been changed to that of Roman provenance, December 25.

Aquileia

A list of Gospel readings from the early seventh century testifies to four Sundays of Advent in Rome at that time, though historians have suggested that at an earlier stage there might have been five Sundays. The evidence is scant, but perhaps the earlier stratum bears the remnant of a period of preparation for baptism at Epiphany, and — once initiation at Epiphany was gone and the process of initiation was itself anchored at Easter — Advent became more oriented to the two comings of Christ, in the past coming of Jesus in the incarnation and in the future coming at the end of time, and less celebratory of the present manifestation of the risen Christ in the newly baptized.

The manuscripts of two early medieval Gospel lists or capitularies, the *Codex Rehdigeranus* and the *Codex Foroiuliensis*, are a few centuries after Filastrius, but the Latin texts used in their lists are not Jerome's Vulgate translation (of the late fourth century), thus lending credibility to dating their testimony to the fourth and fifth centuries rather than to the early Middle Ages (sixth or seventh century). The provenance of these capitularies is the church of Aquileia, a city overtaken by barbarian invasions in the fifth century. They are included in this history because they testify to an Advent season of five Sundays, as was observed before the wide reception of a four-week season before Christmas.

---

12. *Diversarum hereseon liber* 149.3; Latin from *Eusebii Vercellensis Episcopi quae supersunt*, ed. Vincentius Bulhart, CCSL 9 (Turnholt: Brepols, 1957): 312; trans. Connell.

The *Rehdigeranus* begins its list with the First Sunday of Advent and this listing: *De Adventum Domini — Prima Domenica evangelium secundum Matth. cap. CCXLVII [247]. Cum videretes aduminacionem,* in translation: "Concerning the Coming of the Lord: The First Sunday from Matthew, chapter 247."[13] The three Latin words *"cum videretes aduminacionem,"* after the citation of the chapter (*CCXLVII*) are the incipit, or first words of the reading that would have let the lector know where in the Bible the liturgy's proclamation began — here at the words of Gospel of Matthew, "When you see the coming darkness" (Matthew 24:15, Old Italian version).[14] This is significant because it testifies to the eschatological character of the season of Advent at its earliest appearance. The simultaneous remembrance of the birth of Christ and the anticipation of the end of the world, still a vibrant part of the theology of Advent in liturgical books, appears here. Though we cannot be certain, the eschatological content of the season of Advent might have been introduced in this church during the time when the end of the world would not have felt distant to the native residents.

In the *Rehdigeranus* the Second Sunday of Advent lists *Venet dominus in civitatem samaria que dicitur sichar,* the incipit for a Gospel passage beginning, "The Lord came to a Samaritan town called Sichar," the story of Jesus and the woman at the well of John's Gospel (4:5). Because, in other churches of the period, this Gospel was one with which the church catechized those in formation for baptism, its appearance in Advent adds weight to the possibility that Advent was once a season of preparation for baptism at Epiphany. (The *Codex Foroiuliensis* also has this story from the Gospel of John in Advent, but there it was proclaimed on the First Sunday of Advent.)

After the eschatological direction and the "initiatory" content of the Sundays at the beginning of the Advent season, both Aquileian codices give witness to the eventual turn of the season to more historical narratives, those of the coming of John the Baptist and the birth of Jesus.[15]

---

13. The chapters and verses used today were not yet introduced. The chapters were the sections of the Gospel, without versification.

14. See Matthew 24:15, though, as above, many of the verses in these codices suggest that St. Jerome's Vulgate translation was not yet used in Aquileia when these readings were listed. In Jerome's Latin translation of the Greek, this verse began with the words, *Cum ergo videritis abominationem desolationis.*

15. In the *Rehdigeranus* the reading incipit from Matthew (11:2) for the Third Sunday of Advent, *Iuhannes cum audisset,* "When John had heard," seems odd at first for it seems to have no eschatological, initiatory, or nativity content. But the reading to follow makes the etiology clearer because there Jesus speaks to the crowds about John the Baptist: "What did you go out into the wilderness to look at? . . . This is the one about whom it is written, 'See, I am sending my messenger ahead of you, who will prepare your way before you.' Truly I tell you, among those born of woman no one has arisen greater than John the Baptist"

For the Fourth Sunday of Advent, both lists have Luke 3:1, "In the fifteenth year of the reign," as the beginning of the Gospel proclamation, and the Fifth (and last) Sunday of Advent has the perennially enduring Advent story, *Mense sexto messus est angelus gabrihel*, "In the sixth month the angel Gabriel was sent," the narrative of the annunciation.

Turin

A few decades after the episcopates of Filastrius in Brescia and Ambrose in Milan, and a little further to the west of Aquileia, one finds a season of preparation for Christmas in the church of Turin, cared for by its bishop, Maximus. Bishop Maximus anticipated the "upcoming feast" because the "birth of Christ the Lord is near."[16] Although it is difficult to ascertain for how many weeks the period anticipating Christmas lasted in Turin, it seems to have been for two Sundays before December 25.[17] The bishop's preaching is lively as he exhorted the church to asceticism as the feast of celebrating the birth of Christ neared:

> Before many days, then, let us make our hearts pure, let us cleanse our consciences and purify our spirit, and, shining and without stain, let us celebrate the coming of the spotless Lord, so that the birthday of Him whose birth was known to be from a spotless virgin may be observed by spotless servants. For whoever is dirty or polluted on that day will not observe the birthday of Christ and fulfill his obligation. Although he is bodily present at the Lord's festivity, yet in mind he is separated by a great distance from the Savior. The impure cannot keep company with the holy, nor the avaricious with the merciful, nor the corrupt with the virgin....
>
> Let us fill his treasuries with gifts of different kinds so that on the holy day there might be the wherewithal to give to travelers, to refresh widows, to clothe the poor. For what sort of thing would it be if in one and the same house, among the servants of a single master, one should vaunt himself in silk and another should be completely covered in rags; if one should be warm with food and another should endure hunger and cold; if, out of indigestion,

---

(11:7, 10–11). In this sequence the reading about the Baptist has a narrative link with the testimony from Peter Chrysologus.

16. These excerpts come from *Sermones* LXI, 4 and LXIa, 3.

17. See Milena Mariani Puerari, "Le feste della chiesa torinese sotto S. Massimo," *Ephemerides Liturgicae* 107 (1993): 381–406, especially 386–391. This is the second of a two-part essay; the first part appeared under the same title at *Ephemerides Liturgicae* 106 (1992): 205–235, and it treats Easter and its seasons; see also Giuseppina Rossetto, "La testimonianza liturgica di Massimo I vescovo di Torino," *Archivio Ambrosiano* 18 (1970): 159–203, especially 165–166.

one should be belching what he had drunk yesterday and another should not have compensated for yesterday's dearth of food?[18]

The bishop's sermon is poetic and exhortative, and his link between the present followers of Christ and the birth of Christ in the past reveals the church's immersion in a life of paschal mystery in every season. His witness is encouraging theologically because he instinctively brings the incarnation of Jesus to the experience of the communal life of the church at worship and in its disciplines of Advent. The bishop made tangible the birth of Christ not only in remembering Bethlehem four centuries earlier, but in seeing the church's birth of Christ in the assembly before him as he preached in Turin.

Ravenna

The greatest bounty of evidence that we have about a period of preparation for Advent comes from the treasury of sermons from the episcopate of Peter Chrysologus, bishop of the church of Ravenna in Northern Italy in the second quarter of the fifth century (bishop ca. 425–450). Peter's exhortations are unique for this time because there are so many extant sermons, and they are so intimately tied to the Gospel text about which he is preaching. As a result the lectionary cycle in ancient Ravenna is able to be reconstructed quite fully.

The period of Advent in fifth-century Ravenna focused on the double annunciation, from Luke's infancy narrative, of the angel to Zechariah about the birth of John the Baptist and of the angel to Mary about the birth of Jesus. This is similar to what we have in the Third and Fourth Sundays of Advent today, when the Third Sunday focuses on John the Baptist (though on his ministry rather than on the annunciation of his birth) and the Fourth Sunday on the annunciation to Mary.

The Ravennese evidence for Advent in the fifth century has, unfortunately, been largely overshadowed by the scholarly attention accorded the *Rotulus* of Ravenna, a collection of Advent prayers from the second half of the seventh century.[19] Although the evidence in the sermons of Peter Chrysologus antedates the prayers of the *Rotulus* by two or

---

18. Maximus of Turin, Sermo 60.3–4; trans. ACW 50 (New York: Newman Press, 1989): 145, 146.

19. For a critical edition of the Rotulus, see Suitbert Benz, *Der Rotulus von Ravenna nach seiner Herkunft und seiner Bedeutung für die Liturgiegeschicte kritisch Untersucht*, Liturgie-wissenschaftliche Quellen und Forschungen 45 (Münster: Aschendorffsche Verlagsbuchlanglung, 1967): esp. 5–16. Earlier studies have considered the parallels between the sermons of Peter Chrysologus and the Rotulus; see, for example, D. F. Cabrol, "Autor de la Liturgie de Ravenne: Saint Pierre Chrysologue et le *Rotulus*," *Revue Benedictine* 23 (1906): 489–520; Klaus Gamber, "Die Orationen des Rotulus von Ravenna: Eine Feier des Advents schon zur Zeit des heiligen Petrus Chrysologus?," *Archiv für Liturgiewissenschaft* 5 (1958):

more centuries, a significantly greater portion of scholarly work has been devoted to the *Rotulus,* and perhaps this is so for the following reasons: first, the unique literary genre of the *Rotulus.* In retrospect, the *Rotulus* looks like it was written with a later readership of scholars and liturgical historians in mind, for its author or copyist collected in one place forty prayers regarding one aspect of the early medieval liturgical year, the anticipation of the Lord's birth. Second, the *Rotulus* is a known quantity of ready-to-use material. The texts do not have to be combed out of long, more than fulsome collections of sermons (as did Maximus's or Peter's above) or out of the many canons of ancient and medieval councils regulating the liturgical year, as does so much of the earliest non-homiletic evidence for studying the origins of Advent.

Of the three traditions for Advent — scriptural, ascetic, eschatological — Peter Chrysologus's rhetoric most closely draws from the readings of Advent, for it is tightly and chronologically based on the infancy narratives of the New Testament, especially on the Gospel of Luke. Bearing in mind again that there was no critical distinction between the historical and the scriptural in this age, we find in the collection eleven sermons commenting on Luke 1, the double annunciation of the angel to Zechariah and to Mary. These are almost evenly divided into two groups.

Franco Sottocornola, in his engaging study of the sermons of Chrysologus, orders these consecutively as follows: two series — Sermons 86–91–92 and 87–88–90 — for Luke 1:5–25, and Sermons 140, 141, and the series 142–143–144 for Luke 1:26–38.[20] What we have, then, are five occasions of preaching, three of these each with three sermons preached consecutively, and two additional occasions with just one sermon. Sottocornola also suggests that the Advent sermons were preached on consecutive Sundays, with the Gospel of the annunciation to Zechariah proclaimed two Sundays before Christmas and that of the annunciation to Mary on the Sunday before the nativity feast itself. This configuration is wholly compatible with the preparation in Turin, extending back before Christmas for two Sundays. Maximus, however, was not as attentive to the readings, so the pericopes of the liturgy in Turin are not as determinable from his preaching as they are from the sermons of Peter in Ravenna.

So, what do Peter Chrysologus's Advent sermons reveal about the character of the pre-Christmas season in the middle of fifth-century

---

354–361; and Joseph Lemarie, "Le mystere de l'Avent et de Noël d'apres le Rotulus de Ravenne," *Questions Liturgiques* 42 (1961): 303–322.

20. See his *L'anno liturgico nei sermoni di Pietro Crisologo: Ricerca storico-critica sulla liturgia di Ravenna antica* (Cesena: Centro Studi e Ricerche, 1973): here at 256–266.

Italy? First, the preparation was thoroughly liturgical in character. In contrast to the later domestic ascetic practices of Advent — refraining from food, foregoing sexual intimacy — that will come to mark the Western observance of Advent elsewhere, the Ravennese observance was communal and liturgical, based on the proclamation of the word of God from the Gospel of Luke.

Moreover, the content of the bishop's preaching is decidedly theological and doctrinal. Peter's episcopate in Ravenna spanned (or nearly spanned) the meetings of the last two christological councils, the Council of Ephesus (431) and the Council of Chalcedon (451). In the Advent sermons, then, it is no surprise, really, that we find emphases on the meaning of the incarnation and on how this mystery is to be held in balance with the divinity of Christ, as we do with his contemporary in Rome, Leo the Great.

In a sermon about the annunciation to Zechariah regarding the birth of his son (88), we find the bishop preaching to the faithful about the mystery of the Trinity:

> O heretic, thus is he another person, so that he himself may be the substance; and he is thus the substance so that there be no confusion in the Trinity. That is the reason for the unity of the Trinity: that there be no distance in God. And so he is in himself, such that the whole Trinity cannot exist without him, so that the definite personality stands together in the Father and the Son and the Holy Spirit, not a separate divinity.[21]

Such dense theological discourse might seem out of place in a sermon for this short period of preparation for Christmas, yet the emergence of a feast remembering the nativity of Jesus coincided with some of the most virulent theological debates about Jesus Christ. In many ways, the image of the savior in the manger ran against the high Christologies of the orthodox councils of the same period. The simultaneous confession of the Son as consubstantial with the Father and the memory of him in the vulnerability of infancy presented a challenge to the preachers of late antiquity. This tension between the theology of the Trinity and the narratives of Jesus' infancy led to the omnipresent emphasis on the new christological and theological teachings in Advent sermons.

---

21. Sermo LXXXVIII.6: *Haeretice, sic est alius persona, ut sit ipse substantia; sic est ipse substantia ut, nulla sit confusio trinitatis. Sic est unitas trinitatis, ut nulla sit in deitate distantia. Sic in se est, et sine se tota trinitas non est, ut insit in patre et filio et spiritu sancto personalitas definita, non separata diuinitas;* trans. Connell.

In Sermon 144 we hear Peter Chrysologus making this odd juxtaposition apparent:

> O heretic, what is it about injury, about infancy, about age, about time, about giving and receiving, about littleness, about death — if you understand these to be not of divinity but of the body, you bring no injury to the son, you make no distance in the Trinity. But we turn to ourselves, and speak of what is ours.[22]

The Council of Ephesus in 431 — with its debates and decisions about the instrumentality of Mary in the birth of Jesus — would have shaped the vocabulary speaking of Mary's pregnancy and the infancy and childhood of Jesus common for this period in the second quarter of the fifth century, the time of Peter's episcopate in Ravenna.

Advent in Spain?

Some scholars of the liturgical year and its origins have supposed that evidence for Advent can be found in a three-week span in Spain.[23] The evidence highlighted in their studies is a canon from the Council of Saragossa in 380 that mandated penitential practices in anticipation of Epiphany. The fourth canon of the council ordered that

> for twenty-one days in a row, from December 17 until the day of the day of Epiphany, which is January 6, for continuous days no one should be absent from church or stay hidden at home or escape to the country or to the mountains or run around in bare feet, but all should come together in church.[24]

This canon was reintroduced to scholarship of the liturgical year with the publication of Thomas Talley's *The Origins of the Liturgical Year*, but Talley drew more from the canon than the text itself can bear, as he wrote:

> That canon urges the constant presence of the faithful in the church, calling on them not to stay at home or run off to the

---

22. Sermo CXLIV.7: *Haeretice, quod est iniuriae, quod infantiae, quod aetatis, quod temporis, quod dati, quod accepti, quod minorationis, quod mortis, si intellexeris non esse diuinitatis, sed corporis, tu nullam filio inrogabis iniuriam, nullam tu facies in trinitate distantiam. Sed reuertamur ad nos, et quae sunt nostra iam loquamur;* trans. Connell.

23. Talley, *The Origins of the Liturgical Year* (New York: Pueblo, 1986): 150.

24. Mansi III: 634; trans. Connell from "The Origins and Evolution of Advent in the West," in Maxwell E. Johnson, ed., *Between Memory and Hope* (Collegeville, MN: Liturgical Press, 2000): 349–371.

country or the mountains during a period of twenty-one continuous days, beginning from December 17 and reaching to the
Epiphany.[25]

Yet he continues a bit later,

> It is altogether likely... that both festivals [Christmas and Epiph-
> any] were already being observed at the time of the synod of
> Tarragona in 380,[26] and thus the period mentioned there was not
> simply oriented toward the Epiphany, but included Christmas.[27]

The problems with Talley's reasoning here are many; I mention just
a few.[28] First, there is no confirmation anywhere of the celebration of
Christmas in Spain in 380 or before in any church or any text contemporary with the Council of Saragossa. Talley used this canon not only
as evidence for Advent, but as the first evidence of Christmas outside
of the church of Rome. Second, as one can see by the canon itself,
there is actually no mention of Christmas at all in the text. Yet, as
with his hypotheses about Christmas in the third century, the absence
of evidence does not impede Talley's speculation that will eventually
be assumed as fact.

The disciplines listed in the canon clearly portray an ascetic character for this period from December 17 to January 6, and the canon
itself is clear in specifying that the disciplines continue between those
dates "without interruption," *continuis diebus,* in the Latin of the
time. Surely if there had been a cardinal celebration of the birth of
the Lord on December 25, the canon would not have described the
penitential span as one observed "without interruption." That Talley
would find a celebration of Christmas implied in this text when the
verbally spare canon itself specifies that the season is continuous is a
problem with his work on Advent. In 380, there is as yet no evidence
that Christmas was celebrated anywhere in the West except Rome.

In 1928 Dom Gabriel Morin published the critical edition of a letter
written by, as he called her, "a Spanish ascetic." The manuscript is of
the ninth century, but Morin hypothesized that it had been written in

---

25. Talley: 150.
26. I assume that Talley's "Tarragona" here was supposed to be "Saragossa." He had just
referred to a letter to Himerius of Tarragona, but the council in this segment of Talley's
argument was in Saragossa.
27. Talley: 150.
28. For a closer examination of Talley's work on Christmas and Epiphany, see Martin
Connell, "The Origins of Christmas in the West: Did Ambrose's Sister Become a Virgin on
December 25 or January 6?" *Studia Liturgica* 24 (1999): 145–158.

the region of the Pyrenees near the year 400.[29] The author of the letter
was a visionary, and she wrote that between her tenth and eleventh
visions she prayed and fasted *tribus ebdomadis,* "for three weeks,"[30]
and these are again described as a span of "fasting and prayer."[31]

Later she wrote of "our Jesus put in the manger by the prophet himself, and in swaddling clothes,"[32] which, combined with a mention of
"two proximate solemn festivals," might have been what led Morin to
suppose that she was referring to Epiphany and Christmas. However,
she never speaks explicitly of Christmas, by name or by indicating its
date, though she does mention Epiphany, *Ipsius Epiphaniae dies latine manifestationem dicitur indicare,* "in Latin the day of Epiphany
itself means 'manifestation.'" Moreover, the phrase in which she wrote
of the two festivals is *inter duas sanctorum dierum proximas festivi-
tates sollemnitas,* which could as likely be translated as "between the
two proximate solemn festivals of the days of the saints," referring to
saints' feast days rather than to Christmas and Epiphany.

Although the letter itself might not bear much weight, the scholarship resting on it has. Morin located the ascetic in Spain because of
the earlier-mentioned fourth canon of Saragossa; yet, if Christmas had
not been received by any church except Rome, the letter could have
come from any number of regions in late fourth-century or early fifth-
century Latin Christianity. The attribution of the letter to a Spaniard
circumscribes the region in which Epiphany was still observed without
Christmas, so there is still no evidence of Christmas in Spain in the
fourth century.

The supposition of historians of the liturgical year has been that
Christmas was received in the Eastern churches at the end of the fourth
century. Yet outside of Rome, there is no evidence that Christmas was
received and celebrated in the West any earlier than it was in the East.
With this so, based on the evidence about Epiphany and the absence
of any sure testimony to Christmas, the ascetic who wrote the letter might have been from any church of Latin Christianity in the late
fourth century except Rome, and perhaps North Africa. The argument
about the origins and history of Christmas influences, of course, hypotheses about Advent. Christmas has been inserted into texts before
there is evidence of a preparatory season at this time of the year, even

---

29. See D. G. Morin, "Pages inédites de deux pseudo-Jérome des environs de l'an 400,"
Revue Bénédictine 40 (1928): 289–318, here at 304; trans. Connell for both the visionary's
Latin and Morin's French.

30. Morin: 300, line 10.

31. Ibid.: 301, lines 5–8.

32. Ibid.: 300, lines 27–28.

though the texts that mention the season, such as this ascetic's letter, never mention Christmas and were more likely seasons of preparation for Epiphany or for the feast days of saints.

Part Two:
The Variety of Time Spans for Advent

Three Weeks

The close examination of the canon of Saragossa above served to exclude it as proof of a season of preparation for Christmas. At the same time, the canon does testify to a three-week span in anticipation of Epiphany.[33] The letter from the ascetic woman visionary also mentioned a three-week period, though — except for the similar duration of the spans — there is no other reason to see these as testimonies to the same liturgical season; possible, but not certain.

One can suggest, however, that there were time spans of preparation linked to certain rites even before those rites themselves were locked into feasts or seasons of the year. For example, with the three-week span, there was the narrative of the woman at the well in the capitularies of Aquileia. Other Gospel lists in the Middle Ages have a three-week span of consecutive readings from the Gospel of John in preparation for baptism, that is, the Gospels of the woman at the well (John 4), the man born blind (John 9), and the raising of Lazarus (John 11), the Sundays that today are known as the Scrutiny Sundays of Lent in churches that celebrate the Rites of Christian Initiation for Adults (RCIA).

The history of Epiphany on January 6 reveals that in its first appearances in the third and fourth centuries, that feast was a celebration of the baptism of Jesus, which may or may not have been a time for celebrating the baptism of new members of the church. Although it is merely speculative, might there have been a three-week span of preparation for baptism that proclaimed those readings from John (or possibly from another Gospel, depending on the local churches) before the celebration of baptism was set on a particular day of the year?

If this is so, then the three weeks of the Saragossan council, the three weeks of the readings from the Gospel of John, and the longer spans evident in capitularies of Aquileia might give some evidence of a period, just before its eclipse, when rites were linked to the narratives of

---

33. Talley: 150.

scripture (the Gospels, in particular) before the narratives were themselves set in the year. The liturgical year took its shape in the fourth
and fifth centuries; yet these remnants might give a glimpse back to a
more primitive period when the linking of rites and narratives preceded
the linking of rites and dates or seasons.

Forty Days

As with the history of Lent — a season whose length changed many
times through the Middle Ages[34] — so the length of Advent was of
different lengths in different places and sometimes changed within the
same place.[35] The late fifth-century bishop of Tours, Perpetuus (died
490), described the fasting of his church leading up to Christmas. The
Advent period began on November 11, the feast day of his predecessor
in the episcopate there, Martin of Tours, who died in the year 397.
Though the existence of this span is known from Perpetuus, he reveals
nothing about Advent as a period of preparation; drawing from the
name of the earlier bishop, Perpetuus called the period "St. Martin's
Lent" and it lasted from November 11 until Christmas day. It has
been suggested by some that if the span that became "St. Martin's
fast" antedated the reception of Christmas in the fourth century, the
span at its origin might have been the eight weeks from November 11
to January 6. Since the church at Milan did not fast on Saturdays
and Sundays in Lent, the span of eight weeks of fasting from Monday
to Friday might have been the inculturation of a forty-day period of
preparation for Epiphany.[36] But this adds too much to the little that
can be known from Perpetuus's testimony with certainty.

A century later, another bishop of the church, at Tours, Gregory,
writes his *History of the Franks*, in which he mentions a preparation for
Christmas, ascetic in character and forty days in length. He writes of it
as a kind of winter Lent that would last "from the death of Martin until
the feast of the birth of the Lord, a period of seven weeks."[37] And in

---

34. See Volume 2, Chapter 2, "Lent."

35. Studies of the medieval testimonies to the season of Advent are found in a three-part
series of articles by Walter Croce. The three have the same title, "Die Adventmessen des
Römischen Missale in ihrer geschichtlichen Entwicklung," and they appear in *Zeitschrift für
Katholische Theologie* 74 (1952): 277–317; *Zeitschrift für Katholische Theologie* 76 (1954):
257–296, and *Zeitschrift für Katholische Theologie* 76 (1954): 440–472. A wealth of information is also cited in Josef Andreas Jungmann, *Advent und Voradvent: Überreste des
gallischen Advents in der römischen Liturgie* (Innsbruck and Leipzig: Felizian Raugh, 1937),
a reprint of what appeared first in *Zeitschrift für katholische Theologie* 61 (1937): 341–390.

36. Adam, *The Liturgical Year: Its History and Its Meaning after the Reform of the Liturgy*,
trans. Matthew J. O'Connell (New York: Pueblo, 1981): 130–131.

37. History of the Franks, X.31: *A depositione domni Martini usque Natale Domini terna
in setimana jejunia* (PL 71:566); trans. Connell.

another place Gregory describes an abbot who wanted to be in solitude for the rest of his life: "He did not want to see any human faces. We persuaded him not to make his withdrawal forever, but that he restrict it to the days between the death of St. Martin and the solemnity of the Lord's birth, or in the same way, according to the authority of the fathers, to the forty days period of abstinence leading up to the feast of Easter."[38]

What Gregory described was confirmed by the regulations from the Frankish Council of Mâcon, held in 582, which ordered that between the feast of St. Martin and Christmas Mondays, Wednesdays, and Fridays would be days of fasting, and that during this span the liturgy would be celebrated as during Lent.[39] The link between asceticism and worship in the seasons of Advent and Lent continued even after Easter was no longer the primary time for baptism. In the time of Charlemagne, for example, the feast of St. Martin itself grew more celebratory because the next day would begin the asceticism, not unlike the indulgences of *Mardi Gras* that then and today precede Ash Wednesday. Advent continued as a span of asceticism and obligatory fasting until the promulgation of the Code of Canon Law in 1917. This fast probably preserved some aspects of the ancient time when Epiphany was a time for baptism, but there is virtually no remnant of that corporal, preparatory ritual behavior in the church's celebration of it today.

In the tenth century a monk of Gaul, Ratherius (who died in the year 974), was named bishop of the church of Verona, and, writing to his priests about the season of Advent, he instructed: "Keep the forty days equally, except for Sundays. For if you fast on one day and are hungover the next, you observe not forty days, but only twenty." But there is also an indication that the four weeks before Christmas was still a key span, for, encouraging his priests to refrain from flesh, dead or alive, he added: "During Advent, unless it is a feast, abstain from meat-eating and intercourse for four weeks."[40] Although the four-week Advent was also widely observed, the forty-day observance from the feast of Martin to Christmas seems to have endured to some extent in

---

38. *et ille ita se duxit includere, ut nunquam humanis aspectibus appareret, consilium suasimus, ut non se perpetuo in hac conclusione constringeret, nisi in illis duntaxat diebus, qui inter depositionem sancti Martini, ac dominici Natalis solemnitatem habentur, vel in illis similiter quadraginta diebus quos ante Paschalia festa in summa duci abstinentia patrum sanxit auctoritas* (PL 71: 1072B–1072C); trans. Connell.

39. Canon 9: *Ut a feria S. Martini usque ad natale domini, secunda, quarta, & sexta sabbati jejunetur, & sacrificial quadragesimali debeant ordine celebrari.* Mansi, volume 9 (Paris and Leipzig: H. Welter, 1901): column 933.

40. PL 136:565–566; trans. Connell.

the tradition for centuries. One finds, for example, in the disciplines of the Council of Saltzburg — convened in 1281, during the time of archbishop Frederick and the papacy of Martin IV — a regulation about fasting, and it iterates that a fast is to be observed by all religious people from the feast of St. Martin until Christmas.[41]

Although this span of forty days has not been observed in the Roman Catholic tradition for centuries, it continues in Orthodox churches. In the calendars of the Eastern traditions, of course, the "Christmas fast" does not begin with the feast of Martin, a saint of the Latin tradition, but Advent begins on November 15. (Like the "St. Martin's fast" in the West, the Eastern Advent is sometimes called "St. Philip's fast," for the feast of the apostle Philip is on November 14 in the Eastern traditions.)

Even in the Orthodox churches that celebrate Christmas, Advent is as much or more of an anticipation of Epiphany as it is of Christmas. The theology of illumination that has long characterized Epiphany in the Byzantine tradition is integrated into the liturgical texts of the season of preparation, as the church prays for the coming light in its midst. Perhaps because of the different degrees of reception of Christmas in the Orthodox traditions, the origin of the forty-day span is uncertain. There is evidence that Greek Christians maintained the fast from November 15 until Christmas, but there is no rhetoric about the Nativity of Christ from that time to demonstrate that the period was one of anticipating the birth narrative at Christmas.

Although the Latin and Eastern traditions share the two-fold theology of Advent, juxtaposing anticipation of the end of the world and the birth of Christ, the readings in the Orthodox traditions that support this juxtaposition are unique, at least up to the infancy narratives proximate to Christmas itself.[42]

Six Weeks

Roman liturgical books before Pope Gregory the Great (bishop of Rome from 590 to 604) testify to a six-week span leading up to Christmas, though the earliest evidence dates back only a few decades before Gregory's pontificate. The books from the pre-Gregorian sixth century church of Rome testify explicitly to only five Sundays *de adventu*, but

---

41. The disciplines of the Council of Saltzburg (1281) are found in thirteenth-century papal correspondence, here during the papacy of Martin IV; see *Martini P. IV. Epistolae*, columns 395–404: *De jejunio religiosorum. Item a festo Martini ab omnibus religiosis usque ad Nativitatem Domini jejunium observetur.*

42. See *The Year of Grace of the Lord: A Scriptural and Liturgical Commentary on the Calendar of the Orthodox Church*, trans. Deborah Cowen (Crestwood NY: St. Vladimir's Seminary Press, 1980): 45–65.

there was a *dominica vacat,* a "missing Sunday," on the Sunday before Christmas, which marked that Sunday as an Ember-Day celebration (an agricultural feast) for the month of December; it did not count therefore as one of the Sundays of Advent. The five Sundays *de adventu* plus the *dominica vacat* contribute to six Sundays for the span of the Roman season before Gregory the Great's episcopacy there. Among the witnesses to this span are the Capitulary of Würzburg and the Gelasian Sacramentary.

Gregory the Great reduced the number of Sundays in Advent from six to four. Though the length of six Sundays may have originally characterized Advent because of the baptismal associations with Epiphany in churches that celebrated the birth of Jesus on January 6, there is no evidence that the church in Rome ever celebrated the birth on that date. Such baptismal associations, therefore, would not have been known in Rome. Perhaps this is why Gregory, perhaps unaware of the baptismal imagery that elsewhere marked Epiphany, was inclined to shorten the season to four weeks. After Gregory, in the late seventh and early eighth centuries, there was a further impulse to temporally restrain the season of Advent to the month of December alone. This would have meant that, in four of seven years, Advent would have had only three Sundays — that is, in the years when the First Sunday would have fallen on one of the days from November 27 to 30. In the end the church of Rome stayed with the season of four Sundays before Christmas, with the first one sometimes at the end of November and sometimes at the beginning of December, as it still is today.

Even though the church of Rome reduced the season of Advent to four weeks, the tradition of observing the season from the date of the death of St. Martin of Tours endured for some time beyond Gregory's pontificate in Rome, as chronicled above. The four-week Roman practice was received in most places in the West during the first few centuries of the Middle Ages. But as late as the thirteenth century, Gallican church councils still bear witness to a forty-day Advent, with different degrees of ascetic practices from place to place. In some churches both the four-week and forty-day spans were observed.

Roman liturgical books started to have a greater influence in shaping the length of Advent in the ninth and tenth centuries as they were introduced, used, and inculturated in northern churches after the decline of the city of Rome. Moreover, graduals and antiphonaries placed the season at the start of their lists, signaling that this span began the new cycle of the church's year.

Part Three:
O Antiphons

Independent of the season that began on a Sunday, a tradition of a pre-Christmas span beginning on a date rather than a day of the week also emerged in the Middle Ages. This span lasts from December 17 until Christmas Eve and is sometimes called the "Golden" span.[43] This eight-day period is marked liturgically by the singing of the "O Antiphons." These antiphons were originally sung before the Canticle of Mary at evening prayer, and, though they remain there in the Liturgy of the Hours, they have become popular enough in pastoral life that they are often sung in church apart from evening prayer.[44] The popular Advent hymn "O Come, O Come, Emmanuel" is itself a translation and paraphrase of the O Antiphons.

Each of these scripturally based antiphons has a two-part literary structure: the first part is a call to the Messiah with the introductory "O" followed by a title given him. The second part is a short prayer in anticipation of his coming. (The Latin imperative *veni*, or "come!," bridges the invocation and the supplication in each antiphon.) The O Antiphons appear in the traditions of various religious communities, the Benedictines and Cistercians in particular, but their reception was wide and eventually they were integrated into the antiphons of daily prayer for the church in Roman Catholic and Protestant traditions. They also appear in the oldest extant Antiphonal, the *Liber Responsalis S. Gregorii Magni*, from the end of the ninth century, though the attribution to Gregory the Great is not likely indicative of their Roman origin or of a late sixth- or early seventh-century provenance.[45] Amalarius of Metz (died ca. 850) wrote of them as antiphons used uniquely before the chanting of the evening prayer canticle, the Magnificat, and by the twelfth century there is Roman testimony that they were also sung before the morning prayer canticle, the Benedictus.

---

43. As seen above in the Spanish evidence, the span from December 17 to January 6 is three weeks, a period that is not without importance in the history of preparation for initiation. Though not secure, perhaps the earlier evidence of a three-week period in Saragossa bears something of a three-week period of preparation for what used to be a baptismal feast at Epiphany in Spain, and that a remnant of this remained even after Christmas was received in other places in the beginning of the O Antiphons on December 17. This specaulative possibility is raised because of the common time increments; no calendar reflects the coincidence of the beginning of the three-week span and the first uses of the O Antiphons.

44. M. Huglo, "O Antiphons," *New Catholic Encyclopedia*, volume 10 (New York: McGraw-Hill, 1967): 587–588.

45. A. Hollaardt, "O-antifonen," in *Litugisch Woordenboek*, volume 2 (Netherlands: Roermond and Maaseik, 1966): 1914–1917.

As with all of the feasts and seasons, the various ritual elements appearing in the history of Advent were not likely observed in all churches, but were rather the practices of particular local communities that shared customs with one another. Among these local Advent traditions that became universal were the O Antiphons, the omission of singing the Gloria during the Sunday Eucharist, and the wearing of penitential vestments. The customs of Advent thus reveal the often adhesive nature of liturgical exchange throughout Christian history, with later maintenance and winnowing as part of their history.

An Academic Myth about the Origin of the O Antiphons?

The O Antiphons are now quite popular in liturgical churches but perhaps not always for the right reason. The antiphons are themselves translations of Latin verses, all of them, as noted already, beginning with a vocative address to Christ and each with a different emphasis on a manifestation of his appearance. As they are part of the liturgy today, we find the following names:

> December 17: *O Sapientia!* — O Wisdom!
> December 18: *O Adonai!* — O Almighty Lord!
> December 19: *O Radix Iesse!* — O Root of Jesse!
> December 20: *O Clavis David!* — O Key of David!
> December 21: *O Oriens!* — O Rising Sun!
> December 22: *O Rex Gentium!* — O King of the People!
> December 23: *O Emmanuel!* — O God-with-us!

The antiphons take the church up to Christmas Eve, when most churches celebrate a Vigil Mass (on the night of December 24) or the Midnight Mass of Christmas (after the turn of the date, so December 25). Some historians of the liturgical year suggest that there might be a kind of secret message in the O Antiphons. If one takes the first letter of each of the Latin names above — S-A-R-C-O-R-E — and reverses these letters — E-R-O-C-R-A-S — the result can be taken as two Latin words, *ero cras*, meaning "I will be [or come] tomorrow."

While, perhaps, this is a clever message for the end of the Advent season of expectation of Christ's coming at the end of time, there is little or no support in the sources that this is anything more than a coincidence. Such a cryptic medium is not a common quality of liturgical practice and theology. Moreover, the number of O Antiphons varied from church to church and from religious community to community, and those without ERO CRAS did not fashion their antiphons to construct a cryptic message.

Such clever, inventive explanations can feed into a popular tendency to think of God's word to humanity or of the church's medium in worship as encrypted messages that need to be complexly untangled. But in the whole of the liturgical tradition there has been no tradition of such a labyrinthine way of mediating what God communicates to humanity in his Son. Most people have difficulty accepting the generosity of God in giving the world his Son incarnate, and such labyrinthine media are ways of distancing the message of God that was and is generous and clear in his Son. The encrypted message that he will "come tomorrow" is not characteristic of how the church brings its worship traditions to light.[46] Neither God nor the church hide the message of the good news of God's inexplicable generosity to the world in the gift of the Son.

Part Four:
The Theology of Advent

Often Advent preaching posits that the Son of God was once fully present and will, at the end of time, be fully present again. This kind of theology, sometimes called "already but not yet," can be a consolation to believers who do not feel that God or the risen Christ is present and active in their lives, that humanity languishes during this time "between" those moments of salvation. It solves the enigma about why in the active ministry of Jesus people were cured of diseases, dead people were raised, and seas were calmed at Jesus' command, but it also closes the eyes of believers to the extraordinary and miraculous presence of God in their day-to-day lives. Though the baptized do indeed live in the now long span between the incarnate life of Jesus of Nazareth and the second coming of Christ at the end of time, in church they are present to the incarnate and risen Christ, whose ministry and miracles are wrought in the community of faith.

The *Constitution on the Sacred Liturgy* (1963) taught that there is a four-fold presence of Christ in the celebration of the Lord's Supper: Christ is present in the assembly gathered in church; in the person of the priest, who leads the assembly in its prayer; in the word proclaimed and preached; and in the consecrated bread and wine.[47] If the already-but-not-yet theology is indeed correct, one assumes that the presence

---

46. I welcome any contradiction of my suspicion here, but it would have to be from a primary source, not from a commentary or secondary source, where this labyrinthine explanation is very common.

47. *Sacrosanctum Concilium* #7.

of Christ in the celebration of the sacraments in the church is wanting, is an imperfect manifestation, a gift not fully given; yet none of these is true. In church teaching and in the experience of the baptized gathered to celebrate the sacraments, at Advent and at any time, God — by the power of the Holy Spirit and manifest in the person of his Son, the risen Christ — is fully present.

The Holy Spirit

In the theology and liturgy of Western Christianity, the active role of the Holy Spirit is underappreciated. Some of the problem, no doubt, is that, for those Christians whose Sacrament of Confirmation took place years after their baptism into the church, there is an inclination to regard the presence of the Holy Spirit as an "add-on," as not necessary to the life of God as experienced in Christian life. Yet the readings proclaimed in Advent alert believers to the role of the Holy Spirit in the incarnation of God in Jesus of Nazareth and in the life of the church today.

The Gospel story on the very Sunday before Christmas, the Fourth Sunday of Advent, in particular, illuminates the role of the Holy Spirit in salvation. As often in Year A, one finds a Gospel narrative from Matthew (1:18–24), and the story proclaimed is this: "Now the birth of Jesus Christ took place in this way. When his mother Mary had been betrothed to Joseph, before they came together she was found to be with child of the Holy Spirit." In a dream, the angel of the Lord explains how this could be so to the bewildered Joseph: " 'Joseph, son of David, do not fear to take Mary your wife, for that which is conceived in her is of the Holy Spirit.' " The role of the Holy Spirit, according to this account, is primary in time and salvation; the Spirit is the instrument of the incarnation, the Word made flesh dwelling in humanity.

The theological tradition is constant in teaching that — as the Holy Spirit worked in the incarnation of the Son, in the Son taking on flesh — so does the Holy Spirit work in the body of Christ of the church and its sacraments, knitting together sinful individuals and raising from them the sinless people of God. The community of faith is wrought by the power of the Holy Spirit, as was the body of Jesus knit together in Mary's womb two millennia ago.

In Advent, then, the church is called to be more vigilant in discovering the role of the Spirit in humanity in general and in the life of the church in particular. The Holy Spirit is the mover, the divine impetus that diverts people away from other options for a Sunday morning so that they might celebrate the presence of the living God, embodied in the life of Jesus in first-century Palestine and now embodied in the assembly gathered at prayer. The body of the church is brought together by the Spirit, nourished in word and sacrament, and sent forth to attend to the needs of humanity, as this intercessory oration for Advent from the Presbyterian *Book of Common Worship* expresses:[48]

> Strengthen us, O God, in the power of your Spirit
> to bring good news to the poor
> and lift blind eyes to sight,
> to loose the chains that bind
> and claim your blessing for all people.
> Keep us faithful to your service
> until Christ comes in final victory,
> and we shall feast with all your saints
> in the joy of your eternal realm.

The End of the World

From its origins, the season of Advent has maintained an anticipation of the end of the world, with ambiguity about whether it be near or far. The church's prayer in Advent prepares the baptized not just for the end of the world, but for the end of their own individual lives, an end that is blithely ignored or peripheral in U.S. culture. In Advent the sober reality of death and the end of the world is vibrant and frightening, as it was and is in St. Paul's First Letter to the Corinthians, proclaimed on the First Sunday of Advent (Year B): "[God] who will sustain you to the end, guiltless in the day of our Lord Jesus Christ. God is faithful, by whom you were called into the fellowship of his Son, Jesus Christ our Lord" (1:8–9).

The unpredictability of the final time is proclaimed from the Gospel of Luke (First Sunday of Advent, Year C), as the evangelist warned about the precarious end of the world and the inexplicability of God's judgment: "Take heed to yourselves lest your hearts be weighed down with dissipation and drunkenness and cares of this life, and that day come upon you suddenly like a snare; for it will come upon all who dwell upon the face of the whole earth. But watch at all times, praying that you may have strength to escape all these things that will take place, and to stand before the Son of man" (21:34–36). So, too, from the Gospel of Mark (First Sunday of Advent, Year B): "Of that day or that hour no one knows, not even the angels in heaven, nor the Son, but only the Father. Take heed, watch; for you do not know when the time will come" (13:32–33).

---

48. *Book of Common Worship* (Louisville: Westminster/John Knox, 1993): 171.

Advent is a time of reckoning, when a believer, the parish, or the church universal might face their ends, might prepare for death. Only in a posture of preparedness can one truly celebrate the life incarnate in the Son, whose birth is celebrated at the season's end. Such an apocalyptic theology of Advent, waiting for the divine Judge at the end of time, is usually overshadowed by the more sentimental waiting for the infant at Christmas, but the readings do not pull back from death in the first few weeks of Advent. As Mark Doty wrote candidly in the face of the death of his loved one, so does the church face death and the end squarely in Advent: "Apocalypse is played out now on a personal scale: it is not in the sky above us, but in our bed."[49]

Doty's chronicle written in proximity of death raised the issue starkly about how people are more intensely themselves in the face of death, an apt representation of what the theology of Advent might be for the church:

Watching Wally, watching friends who were either sick themselves or giving care to those who were, I saw that they simply became more generous or terrified, more cranky or afraid, more doubtful or more trusting, more contemplative or more in flight. As individual and unpredictable as this illness seems to be, the one thing I found I could say with certainty was this: AIDS makes things more intensely what they already are. Eventually I understood that this truism then must apply to me, as well, and, of course, it applied to my anxiety about the future.

Because the truth was I'd *never* really believed in a future, always had trouble imagining ongoingness, a place in the unfolding chain of things. I was raised on apocalypse. My grandmother — whose Tennessee fundamentalism reduced not a jot her generosity or spiritual grace — used to read me passages from the Book of Revelation and talk about the immanence of the Last Days. The hymns we sang figured this world as a veil of appearances, and sermons in church characterized the human world as a flimsy screen behind which the world's real actors enacted the struggles and dramas of a loftier realm. Not struggles, exactly, since the outcome was foreknown: the lake of fire and the fiery pit, the eternal chorus of the saved — but dramatic in the sense of scale, or scope. How large and mighty was the music of salvation![50]

---

49. *Heaven's Coast* (New York: Harper Perennial, 1996): 4.
50. Ibid.: 3–4.

Advent proclaims that *now* is the time for humanity to be what God made it. On the Second Sunday of Advent (Year A), the church reads from Paul's Letter to the Romans:

> You know what hour it is, how it is full time now for you to wake from sleep. For salvation is nearer to us now than when we first believed; the night is far gone, the day is at hand. Let us then cast off the works of darkness and put on the armor of light; let us conduct ourselves becomingly as in the day, not in reveling and drunkenness, not in debauchery and licentiousness, not in quarreling and jealousy. But put on the Lord Jesus Christ, and make no provision for the flesh, to gratify its desires. (13:11–14)

The prophetic stand of the church in Advent, encouraging people to be brave in the face of death and the end of the world, would be a significant counter to the untruth of the culture, in which death is erased and hidden. The church is called to such prophecy at all times, for, as proclaimed from the Second Letter of Peter (Second Sunday, Year B), "the day of the Lord will come like a thief, and then the heavens will pass away with a loud noise, and the elements will be dissolved with fire, and the earth and the works that are upon it will be burned up" (3:10).

The Lord's Reign of Justice and Peace

Though the apocalyptic character of Advent is potent, the eschatological is balanced with a theology of the realization of God's kingdom today. With one of Advent's most poetic proclamations, the church draws from the prophet Isaiah, whose words are found frequently throughout the season (Second Sunday of Advent, Year A):

> The wolf shall dwell with the lamb,
> and the leopard shall lie down with the kid,
> and the calf and the lion and the fatling together,
> and a little child shall lead them.
> The cow and the bear shall feed;
> their young shall lie down together;
> and the lion shall eat straw like the ox.
> The sucking child shall play over the hole of the asp,
> and the weaned child shall put his hand on the adder's den.
> (11:6–8)

So, too, from First Thessalonians (Third Sunday, Year B): "May the God of peace himself sanctify you wholly; and may your spirit and soul and body be kept sound and blameless at the coming of our Lord

Jesus Christ" (5:23). The message of peace fits in tension with the apocalyptic character at the start of Advent. The latter is threatening as the former is irenic and calming. The tension captures the enigma of the season and of the Lord's coming, celebrated in the four weeks of the season.

The Book of Blessings and the Advent Wreath

The progress of time during the season is marked in Advent's unique ritual practice, the lighting of candles on the Advent wreath. The wreath traditionally has four candles, one for each Sunday of the season leading up to Christmas. Its use was appropriated late in Christian ritual tradition, usually dated to the sixteenth century, but even in that period documentation is weak. Most suppose that its appearance is the Christian adoption of a pre-Christian custom of northern Europe, where people lit candles on wagon wheels or wheel-shaped bundles of evergreens at the darkest time of the year as they waited for the lengthening of days after the winter solstice. Wreaths were also used by Eastern European Catholics, and eventually the custom spread to most Christian churches in the West.

Although the Sacramentary does not have a rite for the wreath, the *Book of Blessings* provides an introduction, rubrics, and an outline for blessing the wreath during the Sunday Eucharist or within a Liturgy of the Word. According to the *Book of Blessings*, "the use of the Advent Wreath is a traditional practice which has found its place in the Church as well as in the home. The blessing of an Advent wreath takes place on the First Sunday of Advent or on the evening before the First Sunday of Advent."[51] The *Book* instructs how the wreath might be made: "Customarily the Advent Wreath is constructed of a circle of evergreen branches into which are inserted four candles. According to tradition, three of the candles are violet and the fourth is rose. However, four violet or white candles may also be used."[52]

The constancy of vigilance in the church and at home during Advent links the rites of the church and the rites of families, the domestic church, in which the risen Christ is manifest and the Holy Spirit active. Within Mass, the rite for the blessing of the wreath follows the general intercessions, which themselves reveal a strong theology of light in the season:

---

51. *Book of Blessings: Study Edition* (Collegeville, MN: Liturgical Press, 1989): #1509.
52. Ibid.: #1510.

Christ came to bring us salvation and has promised to come
again. Let us pray that we may be always ready to welcome
him. *R.* Come, Lord Jesus.

That the keeping of Advent may open our hearts to God's love,
we pray to the Lord. *R.*

That the light of Christ may penetrate the darkness of sin, we
pray to the Lord. *R.*

That this wreath may constantly remind us to prepare for the
coming of Christ, we pray to the Lord. *R.*

That the Christmas season may fill us with peace and joy as we
strive to follow the example of Jesus, we pray to the Lord. *R.*

With longing for the coming of God's kingdom, let us offer our
prayer to the Father: *R.*

Our Father . . .

Then the celebrant, with hands outstretched, says the prayer of
blessing:

Lord our God,
we praise you for your Son, Jesus Christ:
he is Emmanuel, the hope of the peoples,
he is the wisdom that teaches and guides us,
he is the Savior of every nation.
Lord God,
let your blessing come upon us
as we light the candles of this wreath.
May the wreath and its light
be a sign of Christ's promise to bring us salvation.
May he come quickly and not delay.
We ask this through Christ our Lord.
R. Amen.[53]

The *Book of Common Worship* has a verse from the prophet Isaiah
shaped for each week's candle-lighting:

We light this candle as a sign of the coming light of Christ. Advent
means coming. We are preparing ourselves for the days when . . .

---

53. Ibid.: 573–582.

First Sunday of Advent

Nations shall beat their swords into plowshares,
and their spears into pruning hooks;
nation shall not lift up sword against nations,
neither shall they learn war any more [Isaiah 2:4].

Second Sunday of Advent

The wolf shall dwell with the lamb,
the leopard shall lie down with the kid,
the calf and the lion and the fatling together,
and a little child shall lead them [Isaiah 11:6].

Third Sunday of Advent

The wilderness and the dry land shall be glad
the desert shall rejoice and blossom;
like the crocus it shall blossom abundantly,
and rejoice with joy and singing [Isaiah 35:1].

Fourth Sunday of Advent

The Lord will give you a sign,
Lord, the young woman is with child
and shall bear a son,
and shall name him Immanuel (God is with us) [Isaiah 7:14].

The rite concludes with the antiphon, "Let us walk in the light of
the Lord," emphasizing the once mobile, stational quality of church
practice with the wreath.[54]

Conclusion

At the beginning of Advent, the church proclaims the message of the
world's proximate end and the story of the proximate celebration of
the world's salvation in the birth of Jesus Christ, so the season bears
the bittersweet theology of proximate ends and new starts. T. S. Eliot's
"Journey of the Magi" captures the same feelings as he portrayed one
of the wise men reminiscing about the trip the trio of magicians took
in "the very dead of winter," a time befitting Advent's location in the
natural year. In the first stanza the magus recounts what they sacrificed
for the journey, what they forsook in the old life as they risked the trip
to the new: "There were times we regretted / The summer palaces

---

54. *Book of Common Worship*: 165–166.

on slopes, the terraces, / And the silken girls bringing sherbet."[55] The second stanza recounts a later time, after their arrival at the place of the holy birth, "With a running stream and a water-mill beating the darkness," still in the dead of winter.

Then, in the third and final stanza, he looks back over the distance of years on what the journey had begotten:

> All this was a long time ago, I remember
> And I would do it again, but set down
> This set down
> This: were we led all that way for
> Birth or Death? There was a Birth, certainly,
> We had evidence and no doubt. I had seen birth and death,
> But had thought they were different; this Birth was
> Hard and bitter agony for us, like Death, our death.
> We returned to our places, these Kingdoms,
> But no longer at ease here, in the old dispensation,
> With an alien people clutching their gods.
> I should be glad of another death.

Although the narrative is that for Epiphany, the poem's theology aptly captures the bittersweet reality of the season, for Advent is indeed a time during which Birth and Death are held together, inseparable and indistinguishable sides of the same divine-and-human coin.[56] Death and birth are paired not only in the tradition of the season's prayers and readings, but in the plight of believers who wait for the coming of the Christ with patience and sobriety as Christmas shopping's consumption and excess crushes and overwhelms them.

Like the magi, people of faith — or people of "no doubt," in the poet's phrase — know that there has been a Birth. But it was not the Birth they would have imagined or expected, for, as ever in human life, "this Birth was / Hard and bitter agony for us, like Death, our death." Christian faith always embraces such complementarily wonderful realizations and difficult memories. In Advent, a dark and cold time of the year, believers remember the cold and darkness of life without Christ, as the magus reconsidered the comforts and sherbets they relinquished in the old order. And like the wise men, believers await the life to come without looking back with regret at what was left behind.

---

55. *The Norton Anthology of Modern and Contemporary Poetry*, volume 1, ed. Jahan Ramazani, Richard Ellman, Robert O'Clair (New York: W. W. Norton, 2003): 487–488.
56. T. S. Eliot, *The Complete Poems and Plays* (New York: Harcourt, Brace, 1952): 69.

Of a completely different literary style and sensibility — but confirming the church's celebration of death and birth in the assembly's disposition during Advent — is a poem by Franz Wright:[57]

I For One

I for one never asked
for my youth back; when I was young
I was always afraid.
Like somebody in a war

with no allegiance
I was terrified
of everyone.
But now

now I am amazed
and grateful every day.
I don't know how that happened.
I am so glad

there is no fear,
and finally I can

ask no second life.

For those within the church's embrace after baptism, there is no going back on the compelling truth, beauty, and affections of faith. Many believers discover the gifts of lives for themselves that none before would have been able to imagine, and often with unexpected results. As with Eliot's magus, who would have done it all over again, Christians too are glad to be there again and again, for their lives were irreversibly changed when they became members of a body larger than their individual corpus and flesh. Christians do not necessarily live lives any holier than their unbaptized peers, but the traditions of the faith enable them to open their eyes more widely to see what God's illuminated world bares to the vision of faith. "But," in Wright's words, "now //
now I am amazed / and grateful everyday // I don't know how that happened."

During Advent members of the church ask themselves: Who deserves the grace of God's love or the illumination of faith in a dark world misshapen by the advent of the devil and his wiles in the world? Advent reorients the faithful's recognition that in Christ the world has

---

57. *The Beforelife* (New York: Knopf, 2002): 36.

been changed, and they remember how to see things with brighter eyes
as they await the birth and death that comes with the Body of Christ at
Christmas. The simplicity of "I For One" recalls the abandonment of
a life before its communion in the body of the church. Before baptism,
each person existed constitutionally as an individual, but the washing
in holy waters inexorably changes that existence, for individual bodies
are no longer apart from the human race as a whole; the branch that
was lifeless and cut off was engrafted into the vine that is Christ. "I
am so glad," for that believer would by now have died apart from the
life of faith, no matter how august its successes apart from Christ, in
that dark time when the ignorant — no matter how loved by family
and friends, no matter how deeply involved in society and culture, no
matter how successful in the world — languish without Christ.

Because the nativity feast of Epiphany was changed when the Eastern churches adopted the Roman date of Christmas and its theological
emphases for initiation at Easter, the tradition of the season of Advent
has not emerged strongly in the Eastern traditions of Christianity, for
the theology of birth was separated from the narrative of the baptism
of Jesus, and this link had been deep in the baptismal theology of
many Eastern churches. Great was this loss and some of it the result
of the separation of paschal theology from natal theology,[58] separating
Death from Birth. In that separation the role of Adam and Eve, and of
Jesus as the New Adam and Mary as the New Eve, was separated —
not completely, but in large part — as have experiences and mysteries
of pregnancy and birth often been separated from the paschal mystery celebrated in the church. Such a separation would also have been
exacerbated by the winnowing out of married people from preaching
ministry of the church, for priests would have not have experienced
these mysteries of God in humanity. A balance in the tradition would
be restored if the preaching tradition reconsidered the paschal theology
of Advent, taking up the ancient theology of Epiphany from teachers like Ephrem of Syria,[59] or contemporary theology from poets like
Robert Frost, in his "Never Again Would the Birds' Song Be the Same":

> He would declare and could himself believe
> That the birds there in all the garden round
> From having heard the daylong voice of Eve
> Had added to their own an oversound,
> Her tone of meaning but without the words.
> Admittedly an eloquence so soft

---

58. See Volume 1, Chapter 4, "Epiphany."
59. See Volume 1, Chapter 4, "Epiphany."

Could only have had an influence on birds
When call or laughter carried it aloft.
Be that as may be, she was in their song
Moreover her voice upon their voices crossed
Had now persisted in the woods so long
That probably it never would be lost.
Never again would birds' song be the same.
And to do that to birds was why she came.

Here the poet or the reader views the scene from the vantage of Eve's companion, Adam, and he, with Frost's keen words, appreciates the wonder of his mate and companion — "her daylong voice," her "tone of meaning," her "eloquence so soft" — and the effect of her voice on the music of birds.[60] Such an experience of paradise before the fall is what people of faith await in the season of Advent, yet the natal theology that the figure of Eve bears is no longer as manifest as it was before birth and baptism narratives were separated. The church's anticipation of Christ can see him as the new Eve for he bears life to humanity in his coming, which is marked at the season's end.

In Advent the church reminds itself of God's "daylong voice," as the days themselves dim and as the church awaits the Light and Word of God at Christmas, born of the community of faith that ever stands at the brink of Birth and Death. Advent startles the church by its sober accounting of the state of the world standing in the face of its end, and of the prophetic and clear contradiction that Christian faith poses to a manic, consumptive, and rapacious society. Faith consoles in Advent because it is shared and thereby given voice.

As the church anticipates the joys and wonder of Christmas, it re-lives in a way the eons, millennia, centuries, and minutes in which the world waited for the fullness of revelation, lost in Eden and revealed in Christ. Even after the incarnation in Jesus, humanity has not escaped, indeed cannot escape, the ugliness of the original sin that marks its existence in a fallen world and self-absorbed species. Members of the church after baptism are not excised from the world and society of sin, but the waiting of Advent is one of a joyful anticipation, yes, but also of a sober awakening to the quotidian impediments to the fullness of life proffered by God but often not perceived by a blinded humanity. Advent is a time of reckoning during which the community of faith remembers the days before the incarnation that opened its eyes and before the sacrament of baptism mediated the nascent miracle.

---

60. Robert Frost, *The Poems of Robert Frost* (New York: Modern Library, 1946): 394.

Returning to the expressions of Wright, each of the unbaptized is indeed "always afraid," necessarily afraid because each is without hope, anchor, direction, or succor; without the fullness of love wrought by initiation into the church. The foretime was "Like somebody in a war / with no allegiance." The coming of Christ brings that irreversible allegiance, but it does not erase the effects of sin, for members of the body after baptism remember the fear of days past. God's grace, recognizable with the eyes of faith, finds believers not ignorant, but corporally "amazed and / grateful everyday." The season of Advent is a time to reflect on the old dispensation, on the inexplicability of happenstance that led to this moment, to this Advent, during which the community gives thanks as it considers the end of the world at the final reckoning with Christ's coming.

Those who celebrate in Advent and hear the readings of the season know the debilitating annual rub between U.S. consumerism and Christian faith. Manic shopping and depressing holiday tunes are all around as they yet hear proclaimed the sobering, true, and at times frightening lections about the end of the world and the coming judgment. Yet the season also piques the church to look again for the supreme manifestation of God in the flesh, in the church's memory of Jesus of Nazareth, born in Bethlehem, and the church's celebration of the risen Christ, born in the church assembled and shared in the tangibility of the sacraments. Advent reminds believers of the choice of faith they make from year to year, the choice of this religious tradition over another, of this community of faith over another, of faith over despair, of Birth and Death over indifference and mediocrity. By God's grace, the world is turned, changed by Christ's presence, and in Advent believers can mourn what is left behind with the full knowledge that the changes wrought in Christ's coming makes them "grateful everyday."

As the church waits for Christ in Advent, so believers might recall the words of Walt Whitman as he recounted his state on waiting for the arrival of a friend:[61]

> When I heard at the close of the day how my name had been
>   receiv'd with plaudits in the capitol, still it was not happy
>   night for me that follow'd;
> And else, when I carous'd, or when my plans were accomplish'd,
>   still I was not happy;

---

61. Walt Whitman, "When I Heard at the Close of the Day," *Leaves of Grass* (1891–92), in *Complete Poetry and Collected Prose* (New York: Library of America, 1982): 276.

But the day when I rose at dawn from the bed of perfect health,
    refresh'd, singing, inhaling the ripe breath of autumn,
When I saw the full moon in the west grow pale and disappear
    in the morning light,
When I wander'd alone over the beach, and undressing, bathed,
    laughing with the cool waters, and saw the sun rise,
And when I thought how my dear friend, my lover, was on his
    way coming, O then I was happy.

So with believers: No matter how broken or successful before the coming of Christ into the world and into their lives, their fulfillment comes with the new dispensation found in salvation by their reception and incorporation into the Body of Christ. Before, in the old dispensation, they "wander'd alone over the beach," when, undressing, they chose the cool waters of baptism and "saw the sun rise," anticipating the Advent of Christ, dear friend and lover, who is ever near, ever "on his way coming."

Chapter 3

CHRISTMAS

Critical study of the New Testament after the Enlightenment has yielded many fruits, among them a reconsideration and reconstruction of the origins and sources of the narratives of the life of Jesus. For better or worse, such studies continue to labor at discovering the revelatory truth in the narratives of each Gospel as it might been found within a continuum that extends, on the one side, from the history of the life of the man Jesus of Nazareth, to, on the other, the faith of the late first- and early second-century communities from which the Gospel narratives were born. Contrary to some of its loudest scholars, advocates, and cheerleaders, the historical-Jesus side of the potentially animating tension need not always be set in opposition to the work of theologians, for truths are wrought and apprehended in human life by different media — literary and liturgical, rhetorical and theological — and the complexity of the search for truth is itself a fruit of the tensions of academy and church, or, more broadly, of thought and belief.

A characteristic of early Christian faith that has been illuminated by post-Enlightenment studies is that living communities of faith after the death of Jesus expressed their fear of abandonment and their experiences of the presence of God in a variety of artistic and literary forms, among which was the genre of the infancy narrative. The first two chapters of the Gospels of Matthew and Luke brought the stories of the conception and birth of Jesus, and these evangelists supplied the wonderfully odd and delightfully surprising and prophetic narratives proclaimed in the liturgies of Christmas and its seasons of preparation (Advent) and celebration (the Christmas season, which is observed from the Christmas Vigil to the feast of the Baptism of the Lord, the First Sunday of Ordinary Time).

By the criteria of historical criticism, the infancy narratives have not fared well as biographies or historical testimony to the earliest years of the incarnate Savior; yet by the criteria of theological richness they are among the strongest and most memorable elements of the whole Christian tradition, reflecting truths of the life of faith as intricate as they are compelling.[1] The faith of some has faltered, perhaps, on learning that Bethlehem was chosen by Matthew as the site of the birth because the evangelist wanted to have Jesus born in the city of King David for his Jewish-Christian hearers (Matthew 2:1; Luke 2:4), or that it was logistically impossible for the holy family to have traveled to Egypt in flight from Herod (Matthew 2:13–21). But by the measure of faith, these narratives inspire faith and build up human society by the church's proclamation of the tales and by the engagement of imaginations in the communal acts of worship that flow from the delivery of the narratives. The echo of the proclamations through centuries of faith and conversion is a measure of their truth, which moves people to strength, conversion, and social cohesion, which in turn gradually beget the transformation of the world.

Extremely detailed studies of the historical Jesus, though important in the academy, have not moved people to strength and cohesion as have the simpler stories of shepherds and wise men, of a heavenly choir of angels and unexpected pregnancies in youth and old age, which does not negate the contribution of critical study, but qualifies its efficacy in forming people in faith. The truth of Christian worship — and of the narratives that shape Christmas and its mysteries — is in how well the proclamation of and preaching about the narratives of the Bible prompt people to find God in persons, places, times, and situations where before they had not. Such transformation — in individual lives and in the life of the world outside the community of faith — is the measure for the truth of the narratives as well as of their proclamation in the society of the Christian assembly, however grand or modest. These are narratives of family, courage, trust, and transformation, and as such they have inspired the church from the beginning.

Christmas and Rilke's Letters

The correspondence of Austria-born poet Rainer Maria Rilke (1875–1926), a well-known poet of, primarily, the German language, reveals how deep the stories and symbols of Christmas echoed throughout his life. His references to the feast and how he drew from memories of it are but one example of how much the solemnity engages imaginations and changes people according to their circumstances and experience, which for Rilke reflect some elements of the life of Europe in the first quarter of the twentieth century. His appreciation of the theology and

---

1. See Raymond Brown, *The Birth of the Messiah* (Garden City, NY: Doubleday, 1977): 26–38.

symbols of Christmas and their impact on him through the years of his life can inspire believers to consider the preparation for Christmas and the holy day itself apart from the cultural mania of Christmas that counters so many fundaments of the theology of Christmas.

A formative influence on Rilke's Christmas memories was a result of his visits to Russia just before and just after the turn of the twentieth century. He traveled there with the formidable intellectual and painter Lou Andreas Salomé (1861–1937), his lifelong friend and confidant. For years his end-of-the-year letters to Salomé would refer to "our two Christmases," testifying to the time when they had together witnessed the nativity celebrated in a culture different from their own. In a letter of December 28, 1911 — when he was thirty-six years into his eventual fifty-one years, and about a decade after their trips together to Russia — Rilke wrote to Salomé, "There is a chance at this time that you are at home and have quiet, for it was always so between the two Christmases."[2]

Though his letters do not describe the Russians' liturgical or domestic traditions Rilke and Salomé witnessed in their time in St. Petersburg, his reference to the *two* Christmases was likely referring to the two different calendars kept in Europe at that time: the Gregorian calendar, utilized in most of western Europe at the end of the nineteenth century, and the Julian calendar observed in Russia, which did not adopt the Gregorian calendar until after the Communist Revolution in 1917.[3] The "two" Christmases might also have referred to the two different dates of celebrating Christmas, since the Russian Orthodox Church celebrated (and still celebrates) the birth of Jesus on January 7, not on December 25, as do churches of the Roman Catholic and Protestant traditions. As in Rilke's deep memory of Christmas in Russia, so Christmas in many churches embraces in itself a plenitude of unique traditions from various cultures.

Nature and Christmas

From a theological point of view Rilke's shared memory with his friend indicates the expansiveness of his spirituality and theology of Christmas. In many of his letters he expresses the breadth of his experience of Christmas — the feast tied as it is to the manifestation of the natural world at the end of the old year and beginning of the new year.

2. Rainer Maria Rilke, *The Letters of Rainer Maria Rilke, 1910–1926*, trans. Jane Bannard Greene and M. D. Herter Norton (New York: W. W. Norton, 1947–1948): 32.

3. See Volume 1, Chapter 1, "On God and Time" on Pope Gregory XIII and the Gregorian calendar.

True to the seasonal impetus, Rilke wrote of Christmas with particular attention to the balance of light and night, to the waning of the daylight, to the moon and to the colors in the winter sky.

The natural and cultural backgrounds for his reflections on faith and Christmas were numerous and various, for Rilke traveled widely throughout his life. The body of his correspondence numbers about 11,000 letters, and the addresses from which letters were sent demonstrate how diverse the landscape of his life and his faith experience was: Prague, Munich, Berlin, St. Petersburg, Paris, Rome, Sweden, Copenhagen, Brussels, Zurich, Geneva, Assisi, Naples, Capri, Venice, Vienna, Bohemia, Tunisia, Algiers, Egypt, Toledo (Spain), and many letters from the Duino Castle in Austria, where he wrote one of his most widely known works, the *Duino Elegies*. This litany of place-names stirs up many moments in the history of the Christian tradition and its worship and thereby helps one over a century later appreciate the richness of his reflections on Christian faith. Quite a number of the places above were sites for his experience of Christmas, and the interaction of faith and nature was ever part of his perspective.

In one of his earliest letters, written when he was just twenty-six, he says, "I feel Christmassy," and then relates the feast to nature as he mentions to his correspondent "the new things and possessions that come to you, as the light of the sun repeats itself over every new little child that was born in the night."[4] A few years later, writing from the Italian island Capri to his wife, Clara (1878–1954), a sculptor and student of Auguste Rodin — to whom he wrote frequently and almost every year reflected on the celebration of Christmas — he described Christmas's "winter light with its entirely new order, with its impatience, its anticipation strained to the limit, which through the little, momentary and tangible fulfillments grew to ever stronger tension."[5] Still a few years later, writing to Clara from North Africa, he observed that here "Christmas is not so unthinkable at all. But even in the morning I am astonished again and again at what the sun accomplishes as it reaches in through the tattered covering of the souks,[6] how, falling here and there, it makes a green transparent, a red hot, a mauve give itself infinitely."[7] The origins of the feast, in the fourth century, show how, in the northern hemisphere, the shrinking light of

---

4. *The Letters of Rainer Maria Rilke, 1892–1910,/* trans. Jane Bannard Greene and M. D. Herter Norton (New York: W. W. Norton, 1947–1948): 54.

5. Ibid.: 250.

6. Souks are Arab market stands.

7. *The Letters of Rainer Maria Rilke, 1910–1926:* 20.

December contributed to what gave the nativity its place in the calendar. The poet's reflections on the light of the time of the year supports the church's intuition in this regard, for nearly all of his reflections on Christmas describe how the changing light was manifested at the time of the celebration.

The Consolation of Christmas

Rilke's Christmas can inspire Christians about the significance of the feast in times of trouble, for today the consumer culture feigns the Christmas mystery as comprised only of smiles and glee, of ease and happy endings. Yet the infancy narratives proclaimed in its season are foreign to this aberrant and exuberant theology of the feast, and Rilke's theology of Christmas is truer to the faith of the church than the mania of the market. His insight in finding Christmas to be a consolation in the midst of strife and hardship is related to his familiarity with death and his philosophy that life and death are one, as he wrote to Countess Margot Sizzo on the feast of Epiphany just two years before his death (in 1923):

> One should not fear that our strength might not suffice to bear any experience of death, even were it the nearest and the most terrible; death is not beyond our strength; it is the measure mark at the vessel's rim: we are *full* as often as we reach it —, and being full means (for us) being heavy...that is all. — I will not say that one should *love* death; but one should love life so magnanimously, so without calculation and selection that spontaneously one constantly includes with it and loves death too (life's averted half), — which is in fact what happens also, irresistibly and illimitably, in all great impulses of love![8]

This issue of the proximity of birth and death in Rilke's theology is one of the anthems of his Christmas missives, a corrective to the merely exuberant Christmas joy that so often eviscerates the church's celebration of the solemnity in cultures of consumption.

The two particular times of Rilke's life when he described how Christmas had buoyed him up through grim times were during his miserable years at a military boarding school in his youth, and in his later years after he had witnessed the ravages of the First World War. His wife would have known of his difficulties in school only by his later

---

8. Ibid.: 316.

accounts of them, but they were clearly among the worst days of his whole life. Before his birth, Rilke's parents had a daughter whose early death came as a tremendous blow. When their son came along, they called him Sophia and dressed him in girls' clothes until he was five years of age. Added to that complexity of his childhood, his father, a military officer, tried to toughen up the son by having him lift weights and play with toy soldiers. Then, much against the boy's protests and even after the parents' marriage had ended, the father forced the son at age nine to go away to a military boarding school.

Yet, reflecting back on Christmas in the misery of those days, he wrote to his wife, Clara, from Italy, "You know...what Christmas was to me in my early childhood; even when the military academy made a hard, unbelievably malicious life, devoid of wonders, appear so real that no other reality seemed possible to me beside that undeserved one; even then Christmas was still real and was that which approached with a fulfillment that went out beyond all wishes."[9] Rilke would take from his experience and comb out what would be a consolation to another, as he did in giving advice from Rome to a young poet just two days before Christmas in 1903. The poet was in the military, and Rilke offered him support in a time of difficulty:

My dear Mr. Kappus,

You shall not be without a greeting from me when Christmas comes and when you, in the midst of the holiday, are bearing your solitude more heavily than usual.... If it frightens and torments you to think of childhood and of the simplicity and silence that accompanies it, because you can no longer believe in God, who appears in it everywhere, then ask yourself, dear Mr. Kappus, whether you have really lost God. Isn't it much truer to say that you have never yet possessed him? For when could that have been? Do you think that a child can hold him, him whom grown men bear only with great effort and whose weight crushes the old?...

Why don't you think of God as the one who is coming, who has been approaching from all eternity, the one who will someday arrive, the ultimate fruit of a tree whose leaves we are? What keeps you from projecting his birth into the ages that are coming into existence, and living your life as a painful and lovely day in the history of a great pregnancy? Don't you see how everything

---

9. Ibid.: 249.

that happens is again and again a beginning, and couldn't it be His beginning, since, in itself, starting is always so beautiful? . . .

Dear Mr. Kappus, celebrate Christmas in this devout feeling, that perhaps He needs this very anguish of yours in order to begin; these very days of your transition are perhaps the time when everything in you is working at Him, as you once worked at Him in your childhood, breathlessly. Be patient and without bitterness, and realize that the least we can do is to make coming into existence no more difficult for God than the earth does for spring when it wants to come.[10]

Rilke had fond memories of how the mystery of Christmas had brightened his life in the dark days of his childhood in a military school, and yet without resentment he hands on the gift of Christmas to another writer, consoling a young poet who ached in the military, constrained from fulfilling his poetic ambitions as Rilke himself had been in his youth.

The other period when Christmas supplied consolation in a time of trouble was not personal but political and social, in the context of the First World War and its aftermath. A week before Christmas in 1920, Rilke wrote to his mother, reflecting on what Christmas brings "after such bad times," the darkness and exigencies of war and bloodshed:

My dear Mama. . . . Now it is a matter not of *reading*, but of *going-into-oneself* and, into one's own heart, for the year's holiest hour of celebration, preparing the manger, so that therein, this hour, and in it the Savior, may with all fervor be born into the world again!

What I wish for you, dear Mama, is that on this evening of consecration, the remembrance of all distress, even the consciousness of the immediate worry and insecurity of existence may be quite checked and in a sense dissolved in the innermost knowledge of that grace, for which indeed no time is too dense with calamity and no anxiety so sealed that in *its own* time — which is *not* ours! — it could not enter and penetrate what seems insurmountable with its mild victory. There is no moment in the long year when one would be able to call so vividly into one's soul its ever possible appearance and then omnipresence, as this winter night, autonomous through the centuries, which, through

---

10. Letter Six from Rilke to Franz Xaver Kappus, trans. M. D. Herder, in *Letters to a Young Poet* (New York: W. W. Norton, 1962): 45–51.

the incomparable coming of that child who transformed all crea-
tures, all at once outweighed and surpassed in value the sum of
all other earthly rights.[11]

So for Rilke, as for fervent and sober Christians at Christmas in all
times, the solemnity does not numb one against life's difficulties and
hardship, but rather provides a backdrop for remembering and celebrating the birth of God's Son in the midst of such calamity and angst. As
for Rilke, Christmas is that

> outwardly unassuming, even poor night that suddenly stands
> open toward the inside, like an all-embracing and warming heart,
> which — with beats of its own bell-toned center — really does
> reply to our hearkening into the innermost cell.
>
> All annunciations of previous times did not suffice to herald
> this night, all hymns that have been sung in its praise did not
> come near the stillness and eagerness in which the shepherds
> and kings knelt down, just as we too, none of us, has ever been
> able, while this miracle-night was befalling him, to indicate the
> measure of his experience.[12]

In closing the letter to his mother, he called Christmas "the night of
radiant depth unfolded." "For you, dear Mama, may it be hallowed and
blessed. Amen. — René." He signed it not Rainer, but with his original given name, René, a reminder of the complexities and hardships
of the life he received, soon after the death of his sister, and against
which the brightness of his Christmas remembrances and celebrations
shines as inspiration for those who consider the history and meaning
of Christmas today.

Christmas as Sacrament and Memory?

Within the first century of Christmas's emergence in Rome, a certain
Januarius inquired of St. Augustine regarding the date of Christ's birth.
Augustine responded by letter (ca. 400), considering the "sacramental
character" of "the day of the Lord's birth." As Augustine recorded it,
Januarius had asked, "Why is it that the annual commemoration of
the Lord's Passion does not come around on the same day of the year,
as does the day on which he is said to have been born?" "Here you
must know," the bishop responded, "that the day of the Lord's birth
does not possess a sacramental character, but it is only a recalling of
the fact that he was born, and so it was only necessary to mark the

---

11. *The Letters of Rainer Maria Rilke, 1910–1926:* 237–238.
12. Ibid.: 238.

day of the year." Augustine's liturgical theology here distinguishes this Christmas "recalling" from the way

> we celebrate Easter, so as not only to call to mind what happened — that is, that Christ died and rose again — but we do not pass over the things about him which bear witness to the significance of the sacraments.[13]

The recalling of the day of Jesus' birth, then, did not for Augustine make the mystery of salvation present for the assembly,[14] quite dissimilar for him from the Three Days of Easter that happened in the spring as the church celebrated the mystery of human salvation wrought both in the life of Jesus of Nazareth and in the paschal font.

Yet this theological understanding of the celebration of Jesus' birth as merely a memorial was not universal. In fact, one can find in the sermons of Pope Leo the Great — bishop of Rome, 440–461, only a half-century after Augustine — a theology in which the sacrament of salvation was clearly one with the celebration of the nativity. Leo's Christmas sermons indeed bear a deep paschal theology. Leo made frequent links between the annual nativity feast and the celebration of Christian baptism, such as the one he made in the Christmas sermon of the year 450:

> That infancy, which the majesty of God's Son did not scorn, was eventually brought to perfect manhood with the increase of age. When the triumph of his Passion and Resurrection had been brought to completion, all the activities of the lowliness he had undertaken for our sake passed away. Today's feast, nevertheless, renews for us the sacred beginnings of Jesus' Birth from the Virgin Mary. As we worship the Birth of our Savior, we find ourselves celebrating our own origin as well. For the Conception of Christ is the origin of the Christian people, and the birthday of the Head is the birthday of the body.
>
> All of the elect have their own special place, and the Church's children are set off from one another by the passage of time. Yet all of us, the whole sum of believers who have sprung from the baptismal font, just as we have been crucified with Christ in his Passion, been raised with him in his Resurrection, and been set

---

13. Augustine, *Letters*, trans. Sister Wilfrid Parsons (New York: Fathers of the Church, 1951): 260–261.

14. P. Jounel, "The Year" in *Liturgy and Time*, The Church at Prayer, volume 4, ed. A. G. Martimort et al. (Collegeville, MN: Liturgical Press, 1986): 77–86.

at the right hand of the Father in the Ascension, so too have we been born along with him in his Nativity.[15]

This theological spectrum — on the cusp of late antiquity and the early Middle Ages — regarding how the celebration of the birth of Christ participates in the paschal mystery (or not) was likely to be a major factor in the development of the solemnity throughout the Middle Ages, so the poles of Christmas' celebration as memorial (Augustine) or as sacrament (Leo) and the span between these are necessary to bear in mind in studying the emergence and development of Christmas.

In this chapter three parts will follow:

1. The History of Christmas
2. Christmas and Society
3. The Theology of Christmas

Part One:
The History of Christmas

The Origins of Christmas

The celebration of Christmas is a major part of winter in North American culture. The birth of Jesus was a narrative so strong that it grew to be deeply embedded in the tradition, extending back to the earliest days of the Christian faith, at least as far back as the writing of the infancy narratives of the New Testament, in Matthew and Luke, written at the end of the first century. But the birth of the child, the story of that birth in the New Testament, and consensus on a date when that story would be remembered are three separate moments in the tradition.

The date of December 25 for the feast did not emerge in the Christian tradition until the fourth century, and it was not universally received right after the first evidence for the feast in Rome. Some churches of the Eastern traditions still resist the date and maintain January 6 (or January 7) as the date for the nativity, which is as likely an issue of ecclesiology as of calendar.[16] Even in the Latin tradition there were some churches in late antiquity and in Protestant Europe that did not find the celebration of Christmas fitting to the faith. When

---

15. St. Leo the Great, *Sermons*, trans. Jane Patricia Freeland and Agnes Josephine Conway, FC 93 (Washington, DC: Catholic University of America, 1996): 76–131.

16. See Volume 1, Chapter 1, "On God and Time," for the interaction of time-keeping and belief.

Puritanism ruled in England, in the middle of the seventeenth century, Christmas was abolished,[17] and, on the other side of the Atlantic, Christmas was not part of the expression of religious freedom sought in the United States by the pilgrims who migrated there in the seventeenth century.[18] Celebrating Christmas in the United States was still illegal in some places until as late as the nineteenth century.

Scholars, historians, and theologians have tried strenuously — some too much — to find evidence for Christmas in the earliest three centuries of the church, but the earliest firm datum for the feast of the birth of the Savior on December 25 is from a Chronograph (or list of dates) of 354 A.D.; the list itself contains the dates of the anniversaries of various martyrs, *depositio martyrum*, and this list contains the abbreviated Latin phrase: *VIII Kal. Ianuarii natus Christus in Bethleem Iudeae*, "On the eighth kalends of January [December 25] Christ was born in Bethlehem of Judea." As one examines the names added to the list over the years in the second quarter of the fourth century, the list of martyrs appears to have been composed in 336, so the celebration of Christmas in at least one of the churches of the city of Rome has origins from at least that year. But one church in one city is a modest beginning, for it would be four, five, or six decades after 336 until there is any reliable evidence of Christmas outside of Rome.

The theological climate of the period needs to be kept in mind as one considers the emergence of Christmas in Rome at the beginning of the fourth century. The raging theological debate throughout the fourth century was about the relationship of God the Father and his Son, Jesus Christ, about whether they were equal or not. The crisis was pressed on the church by the presence of the Arians, who are usually portrayed retrospectively — and erroneously — as enemies of the true or orthodox church. But the documentation from the time of the crisis reveals that there was no clear winner when the christological debates raged, and there was no clear Christology that was obviously correct or orthodox.

What became the theologically orthodox faith — led in the East by Athanasius of Alexandria, and in the West by Ambrose of Milan — sought to preserve the unity of the Father and the Son, while the Arians sought to preserve the unity of the Son and humanity. The Arians argued for the Son's beginning in time not because their goal was to

---

17. Clement A. Miles, *Christmas Customs and Traditions: Their History and Significance* (New York: Dover, 1976), reprint of *Christmas in Ritual and Tradition, Christian and Pagan* (T. Fisher Unwin, 1912): 182–186.

18. Ibid.

perniciously demote the Son's divinity, but because they wanted to preserve the salvation the Son gained and shared with all other created things, all of which have a beginning in time, and so the Arians predicated such a beginning on the Son as well. The Arian slogan, "There was a time when the Son was not" — that is, there had been a time when the Son did not exist — preserved an important anthropological datum regarding all other human life: that it has a start.

The theological context is important in considering the origins of Christmas because the early rhetoric of the feast faced the simultaneous challenge of introducing a feast in which the Son is portrayed as a weak, vulnerable infant swaddled and laid in an animal feeding trough, on the one hand, and, on the other, a theology in which — for those opposing the Arians — the Son was portrayed as "one in being with the Father," in which he is eternal, omnipresent, omniscient, and omnipotent. Sermons from the period bear witness that the narratives of Christmas from Matthew and Luke were awkwardly proclaimed and preached about in the fourth century, during which the anti-Arian bishops at the Council of Nicea had defined the Son as *homoousious*, as having the "same being" or same essence (*ousia*), as God the Father. The position of the Arians would have been as strengthened by the portrayal of the Son as a vulnerable infant as the anti-Arian position would have been weakened by such a portrayal.

What I suggest, then, is contrary to the arguments of more than a few historians of the calendar, for example, liturgical-year historian Adolf Adam, who wrote about the origins of Christmas that

> the new feast had spread with astonishing rapidity throughout the West and in many of the Eastern Churches before the fourth century was over. The reason is probably that the struggle against the Arian heresy focused greater attention on the person, and not simply the work, of the God-man, and that a feast of Christ's birth would give a suitable liturgical expression to the profession of faith drawn up at Nicea, the Council which condemned the Arian heresy in 325.[19]

Others have proposed similar suggestions about the rapidity of the spread of the date of Christmas, but the evidence does not support this conclusion. While the feast did indeed spread quickly at the start of the fifth century, one is hard-pressed to find sure evidence for its spread outside Rome before the end of the fourth century, though both Adam

---

19. Adolf Adam, *The Liturgical Year: Its History and Its Meaning After the Reform of the Liturgy,* trans. Matthew J. O'Connell, (New York: Pueblo, 1981): 124.

and Thomas Talley have argued for widespread reception of Christmas in the middle of the fourth century, to which this chapter will return.[20] Rather than demonstrating an "astonishing rapidity" for the spread of Christmas, as Adam did, it is clear that there was considerable and protracted resistance to receiving Christmas in any church outside of Rome for about a half-century because, I am arguing, the narrative of Christmas was so contrary to the Christology of anti-Arian theology of the Son as "one in being with the Father."

Adam also asserted above "that a feast of Christ's birth would give a suitable liturgical expression to the profession of faith drawn up at Nicea," but this is contrary to the high theological aims of the anti-Arian agenda, which drew up a supremely lofty, celestial, other-worldly portrait of the Son. Against the low Christology of the Arians, the anti-Arians asserted an extremely high Christology.[21] The introduction of Christmas and its narratives from Matthew and Luke would not have supported such a high Christology but would rather have bolstered a low Christology in which the Son is portrayed as an infant.

Why December 25?

The birth of Jesus was not at first celebrated on December 25, and there had been other dates when the event was celebrated in the first few centuries, before the general shape of the Christian year was standardized — at least in the Roman tradition — in the fourth and fifth centuries. For, unlike the narratives of the death and resurrection of Jesus, set on or near the observance of Passover, the Gospels lend no clues or indications regarding the date of his birth.

Though a great deal has been written about the origins of Christmas, and many speculations and hypotheses put forth as facts, the concrete evidence supporting them is simply not dependable as referring to December 25. In the studies of the development of the liturgical year, two hypotheses predominate regarding when, why, and how the date December 25 was established for commemorating and celebrating Jesus' birth. Each hypothesis is presented below with a description of factors contributing to the emergence of the feast and of those who support the one hypothesis over its alternative. There has been some deliberation about the reception of each hypothesis in the academy of liturgical studies for over a century.

---

20. The early evidence for Christmas outside of Rome is laid out in Martin Connell, "When Did Ambrose's Sister Become a Virgin? December 25 or January 6?" *Studia Liturgica* 24, no. 2 (1999): 145–158.

21. This is argued at length in Volume 2, Chapter 3, "The Three Days."

History-of-Religions Hypothesis. The first hypothesis for explaining the origins of December 25 as the date of the birth of Jesus derives from the circumstances of a feast of the Roman Empire. In the year 274 the Roman emperor Aurelian (214–275, reign 270–275) established a feast celebrating the Syrian sun-god Emesa, and titled it *Dies Natalis Soli Invicti,* the "Birthday of the Unconquered Sun." December 25 was the date chosen because it approximately coincided with the time of the winter solstice, the time of the year with the shortest days (in the northern hemisphere) and therefore a time to remember that the sun would be "unconquered" and born again in the lengthening of the daylight. For the emperor, the establishment of the festival was an attempt to unite the empire, bringing a feast of the Syrian tradition to the Roman Empire at large.

It is thought that Christianity adopted this pagan chronology as a way of drawing on the success of the pagan feast to bring pagans from their religious practice to Christianity. The emperor Aurelian's effort was still about a half-century before Christianity would gain legal status under the emperor Constantine, but as Christianity began to rise to prominence, Christian church leaders sought to drawn pagans away from their ritual and calendrical traditions. This theory is called "history of religions" as it depends on the historical intersection of the Christian cult of Jesus' birth and the pagan cult of *sol invictus.*

Such adoptions of pagan ritual traditions were not as unlikely as one might think, for there are extant sermons of the fourth century that show how the fathers sought to interpret the pagan polytheistic zodiac with images from the life of Jesus or with typological precedents for his life in the Old Testament. Consider, for example, this from a sermon of Zeno of Verona, of the mid-fourth century:

> I recognize your curiosity. Because of the habit of your earlier life, which is no longer beneficial for you, perhaps you also need to know from us under which of the many and different signs your mother gave birth to you. As is done for babies, so will I explain to you briefly all the mysteries of your sacred horoscope. This is your beginning, brothers, for you were welcomed not by the Ram [Aries, the first sign of the zodiac], but by the Lamb who does not turn away from anyone who believes in him. He clothes your nakedness with the snowy whiteness of his garment, and bountifully pours his blessed milk on the lips that opened when you cried.[22]

---

22. Tractatus I, 38, *Tractatus de Duodecim Signis ad Neophytos,* ed. B. Löfstedt CCSL 22 (Turnholt: Brepols, 1971): 105–106, trans. Connell; for a study of the tract, see Wolfgang

The bishop continues through the pagan calendar with its signs, but clearly not all of the signs were easily adopted for Christian interpretation, as when he gets to Saggitarius: "No one will have to be afraid of the fierce Archer, armed with red-hot arrows, who at any moment will bring terror to the hearts of the whole human race!"

As Zeno and others played with the zodiac as a way of gaining pagans into the church's fold, so too they adopted the sun imagery of the pagan feast in December and applied it to the birth of Jesus Christ, the new unconquered sun, as in this passage from the same Zeno of Verona:

> Here is our God, the coeternal Son of the eternal God. He is both human and God, for he stands between the Father and humanity, proving the flesh by his infirmities and proving majesty by his strengths. He is our sun, the true sun, who with the fullness of its clarity inflames and joins the bright fires of the world and of the shining stars of the sky.[23]

Zeno's episcopate in Verona came just a short time after the emperor Julian the Apostate (reign 361–363) tried to abandon the empire's link with Christianity, and one of his efforts in this regard was to speak of the sun itself as the divine Word, drawing power from the theology in John's Gospel of Christ as the Word. So the fathers of the church linked Christmas and the sun perhaps as a way of reversing the anti-Christian effort of the short-lived apostasy under Julian.

Unlike the image of a vulnerable infant burbling in Bethlehem, that of the sun was powerful and commanding for preachers and believers. So even as Christmas was introduced to churches outside of Rome at the beginning of the fifth century, the cult of the sun provided the opportunity for anti-Arian church fathers to wax about the birth feast in balance with the regality of the Son, as in the rhetoric of Maximus of Turin on Christmas:

> While the world dreads having its course come to an end because of the shortness of the hours in the day, it shows by its hope that the year is about to be formed anew. This anticipation on the part of creation, then, also persuades us to anticipate that the new sun, the risen Christ, may cast light upon the darkness of

---

Hübner, "Das Horoskop der Christen (Zeno 1,28 L.)," *Vigiliae Christianae* 29 (1975): 120–137.

23. Tractatus II, 12, *De nativitate domini et maiestate*, CCSL 22:185–186; trans. Connell.

our sins, and that by the power of His birth the sun of justice may scatter the protracted gloom of sin in us.[24]

Calculation Hypothesis. The date of the birth of Jesus clearly was not a concern for believers in the earliest period of church history, as the New Testament gives no indications in this regard. Only in the late third and early fourth centuries did Christians begin to be concerned with plotting out the times and places of the life of the incarnate Son of God. Primary among these were the place and date of his birth.

The Calculation Hypothesis dominated the field of the study of the origins of Christmas in the middle of the twentieth century, particularly after the publication of a critical study by Bernard Botte, OSB, *On the Origins of Christmas and Epiphany.* Botte's study provided an appendix that included a sermon supporting the history-of-religions theory, entitled "On the Solstices and Equinoxes of the Conceptions and Births of our Lord Jesus Christ and John the Baptist."

Botte's publication of the Latin sermon in the appendix of his work was, as he candidly confesses in the study, not an exhaustive critical edition, but a version published based on only three manuscripts and three printed editions of the sermon. The manuscripts were from the ninth century (Berlin), tenth century (Brussels), and fifteenth century (also Brussells), and the printed editions were all from the middle of the sixteenth century. With two other scholars of the liturgical year, D. Wilmart and H. Lietzmann, Botte argued that the sermon was of Roman provenance and from the early part of the fourth century or, as Wilmart argued in particular, from the late third century. They seem to have rightly supposed that the sermon was preached when the feast of Christmas had not yet been instituted on December 25. Though others argued that the sermon was merely a Latin translation of a sermon originally in Syriac, the consensus of these three was that it was of North African provenance, where Latin was the language, though preached or written by someone who was familiar with Syriac or with Syrian Christian traditions and scripture.

The Syrian element comes mostly as a result of the appearance of a curious Latin phrase used by the Latin writer to translate a familiar word of New Testament Greek. The curious translation is from the Lukan story of the angel's greeting to Mary at the annunciation. In New Testament Greek the greeting is *chairé,* or "rejoice." In this sermon the Latin renders this phrase as *Pax tecum,* "Peace [be] with you,"

---

24. Sermo 61a.1, CCSL 23, ed. Almut Mutzenbecher (Turnholt: Brepols, 1962): 249; English translation: *The Sermons of St. Maximus of Turin,* trans. and notes Boniface Ramsey, ACW 50 (New York: Newman, 1989): 150.

which is much closer to *schlom lek,* or "peace to you," from the Syriac New Testament, know as the Peshitta. The preacher argues in the sermon that it was by divine providence that the conceptions and births of John and Jesus coincided with the cosmic events of the solstice and equinox, and he presses the point with a complex concatenation of quotes from the Old and New Testaments.

Although the sermon is too long to supply in full, its content is relevant enough to the origins of the date of Christmas to warrant translation of a few extended excerpts:

> He [Christ] is our light and the true light that coming into this world lights up our hearts.... This is called the birth of the Unconquered [Sun]. Could anyone else be this but our Lord who conquered death? Or what they say of the birth of the sun, he is the sun of justice, about which the prophet Malachi spoke: "unto you that fear my name the Sun of justice shall arise, and [there is] health in his wings" [Malachi 4:2a].[25]

> If he is the beginning of the year [in March], then we ought to count June as the fourth month, September as the seventh, and December as the tenth. The Lord himself spoke to Moses about these: "Three times every year you shall celebrate feast to me" [Exodus 23:14]. To these he added about the fourth month, saying: "Thou shalt keep the feast of unleavened bread. Seven days shalt thou eat unleavened bread, as I commanded thee, in the time of the month of new corn" [Exodus 23:15; 34:18].

> These are the months in which our Lord and John the Baptist were conceived and born, that is, in the four seasons, that is in spring and summer and fall and winter, by which the turning (or changing) of the year is known. And so did the prophet say: "the acceptable year of the Lord" [Isaiah 61:2].[26]

---

25. Ipse enim est lux nostra et vera lux qui veniens in hunc mundum inluminavit corda nostra. [lines 25–26] Sed et invicti natalem appellant. Quis utique tam invitus nisi dominus noster qui mortem subactam devicit? Vel quod dicant solis esse natalem ipse est sol iustitiae de quo malachias propheta dixit: *Orietur vobis timentibus nomen ipsius sol iustitiae et sanitas est in pennis eius* [Malachi 4:2a]. After each of the Latin citations there are the lines from the Botte edition, here lines 434–439.

These excerpts are important because the history-of-religions and calculation hypotheses are not mutually exclusive, as most historians of the calendar have suggested. In this sermon on the calculations, the theology of Christ, the "shining light," is clear.

English translation of the Latin from *The Holy Bible,* Old Testament in the Douay-Challoner Text, New Testament and Psalms in the Confraternity Text, ed. John P. O'Connell (Chicago: The Catholic Press, 1950).

26. Quod si ergo ipse est initium anni, iam utique ab ipso quartum mensem iunium numeraremus et septimum septembrem et decimum decembrem, de quibus dominus ad

Therefore it was, as we said, when this angel announced to Mary on March 25, which was also the day of the equinox and the appearance of the light. For our Lord was conceived on eighth kalends of April [March 25], in the month of March, which is the day of the Lord's passion and his conception. For on this day he was conceived and on the same day he suffered.[27]

The Lord was born in the month of December, in winter, on the eighth kalends of January [December 25], when the mature olives are pressed so that unction — that is, chrism — is born, by which the grains are combined with the herbs, when they are born with oil by fire, and the twigs of the vine are cut off with the blades so that the must of sweetness is brought, by which the apostles were drunk by the Holy Spirit.[28]

The birth of John the Baptist is celebrated still as a solemnity in the Roman Catholic tradition at the time of the summer solstice, June 24, a half-year from the solemnity of the birth of Christ, December 25. Before the reform of the liturgical year after Vatican II, the feast of the conception of John the Baptist had been celebrated on September 24. Because the Gospel of Luke says that Jesus and John were conceived six months apart from one another (1:26), mathematics prompted the church to see the fourth part of this configuration in the date of the conception of Jesus, March 25, near the spring equinox. (For Jesus, as for many great leaders of the ancient world, confirmation for the importance of their conceptions, births, and deaths was sometimes found in the positions of the sun, moon, and planets.) In the Roman Catholic church this date still marks the conception of Jesus in the womb

moysen dicit: *Tribus temporibus diem festum agetis mihi.* [Exodus 23:14] Quibus et quartum adiunxit dicendo: *Et diem festum azimorum custodietis; septem diebus manducabitis azima sicut praecepi tibi in tempore mensis novorum.* [Exodus 23:15; 34:18]

Hi sunt menses in quibus dominus noster et iohannes baptista concepti et nati sunt, istis quattuor temporibus, id est verno et aestate et autumno et hieme per quae annus vertens cognoscitur. Et ideo propheta dicit: *Annum acceptabilem domini.* [Isaiah 61:2] [Botte edition, lines 81–93]

27. Fuit igitur ut diximus quando haec angelus ad mariam adnuntiavit octavo kalendas aprilis qui et ipse dies aequinoctialis ad inchoationem lucis. . . . [Botte, lines 222–224] Conceptus est ergo dominus noster octavo kalendas aprilis mense martio quis est dies paschae passionis domini et conceptionis eius. In qua enim die conceptus est in eadem et passus est. [Botte, lines 230–233]

28. Sed et dominus nascitur mense decembri hiemis tempore octavo kalendas ianuarias quando oleae maturae premuntur ut unctio, id est, crisma nascatur, quo seges ab herbis extraneis seritur, cum agni balantes nascuntur, vineae falcibus sarmenta amputantur ut mustum suavitudinis adferant ex quo inebriati sunt apostoli sancto spiritu. [Botte, lines 421–432]

of Mary, a feast that is known by some churches as the Annunciation (when the angel "announces" the news of the extraordinary conception to Mary) and by others as the feast of the Incarnation (when the Son takes flesh). In fact, the March 25 date of the Solemnity of the Annunciation contains an ancient remnant of the Quartodecimans,[29] those early believers who maintained a *date* for Easter each year instead of moving it to a Sunday. Then, the events of Jesus' conception and death were thought to have been coincident in the year, and March 25 bears the remnant of those early centuries when Easter itself was on a date rather than on a Sunday. The complexity of the jumble of dates helps explain why this second theory about the origins of Christmas is called the calculation hypothesis, for the dates of the conceptions and births of John the Baptist and Jesus were calculated to be coincident with the astronomical exigencies of the skies, at least as these would have been known in antiquity.

The liturgies of Christmas do not highlight the childhood and family relationship of Jesus and John the Baptist as the sermon in Botte's research does. Yet the readings of the Advent season, particularly in the last days leading up to Christmas, do make explicit this familial and temporal relationship between the two infants and two preachers of repentance, John the Baptist and Jesus of Nazareth.

The research of Thomas Talley on the origins of the liturgical year revived interest in the Calculation Hypothesis, which had begun to wane after Botte published the sermon with its references to solstices and equinoxes.

The Origins of Christmas in the Work of Thomas Talley

Many scholars of the liturgical year have supposed that the church of Rome's date of the nativity, December 25, was readily received by churches of the West, with a few exceptions in Spain and perhaps Gaul. In the rhetoric of a recent historian:

> Because of its antiquity and its presence in the capital of the now Christian empire, the Roman church often influenced other churches, although in varying degrees. The churches in the western, mostly Latin-speaking part of the empire generally followed Rome. The churches in the eastern, mostly Greek-speaking areas followed their own traditions, although they maintained regular

---

29. On the Quartodecimans and the Quartodeciman Controversy of the date of Easter, see Volume 2, Chapter 3, "Three Days."

and fraternal contact with Rome. Most Eastern churches cele-brated the feast [commemorating the birth of Christ] on January 6 in its Epiphany form and were hesitant about the Roman dating.[30]

Yet few churches of the Latin West accepted Rome's nativity dating after its earliest appearance in Rome. It is hard to know to what church the author refers when he writes that "churches in the western, mostly Latin-speaking part of the empire generally followed Rome." This was not accepted by other churches until close to the end of the fourth century, not soon after 336, when the Roman evidence of Christmas appears.

Suppositions about Christmas's origins are more troublesome in the work of Thomas Talley. Talley turned to a sermon on Epiphany that Augustine (354–430) delivered against the Donatists, in which the African bishop preached:

> With good reason have the heretical Donatists never wished to celebrate this day with us: they neither love unity, nor are they in communion with the Eastern Church where that star appeared. Let us, however, celebrate the Manifestation of our Lord and Sav-ior Jesus Christ on which He harvested the first fruits of the Gentiles, in the unity of the Gentiles.[31]

Talley moved from this *Epiphany* sermon to claim that "Augustine makes no similar claim against the Donatists with regard to Christ-mas, however, neither in that sermon nor in any other, a peculiar circumstance given the greater importance of the nativity itself."[32] This conclusion is unwarranted, for there is no evidence for "the greater importance of the nativity itself." Based on the time of greatest fer-vor about the Donatist debate in North Africa, Talley retrojects his hypothesis about the early celebration of Christmas to the start of the fourth century, but he offers no reliable evidence that any church, even Rome, was celebrating the nativity on December 25 at the time. His argument here, as elsewhere, is built up from an absence of evidence rather than from any extant data.

Talley continued to nudge the date of Christmas's appearance still further back in history: "Since in North Africa as at Rome it seems certain that Christmas was established before the Epiphany, one is

30. Joseph F. Kelly, *The Origins of Christmas* (Collegeville, MN: Liturgical Press, 2004): 69.

31. Sermon 202, as in *St. Augustine: Sermons for Christmas and Epiphany*, Ancient Chris-tian Writers volume 15, trans. Thomas Comerford Lawler (Westminster, MD: Newman, 1952): 170.

32. Thomas Talley, *The Origins of the Liturgical Year* (Collegeville, MN: Pueblo, 1991): 87.

left with the strong sense that the Donatists did celebrate Christmas. In such a case, that festival must antedate the Donatist schism, and the date of its establishment would thus be earlier than 311."[33] The "strong sense" becomes even stronger (yet still based on the absence of evidence) as he moved further back and suggested that his is a rather sober assessment of an early date for Christmas because, he argues, "some have supposed that its observance could date from as early as 300 or even earlier and that the place of the origin of the festival could well have been North Africa, rather than Rome as has most commonly been presumed."[34] I do not contest the possibility that the place of Christmas's origin might have been Rome or North Africa; what I contest is pushing back the date of its appearance far beyond what the evidence permits.

The date of the year 311 was not yet earlier enough, for Talley moved even earlier when he cited a sermon of North African provenance from the year 243 on figuring out the date of Easter, *De pascha computus*. Because that sermon did not refer to Christmas, Talley concludes that 243 would be the earliest date for the origins of Christmas, with 311 being the latest date.[35] Although Talley's argument is filled with a flurry of facts and data from late antiquity and from scholarly works about late antiquity, the sober fact remains that he settled on the span of years 243–311 for the emergence of Christmas in North Africa even though there is not a shred of evidence to support this, only the absence of evidence in sermons where Talley supposed it should have been. As a result of the juggling of data, Talley suggested that Christmas might have emerged as early as the middle of the third century, even though there is no evidence for Christmas outside of Rome until at least 370 or 375, well over a century later than the years Talley posited.

The manipulation of the evidence did not stop with adding it where it was not warranted, for his argument also ignored or cast aside evidence that suggested that Christmas was not yet being celebrated in the late fourth century. When writing about the Council of Saragossa's canon prescribing three weeks of asceticism in anticipation of Epiphany — that is, from December 17 until January 6, with no mention whatsoever of Christmas — Talley argued that "the three-week period mentioned there was not simply oriented toward Epiphany, but included Christmas," even though Christmas is never mentioned in the

---

33. Ibid.: 87. The context of the rhetoric seems to indicate that possessive pronoun "its" refers to Christmas rather than to the schism, as the grammar would indicate.

34. Ibid.: 87.

35. Ibid.: 91.

canons of the council.[36] As with the North African evidence, Talley cited no evidence to support his inclusion of Christmas in the three-week period when the very existence of the three-week period does the very opposite, that is, confirms that Christmas had not yet been received by the church of Spain in 380.[37]

Christmas in Late Antiquity and the Early Middle Ages

Overlooked much of the time in considering the Roman origins and hegemony with regard to the date of Christmas is the rising prominence of the church of Rome and its bishops in the fourth, fifth, and sixth centuries. When Christmas first appeared in Rome, its church did not have the influence that it soon would gain with support from the empire. One indication of the circumspection that other churches maintained regarding the church in Rome is the long resistance to Christmas throughout most of the fourth century, not only in the East, but in Latin Christianity as well.

At the time of the first firm evidence of December 25 as the date for the anniversary of the birth of Jesus in the church at Rome, far more widespread was the date of January 6 for marking the date of the birth elsewhere. How could it have happened, then, that the nascent Roman calendrical configuration came to displace the earlier and more commonly observed practice? The answer to this is very complex, but a few reasons might be suggested to help us come to a better understanding.

First, for the first three centuries, the church of Rome was one of a number of great centers of the Christian tradition. Among other centers were the churches of Jerusalem (in the Holy Land), Antioch and then Constantinople (in West Syria), Alexandria (in Egypt), and Aquileia and Milan (both in Northern Italy), each with a bishop leading the communities of faith in that area, each metropolitan bishop with ecclesial authority, and each region with unique ritual and calendrical traditions. The diversity of ritual practice and traditions of time-keeping did not usually make the regions inimical to one another; the ecclesial and liturgical state was rather a kind of communion of communions, in which the theology and liturgy were naturally inculturated into different places and times, though with enough commonality that there was a sense of unity, if not uniformity, throughout the tradition.

---

36. Ibid.: 150.
37. More on the Spanish situation and the evidence for it is laid out in Volume 1, Chapter 2, "Advent."

In the fourth and fifth centuries, shifting religious, political, and economic exigencies led to greater ecclesial authority accorded the bishop of Rome, and as the faith moved into the Middle Ages many other churches began to depend on the favor of the church of Rome for their survival. Moreover, the advent of Islam, in the seventh century, displaced Christian communities in many places where they had earlier thrived — Egypt, Syria, Spain, North Africa — and for some churches this threat wedded them together more closely to one another's traditions than they had been before. The solidarity of theology and worship brought strength and refuge in a time of questioning and insecurity.

This summary of the state of the church in the fourth and fifth centuries is introduced as a way of understanding how the date of one community — the church of Rome, for celebrating the birth of Jesus on December 25 — came to override the date (January 6) for the observance in the rest of Christianity. There is a sermon from John Chrysostom, who was kindly disposed toward the church of Rome, in which he and his church were acceding to the Roman date of the birth.[38] Even from that time, the late fourth century, when Christmas was received as the date of the nativity in some of the churches of the East, January 6 had still been a remarkably full and fervent celebration. There are still churches of the East with some resistance to celebration of the nativity on December 25, particularly those churches where there is a feeling of lament at the passing of old liturgical and calendrical traditions and feelings of exuberance and pride in their earlier, unique inculturations of the faith.

The Armenian Orthodox church, for example, still resists the Roman date even though most of the other Orthodox communities have acceded to commemorating the birth on December 25. The issue at hand in establishing a date for the birth of Jesus is not that of historical accuracy (for the date of the birth of Jesus in history is not to be found) but of authority in the Christian church. The reckoning of the date for the birth of Jesus is a public concession to authority, for the bishop whose church's date for the birth feast is accepted is seen, consciously or not, as the one with more power. Throughout Christian history, struggles with the calendar show that the one who measures and sets time is the leader.

Christians of the Roman church should be aware that it is not only history that is taken into account in celebrating Christmas, but also an image of the church. The rapid spread of the date of December 25 from its slow nascence in 336 to its near universality by 450 seems

---

38. Sermons of St. John Chrysostom, PG 48:752–753 and PG 49:351–352, 356, 358.

natural to Christians whose origins are in Latin Christianity but would likely be seen as a bitter surrender to many Christians of Orthodox traditions and communions. In the resistance to and later reception of the Roman date of Christmas, one can trace the ascent of Roman authority in the Christian church of the fourth century.

The Roman church was still not much of a political force in 336, when the first evidence of December 25 is manifest. Yet the conversion of Constantine in 312 and the solicitation by later emperors of church involvement in political matters reveals that the fortunes of Christianity and its Latin bishops changed remarkably in the half-century between the first evidence of Christmas and the next. During these decades the influence of the bishops on the citizens of the empire grew, and so the reception of the new date for celebrating the nativity was tied to the ascendancy of the church. Although the rhetoric of the feast as known from the liturgy is about the scriptural narratives of the birth of Christ, the underlying issue that brought these narratives to prominence in the Latin West is not a romantic's tale of a wondrous birth but a historical record of church hegemony, bitter and difficult for all but the winner, the church of Rome.

The Popularity of the Gospel of James in the Middle Ages

As the boundaries of theology were being established in Christianity in the fourth and fifth centuries, various narratives of the birth of Jesus, each with its own theology and Christology, were still being proclaimed. As the theology of the relationship of God the Son to God the Father was fashioned, the resulting Christology was matched by new nativity narratives in which even the infant Son occasioned miracles equal to, or even greater than, those of the adult Son in the synoptic Gospels. The Gospels with the highest Christologies in the infancy narratives was generally from the Syrian churches, which also had high Mariologies. But the new stories of Jesus' infancy were not confined to Eastern traditions.

In the church of Verona, for example, the narratives of the birth of Jesus were not only those familiar to us from the Gospels of Matthew and Luke. Bishop Zeno of Verona also preached on the nativity tale from a non-canonical source:

> What a great mystery! Mary conceived as an uncontaminated virgin, she gave birth as a virgin, and she remained a virgin after the birth. The hand of the faithless midwife — who after the birth wanted to examine her in order to witness having found her a virgin as before — was set on fire. When she touched the

infant, immediately that destructive flame was doused. Thus, after having long admired the virgin woman, that happily curious physician herself admired the infant God, exulting with great joy. She who came healthy, goes away cured.[39]

The narrative recounted here is from the Infancy Gospel of James — often called the Protoevangelium of James — which, after the canonical four and especially in the Syrian communities of late antiquity, was one of the most popularly influential Gospels in the early period and Middle Ages.[40] The interpretation of this other Gospel in the second half of the fourth century demonstrates that the canon of the New Testament was still not cemented in Northern Italy.[41]

The preoccupying presence of heresies and heretics would soon move church leaders to settle the matter of what books were to be included in the canon so that they might proof-text their orthodox theology and counter that of their opponents, yet during the ministry of this Veronese bishop the anti-heretical fervor against the Arians had not reached the pitch necessary for the theological decisions that would be drawn from the sacred scriptures. Although the Protoevangelium of James declined in liturgical use in the early Middle Ages, after papal proscription in the sixth century, its nativity narrative survived in church art for centuries.

Medieval Preaching on the Nativity of Jesus

Even though the infancy narratives of the Gospels of Matthew and Luke supplied for Christmas liturgies might have inspired engaging preaching, many of the Christmas sermons until the twelfth century catechized about theological issues, particularly about orthodox theology on the relationship of the Father and the Son. Christmas, a time when preachers might have engaged the large assemblies with the beautiful narratives, became the time of the year when high theological rhetoric was the norm. Characteristic of this kind of sermon are most of those of Pope Leo the Great, in particular those preached

---

39. Zeno of Verona, Tractatus 1.54.5, CCSL 22, ed. B. Löfstedt (Turnholt: Brepols, 1971): 129; trans. Connell.

40. On the Protoevangelium, see Willem F. Vorster, "James, Protoevangelium of," *Anchor Bible Dictionary*, volume 3 (New York: Doubleday, 1992): 629–632. For English translations of this Gospel, see Ron Cameron, ed., *The Other Gospel: Non-Canonical Gospel Texts* (Philadelphia: Westminster Press, 1982), 107–121; David R. Cartlidge and David L. Dungan, *Documents for the Study of the Gospels* (Philadelphia: Fortress Press, 1980): 107–117.

41. See Lee Martin McDonald, *The Formation of the Christian Biblical Canon* (Nashville: Abingdon Press, 1988): 132–141.

on Christmas day in the years 443 and 452. The latter offers the rationale for why such theological issues are needed when the infancy stories are proclaimed:

> Dearly beloved, the Catholic Faith scorns the errors of barking heretics. Deceived by the emptiness of worldly wisdom, these have withdrawn from the Gospel of truth. Not capable of understanding the Incarnation of the Word, they have turned a source of enlightenment into an occasion of blindness for themselves. In tracing the opinions of almost all those who believe falsehoods — even those which lead to a denial of the Holy Spirit — we realize that practically no one has gone astray who did not disbelieve the reality of two natures in Christ while at the same time acknowledging a single Person.
>
> Some have ascribed to the Lord only his humanity, others only his divinity. Some have said that this divinity was real enough, but that his flesh was only an appearance. Others have declared that he took on real flesh but did not have the nature of God the Father. These, attributing to his divinity what belongs properly to the human substance, have fabricated for themselves a greater and a lesser god, though there can be no degrees in the true divinity, for whatever is less than God is not God.[42]

These sermons continued with philosophical theology at great length, as Leo and his later medieval peers went into detail about each error of the heresies and heretics whose theology tainted the mystery of Christmas — Arius, Mani, Macedonius, Sabellius, Photinus, Apollonarius, Nestorius, Eutyches — contrasting them to the steadfast and orthodox faith of the apostle Peter and of the Apostles' Creed.

Through it all, whatever bishop was preaching on Christmas, it is obvious that the canonical nativity narratives raised ecclesial sensitivities and episcopal insecurities about how to reckon the juxtaposition of the high theology of the Son from the christological councils and the Gospel narratives of a swaddled infant with Mary and Joseph, angels and shepherds, and the whole menagerie of Bethlehem's grange. As Leo himself insisted, with the defensive tone of much of medieval preaching on Christmas, "Corporeal birth did not take anything away from the majesty of God's Son, nor add anything to it, for the unchangeable substance can neither be diminished nor increased."[43]

---

42. Leo, *Sermons*, trans. Jane Patricia Freeland and Agnes Josephine Conway, FC 93 (Washington, DC: Catholic University of America, 1996): 115–121.
43. Sermon 27, ibid.: 111.

This highlights the complexity of Christmas's emergence in the fourth century. The theological identity of the Father and the Son in consubstantiality — established at the Council of Nicea in 325, as a corrective to the errors of the Arians (who didn't believe in the equal divinity of the Son and the Father) — so exalted the supremacy of the Son over all creation and humanity that he was virtually out of touch of the ordinary life of most believers. Christmas sermons throughout the Middle Ages took up the christological issues, perhaps because the object of the feast, the infant Son, was incommensurate with the lofty theology predicated upon him. Yet the high theological rhetoric was complicated by the colorful and engaging stories of Jesus' infancy in the Gospels of Matthew and Luke.

The high Christmas Christology of the early Middle Ages was brought to the political arena when on Christmas morning of the year 800 the coronation of Charlemagne was celebrated in the presence of Pope Leo III, a supreme wedding of church and empire: *Karolo piissimo Augusto a Deo coronato, magno, pacifico imperatori, vita et victoria!* "Life and victory to the most holy emperor Charlemagne, peaceful ruler, crowned by God!" As the theology was raised, and as the distinction between church and empire narrowed, the appeal of the stories for the liturgy waned. Christmas gradually became the remembrance of a birth from long ago rather than a celebration of the present manifestation of God's life in humanity.

Christmas in the Later Middle Ages

The high Christology of Christmas reigned for centuries, starting to be tempered only by the piety of St. Francis of Assisi and his friars. The democratizing spirit of Francis, the prophet of the poor, influenced the shape of Christmas greatly. Affectionate devotion to the infant born in Bethlehem had immediate appeal when brought into worship, and the rhetoric of songs and preaching shifted from this time onward away from the heady theological mode it had been in for centuries.

Early Christmas hymns that expressed the new devotion and theology were not from Francis himself, but a follower born shortly before the death of Francis, Jacopone da Todi (1230–1306), who would become a Franciscan. Jacopone was a poet and hymnist, and his work reflects the change of devotion to the infant Jesus. He employed sweet diminutives in songs to the child Jesus to engage the imagination of the faithful; *bambolino, piccolino, Jesulino,* and *Dio fatto piccino* — "little baby," "tiny little one," "little Jesus," and "God made small" — were among the new tags Jacopone utilized in this touching devotion to the infant expressing the new Franciscan theology of Christmas:

You carry God within you, God and man,
And the weight does not crush you.
Unheard-of birth, the child issuing from the sealed womb!
The infant joyously leaving the castle, through locked gates,
For it would not be fitting for God to do violence
To the womb that sheltered Him.

O Mary, what did you feel when you first saw Him?
Did love nearly destroy you?
As you gazed upon Him, how could you sustain such love?
When you gave Him suck, how could you bear such excess joy?
When He turned to you and called you Mother,
How could you bear being called the Mother of God?[44]

In his songs, Jacopone also fashioned a new, transtemporal approach
to the scene of the birth, engaging Christian imaginations with the
details of that scene in Bethlehem:

> The joyous chorus is that of angels
> Singing sweet songs around the manger
> Before the Christ Child
> The Word Incarnate.
>
> Here, robed in firm faith,
> The singers around the manger
> See the Godhead Incarnate,
> And their hearts leap up in hope.
>
> Led by the soaring voice of Stephen,
> Hosts of martyrs chant the first office of the night—
> The chorus of those who gave their lives
> To Christ, that flower burgeoning with seed.
>
> The second sequence is taken up by the Confessors—
> The voice of John the Evangelist heightens the splendor.
> No voice ever soared to such piercing heights
> In such exquisite melody.
>
> The Holy Innocents sing the third sequence,
> They who for all time abide in the presence of the Child.
> "We praise you, God," they intone,
> "For Christ our Lord is born this day."

---

44. Jacopone da Todi, "The Blessed Virgin Mary," in *The Lauds,* trans. Serge and Elizabeth Hughes (Ramsey, NJ: Paulist, 1982): 70–71.

> O sinners, who have served an evil master,
> Come sing with us — now man can find God,
> Who has appeared on earth as a child,
> And all who seek Him can take and hold Him.[45]

These poems mark a vast change from the christologically weighty Christmas discourse that had characterized the feast and the liturgy from its emergence until the twelfth century.

While the institution of the "manger" — *praesepium* in Latin, *presepio* in Italian — is usually ascribed to St. Francis, this was not a completely new object of ecclesial and liturgical devotion in the thirteenth century. A chapel devoted to the manger had existed in the fifth century in Rome, at the Basilica of Santa Maria Maggiore, which itself had once been called *Beata Maria ad praesaepe*, "Blessed Mary at the Manger."[46] Yet Francis brought devotion to the manger and its context to a popular level.

Francis's devotion to the manger is evident in this account of his visit in 1223, to the Italian town of Greccio, a small village on a mountainside. Knowing that the Franciscan hermitage at Greccio would be too small for the Christmas Mass at midnight, Francis built an altar on a rock near the town square, its *piazza*. St. Bonaventure (died 1274), theologian and early biographer of Francis, recounted what happened in Greccio when Francis was there:

> It so happened that, three years before his death, he decided to celebrate the memory of the birth of the child Jesus with great devotion in the town of Greccio so that the people would appreciate its great solemnity. So that this would not be seen as a kind of novelty, he sought and received permission from the Supreme Pontiff [the pope].

The writing continues with the narrative present-tense:

> He had the manger prepared, the hay scattered around, and an ox and donkey brought to the place. The brothers are called, the people arrive, and the forest resounds with their voices, and that holy night is made bright and solemn with the multitude of lights and with resounding and harmonious hymns of praise. The man of God stands before the manger filled with holiness, awash in his tears, and overflowing with joy. A solemn Mass is celebrated over the manger, with Francis, the priest of Christ, singing the

---

45. da Todi, "A Canticle of the Nativity" in ibid.: 194–195.
46. Miles, *Christmas Customs and Traditions*: 106–107.

holy Gospel. Then he preaches to those present about the birth of the poor King, for whom — whenever he wants to call him — he uses the name the "Child of Bethlehem," thereby revealing the tenderness of his love.

Back to the past tense:

> There was a certain strong and dedicated soldier, John of Greccio, who out of his love of Christ had suspended his worldly military service and become a close associate of the man of God. He claimed that he had seen sleeping in the manger a certain beautiful child, whom blessed father Francis embraced with both arms, and whom he seemed to have awakened from sleep.
>
> Not only does the holiness of the witness make this believable, but the vision of this devoted soldier was afterward confirmed in its truth by later miracles. For the example of Francis, when it awakens the attention of the world, can stir up the hearts of those sluggish in faith in Christ. The hay from the manger was kept by the people for the healing of sick animals and it kept away other dangerous plagues. With all of these wonders and miracles, God glorified his servant and demonstrated the efficacy of his holy prayer and the evidence of the many miracles.[47]

This new Christian piety and spirituality of Christmas was readily received by the church. The start of the church's use of nativity sets, in liturgy and in homes, was rooted in the late medieval foundation from the democratic piety of the saint of Assisi.

Christmas and Society after the Reformation

Although the sixteenth-century Protestant reformers found serious issue with the Roman Catholic cult of relics and objects, the manger and other decorations of Christmas seem to have survived in fits and starts in reformed and evangelical piety, in part because of the testimony in the Gospels of Matthew and Luke, since scripture is ever the criterion for theology and worship in Protestant traditions. Though Martin Luther (1483–1546) found the Roman Catholic church laden with distracting accretions in its crammed calendar and its theology of saints — accretions that took attention from the primacy of the Word of God as the ultimate criterion for what is to take place in church —

---

47. Bonaventure, *Opera omnia*, volume 8, *Opuscula varia ad theologiam mysticam* (Florence: Collegium S. Bonaventurae, 1898): 535; this excerpt is from chapter 10 of Bonaventure's *Legenda Sancti Francisci*; trans. Connell.

he seemed to have readily accepted some observances of the liturgical year, like Christmas, as part of the tradition.

Other Protestant churches have waxed and waned in their reception of the date and traditions of Christmas; in England its reception varied according to the ascendancy of monarchs sympathetic to Roman Catholicism or not. When the Puritans held sway, Christmas was in jeopardy; in England in 1644, for example, Christmas was coincident with a Wednesday, which the House of Lords and Commons had appointed for a "Fast and Humiliation." So Parliament published an "Ordinance for the Better Observation of the Feast of the Nativity of Christ," which mandated:

> Whereas some doubts have been raised whether the next Fast shall be celebrated, because it falleth on the day which, heretofore, was usually called the Feast of the Nativity of the Saviour; the lords and commons do order and ordain that public notice be given, that the Fast appointed to be kept on the last Wednesday in every month, ought to be observed until it be otherwise ordered by both houses; and that this day particularly is to be kept with the more solemn humiliation because it may call to remembrance our sins and the sins of our forefathers, who have turned this Feast, pretending the memory of Christ, into an extreme forgetfulness of him, by giving liberty to carnal and sensual delights; being contrary to the life which Christ himself led here upon earth, and to the spiritual life of Christ in our souls; for the sanctifying and saving whereof Christ was pleased both to take a human life, and to lay it down again.[48]

The ways that Christmas was or was not celebrated from the seventeenth through nineteenth centuries can also be ascribed in part to the varying degrees of biblical literalism and moral rigorism in the ecclesial distinctions of Protestant traditions in Europe and in America. Such fledgling attempts, however, to abolish the celebration of Christmas on December 25 were usually short-lived, because the feast had such a deep and wide place in the Christian imagination, Protestant and Roman Catholic.

Moreover, much of what most people think of as northern European Christmas customs adopted by people in North America were really American inventions, new ways of celebrating the feast, with a few remnants, perhaps, from Dutch and northern European customs. But the American penchant for antiquity is more comfortable

---

48. As in Clement A. Miles, *Christmas Customs and Traditions:* 184–185.

imagining that these customs were imported from the "old world" culture rather than in claiming any pious customs as novel. Within the past two centuries in the United States, the shape of Christmas has changed considerably and, as a result of Christmas's cultural and economic ascendancy, the U.S. celebration has been influential in secular and church traditions elsewhere. American culture has influenced the observance and celebration of Christmas greatly with its unique rituals for marking December 25, though Americans are simply more at ease if they imagine these to have been customs borne from elsewhere rather than invented by American Christian piety.[49]

Apart, perhaps, from the occasional "peace on earth" message of the season, with its origin in the angels' song in the infancy narrative according to Luke (2:14), there is little rhetoric about Jesus' birth in the early American tradition of Christmas. Under the guise of St. Nicholas (or Santa Claus) and in the seasonal mania of the gift-exchange, the feast rather marks the supreme, universal victory of U.S. consumerism far more prominently than the celebration of an infant born into an impoverished family and wrapped in swaddling clothes.

The commixture of December 25 as the memorial day of Jesus' birth and the feast of Santa Claus, the bearer of gifts for family and friends, was a remarkable feat for a few reasons. First, the feast day of St. Nicholas had been — and for some Christians still is — celebrated on December 6, not December 25. Moreover, there is the obvious but little considered shift in the person at the heart of the feast day, from Jesus to Santa Claus. Much of the influence on these two changes is rooted in early nineteenth-century New England culture, and in the creative work of one wealthy Manhattan man in particular, Clement Moore, the author of "A Visit from St. Nicholas."

Most Christians in the United States don't find a conflict between the message of the Christmas liturgy in their churches and the message of Santa Claus with its exchange of gifts with one's family members and intimates, yet there were some well-orchestrated marketing values supporting the shift in the celebration's transformation in the early nineteenth century. In the first few decades of the nineteenth century, earlier American traditions of partying and gift-giving were reshaped to support the consumerist fervor and the new sociology of the American family, as described below on the social values connected to the

---

49. The annual seasonal attribution of U.S. Christmas customs to European — particularly Dutch and German — origin is quite exaggerated. When the Christmas tree, for example, was introduced in the United States, it was contemporary with the same custom in Germany, and at that it was a custom in just one region of the German culture.

Christian tradition of preaching about and celebrating the birth of the
Savior to the world.

Part Two:
Christmas and Society

Social Reversals at the Lord's Coming

Long before Christmas appeared as a feast of the liturgical year, the
theology of the birth of Jesus in the two infancy narratives cast the
birth of the Savior as a reckoning of God's justice in the world's order.
These social and theological strands accompanying the conception,
birth, and infancy of Jesus, especially as depicted in the Gospel of Luke,
are not those on which Christmas sermons in the church after Vatican II usually draw. The Lukan narratives for the Lord's birth reveal
profound social upheavals and compelling surprises, yet little social
change or surprises are occasioned by the church's celebration of the
mystery; surprise gifts in the home are many, but preaching about
social upheavals are few.

There is no New Testament evidence for a date on which the late
first-century churches marked the nativity of Jesus, indeed none appear
before the third (for January 6) or early fourth century (for December 25),[50] yet there was common acceptance of the birth narrative as
vital to the narrative tradition of the faith. The piety of the nativity has
long attended to details of the long infancy narratives in the Gospels of
Matthew and Luke, wonderful and engaging narratives that are among
the most well-known stories of the Bible, known by Christians and
non-Christians alike. The narratives were accepted into the canon as
inspired, and proclaimed for the up-building of the church long before
they were accorded a particular place in the liturgical year. Though lectionaries appear only after Christmas was received in East and West,
the infancy stories were likely proclaimed in early communities.

An even cursory reading of the birth narratives reveals that the coming of the long-awaited Messiah would be accompanied by basic social
reversals and inventions, some toward social justice, some toward social humor. These are more evident in the infancy story of the Gospel
of Luke than that of Matthew, but they are incontrovertibly manifest in
both. The narratives are tales of the rich becoming poor, and the poor

---

50. Epiphany's original narrative, in the third century, was not the birth but baptism
of Jesus; the birth was added later with other manifestations. See Volume 1, Chapter 4,
"Epiphany."

rich; of the strong becoming weak, the weak strong; of the old being rejuvenated, and of the formerly barren bearing children; of women fulfilling God's plans for humanity in ways that had before been for men only.

Humor and Sobriety in the Infancy Stories

On the gender issue, in Matthew's genealogy one finds Tamar, Rahab, the wife of David (Bathsheba, though unnamed at Matthew 1:6); and Mary; and in Luke's account Mary again (in a much longer narrative), Elizabeth, and Anna. What is particularly striking, in relation to liturgical history generally, is the prominent place that such narratives of social upset have had day after day, century after century in the two Gospel canticles for Evening Prayer and Morning Prayer, the *Magnificat* (Luke 1:46–55) and the *Benedictus* (Luke 1:68–79).

In the narrative leading up to the *Benedictus* the parents of John the Baptist, Zechariah and Elizabeth, are far beyond the child-bearing age, yet the reversal begins when an angel announces to the father that he and his wife will bear a son, to be named John. The father is struck dumb because he did not believe the angel's message, because it was so far beyond belief or beyond the constraints of ordinary society: "How shall I know this? For I am an old man, and my wife is advanced in years" (Luke 1:18). So the story is already predicated on such a society of surprise when, indeed, the child is born. The father's dumb state had continued throughout the pregnancy, apparently, and the first words he utters, filled with the Holy Spirit, are the canticle that eventually took a fixed place in daily prayer.

In the canticle put on Zechariah's lips the people of Israel will be saved from those who were enemies, from those who had hated them (1:71). The "tender mercy of our God, when the day shall dawn upon us from on high" (1:78), will be manifest in this late-conceived son, who "will be called the prophet of the Most High" (1:76). This tender-hearted Most High will reverse the lives that had been lived until that day, for, as the canticle foretells, God will "give light to those who sit in darkness and in the shadow of death" (1:79). Their fortunes will be upset, and those who had formerly been cast in lowliness and darkness will live in dignity and light. The fragility of old age did not sentence them to death, but bore new life to the world as a beacon for God's people in the person of the Baptist. The advent of the Savior, the infancy story reveals, will reorder the expectations of society regarding who is who and what place each would have in the world.

This is even more pronounced in the other of the pair of daily canticles, the *Magnificat*, sung during Evening Prayer for most of

Christian history and still today. In the Lukan narrative, Mary has just received word from the angel Gabriel that she had found favor with God and that she will conceive and bear a son, for "with God nothing will be impossible" (1:37), as the angel reveals. Mary goes to Elizabeth's house and there sings of what will happen when the Lord comes. For herself, favor has come to "the low estate of his hand-maiden" (1:48), and in this the Lord "has scattered the proud in the imagination of their hearts...has put down the mighty from their thrones, and exalted those of low degree" (1:51–52). In the advent of the Savior, the Lord "has filled the hungry with good things, and the rich he has sent empty away" (1:53). From the start of the Lukan Gospel, the coming of God into human life will be signaled by the upset of society, when those with and those without will change places, and ordinary expectations will be turned upside down.

The Gospel of Luke has such surprises throughout, but the infancy narrative itself has some of the most engaging and humorous examples of this kind. The child born in Bethlehem — a town name that means "house of bread" — is given a bed in a feeding trough for animals, and he and his parents will not find a room in the inn during the weariness of their itinerancy. And the announcement of his coming is made to shepherds, those who — though romanticized and squeaky clean in the retelling of the tradition and in our crèches — had one of the lowliest occupations of Palestinian society in the first century. The theological and narrative link between the coming of the Son and social surprises and upsets was tenacious in Christianity from the start until the nineteenth century (more below). For this reason the separation of the two in the last two centuries in churches and customs in the United States is lamentable, for this link between God's coming and societal reconfiguration was so deep in the theological and pastoral tradition of Christmas and the turn from the end to the beginning of the year.

Christmas and Society in Italy in the Early Church

The narrative tradition for marking the birth of Christ is hard to separate from end-of-the-year social traditions. A constant issue in the preaching rhetoric at Christmas in the earliest stratum of the solemnity's emergence is about social justice. One finds, for example, that in late antiquity the celebration of the coming of the Son was closely linked to the church's pastoral care of the vulnerable and weak. Bishop Maximus of Turin's impassioned theology of Christmas reveals the need for conversion and repentance at Christmas:

It behooves us, then, to be pure in holiness, clean in chastity, and shining in virtue, so that when we see the festal day approaching more closely we may enter into it more carefully. For if housewives who are about to celebrate some feasts are in the habit of washing the stains out of their clothes with water, why do not we who are about to observe the Lord's birthday all the more wash out the stains of our soul's with tears?[51]

Yet Maximus's theology was not just focused on the individual; in anticipation of Christmas he urged the faith of his church in Turin to take care of those in need during that time of the liturgical year:

Let us fill his treasures with gifts of different kinds so that on the holy day there might be the wherewithal to give to travelers, to refresh widows, and to clothe the poor. For what sort of thing would it be if in one and the same house, among the servants of a single master, one should vaunt himself in silk and another should be completely covered in rags; if one should be warm with food and another should endure hunger and cold; if, out of indigestion, one should be belching what he had drunk yesterday and another should not have made up for yesterday's lack of food? And what will be the effect of our praying? We ask to be freed from the enemy, we who are not generous with our brethren. Let us be imitators of our Lord! For as he wished the poor to be sharers with us in heavenly grace, why should they not be sharers with us in earthly goods?[52]

It is not as explicit here as we will see later, but one can sense in this sermon from Northern Italy that Christmas was a time and season of social reckoning, reversals, and leveling, a time when the poor were raised up and the well-off opened their pockets to balance out the inequalities of society prevalent in the rest of the year. This was not just a social value, but an ecclesial value whose advocates were bishops and preachers. The church at Christmas took up the role of advocate for realizing the kingdom of God in the world, prompting people to go out into the streets and realize the reign of God.

In this the church, in the first centuries until the early Middle Ages, was carrying on the theological tradition of the infancy narratives, yet now the narrative had a particular place in the liturgical calendar, in the sacrament of God's coming, narrated in the infancy stories of the New Testament, at the time of the winter solstice, when the days were

---

51. *Sermo* 61.1, ACW 50: 147.
52. *Sermo* 60.4; ibid.: 146.

short. The church proclaimed narratives of humor and delight and engagement at a time of the year when people sought hope and consolation that things would not always be as they were in the present. And these hopes were realized in the exhortations of the preachers to go out into the world and share resources that, in Christian reckoning, had their source in God alone.

The same Maximus of Turin observes in another sermon at Christmas time: "For a wealthy person who would have disdained to give a beggar a *denarius* [a coin] gives a *solidus* [also a coin] to someone who is rich, and on the kalends someone who came to church on the Lord's birthday empty-handed and without anything hastens to his friend's house laden with gold."[53] An essential aspect of Christmas was the realization of the coming of Christ in the church and in the world in which there was a just distribution of goods. This effort to reverse social and economic norms was a key part of the Christmas tradition for centuries, even in the United States in the country's early years, at least before the middle of the nineteenth century.

As the sacraments are moments when the faithful recognize God's presence in church so that they can then see where God is found outside the church (see Luke 24:13–35; John 20:11–18; 19–23), so is the church the place in which this reckoning of the order of society approximates the tradition's understanding of the kingdom of God and applies it to the society in which it finds itself. An appreciation of this aspect would bear on the theology and liturgy at Christmas still, and liturgical celebrations and preaching for Christmas would be ameliorated with more understanding of the early and medieval rhetoric about God's coming.

Another incentive in shaping the feast as a civil celebration may have been to establish law and social order in a time of the year that was traditionally riotous and disorderly, the end of the old year and beginning of the new. Bishops from the early church frequently preached against social marauding and licentiousness, as, for example, in another sermon of Maximus:

> I have no small complaint against a great number of you, brethren. I speak of those who, while celebrating the Lord's birthday with us, have given themselves over to pagan feasts and, after the heavenly banquet, have prepared a meal of superstition for themselves, so that those who beforehand had taken delight in holiness are afterwards besotted with foolishness. They do not realize that a

---

53. *Sermo* 98.2; ibid.: 223.

person who wishes to reign with Christ cannot rejoice with the world, and that one who wishes to find righteousness must turn away from wantonness.[54]

Maximus's suggested antidote to the "gourmandizing, drunkenness, and licentiousness" of the pagans was the preaching of a Christ "who is abstinence, temperance, and chastity." The Christmas behaviors against which the Italian bishop preached in the fifth century seem to have persisted until the seventeenth century, where in the United States Christmas was still the occasion for riotous drinking binges. Severe penalties were exacted in some states upon anyone who missed work on December 25.

The Middle Ages and the Episcopellus, "Boy Bishop"

The social upsets of the season also found expression in the ministers of the liturgy in Advent and Christmas, particularly in religious communities, where there emerged a tradition of appointing one of the lowest ranked members of the community — an adolescent in formation for membership, for example, or a new member of the community — and giving him the bishop's seat in the liturgy and according him all of the insignia, privileges, and liturgical responsibilities that are usually according a visiting bishop. This lucky lad was called the *episcopellus*, "little bishop," or "boy bishop."[55]

Although this was surely done with humor, it was also a link to the social reversals that were embedded in the theology of Christ's birth from its origins in the New Testament stories. Though Christmas eventually evolved into a celebration of power and domination as the church and empire grew closer together and at times nearly indistinguishable, in a number of churches during the Middle Ages the traditional custom of social reversal was maintained, beginning in some places on the Feast of St. Nicholas (December 6) and ending on the Feast of the Holy Innocents (December 28).

Nicholas was a bishop and caretaker of children in Myra in Asia Minor, so his feast was a natural start for such social reversal. The name of the feast of Holy Innocents in some places had been *Childermas* because of the day's natural link to the young, though the narrative of the slaughter of the young in the Gospel narrative of Matthew [2:16–18] supplies a gruesome link to the association with

---

54. *Sermo* 63.1; ibid.: 155.

55. See Carini, "L'Episcopello nel medio evo," in *Palestra del Clero* (Rome, 1887): 74 and following; Sardi, "La ceremonia del Vescovino negli antichi costume lucchesi," in *Archivio storico italiano* (1902): note 4, page 393; and Roberti, "La cerimonia dell'Episcopello a Padova," in *Archivio storico italiano* (1903): note 2, page 172.

children.[56] The feast of St. Catherine of Alexandria, on November 25, had a similar tradition, at least in some churches in Belgium and England, where young girls would process through their towns and one would be chosen as the patroness of sewers and spinners, clothed in white and brightly colored ribbons. A ditty was sung as the saint- or queen-for-a-day passed by in scepter and crown:[57]

> Here comes Queen Catherine, as fine as any queen,
> With a coach and six horses, a-coming to be seen,
>   And a-spinning we will go, will go, will go,
>   And a-spinning we will go.

As already seen in the sermons of Maximus of Turin regarding the place of the rich and the poor at the end of the year, so in ecclesial life social reversals incorporated a change or reversal in the order of liturgical hierarchy and roles. Though they did not pray the Eucharistic Prayer for the consecration of the bread and wine, some choirboys did preach. It was customary for the Feast of the Innocents to have a choir of children, and in the early Middle Ages, particularly in France, Germany, and Italy, the authorities in communities of religious, canons in particular, would give their usual primacy of place within the choir stalls to the young. The tradition first appears in France in the tenth century, and may have its origins in the school at St. Gall, known for the musical traditions of the church to this day.

The antiphon for December 28, the end of the span, reflected the social values of the birth of Christ in the Gospel of Luke, with the very verse from the Magnificat, *Deposuit potentes de sede, et exaltavit humiles*, "he has put down the mighty from their thrones, and exalted those of low degree" (1:52). The terminus of December 28 for this social mix-up is quite appropriate, of course, since the narrative for that day marked the sanctity of those slain by King Herod in his fervor to kill the infant Jesus.

The applicable point here in the history of Christmas, however, is the link between the manifestation of Christ and social upheaval. God's presence in humanity, these traditions from the earliest Christian days and the Middle Ages remind us, is ever recognizable in social change and a reversal of the normally accepted conventions of society. Lamentably, these customs of ecclesial levity were condemned by councils in the thirteenth and fourteenth centuries, with the threat

---

56. Miles: 315.
57. As from Miles, 213, who cites T. F. Thiselton-Dyer, *British Popular Customs* (London: 1876): 426f.

of severe punishment for any communities that would maintain such practices. In a few places, the humorous customs survived for centuries, with evidence calling for an end to the revelry appearing from Sicily until 1555, from Lucca in 1575, and from Catania until 1668, with still one censure there appearing as late as 1736.

The revelry and humor in such theological and liturgical customs — at Christmas time or ever — was basically vanquished in the antipathies of the Reformation and Counter-Reformation, after which religious traditions were sober, if not outright condemnatory of other traditions. The antagonisms of the sixteenth century divorced religion from humor and fun, a separation that still characterizes most of Christian faith and worship today. It is sad that such customs as the "kid bishop" have died in association with Christmas, for it would be a prime opportunity to nurture vocations to ministry in the liturgy — serving, preaching, presiding — by having some children step into the roles temporarily and having other children's imaginations be sparked by watching kids of their own age ministering at the altar. But elastic and playful imaginations do not characterize church or liturgical life these days, to the detriment of the church as a whole and especially the fostering of vocations.

Reformation and Counter-Reformation

After the castigations of Rome by Luther and later reformers, and after the Council of Trent's condemnations of the reformers, the calendar of Christianity in the West grew in severity and austerity while decreasing in lavishness and celebration. With regard to Christmas, in response to the earlier revelries, the celebration of the feast was downright frowned upon in many places. (Indeed it was *illegal* — a criminal offense — to celebrate Christmas in Massachusetts between 1659 and 1681.) Also, before the nineteenth century, tradition held up Christmas as a time for the wealthy to give tips and gifts to the poor in their employ. Coming so close to the turn of the year, both Christmas and Epiphany featured annual social upsets, both economic and gender upheavals, and in this the tradition was nearest the social calls of the Magnificat and of Christmas in antiquity.[58]

Also, children were given gifts, as they are today, but not because Christmas was itself the domestic celebration that it has become in its decline, but because it was the very season and time for social reversal, a reversal in which children, like the poor and women, were given a higher social status as part of the celebration of the day. Christmas also

---

58. See Volume 1, Chapter 4, "Epiphany."

seemed to be a time for reviving marital relations and sexual coupling, for there was a preponderance of births in September and October.[59]

Christmas Capital in the United States

Regrettably, the tradition of social gift-giving to the poor was reworked in the United States to become familial gift-giving as practiced in the home, among families and friends. The poor and needy were cut out of the celebration as the feast became less riotous, more predictable, and eventually domesticated. Previously, children, domestic workers, and the poor were dependent for their well-being in winter upon the generosity and altruism of the well-to-do.

This was not merely a market-induced change, for a few things in the culture were also new, and these contributed to positive social and economic change. For one thing, the middle class emerged as a social group that had not existed as such before. People earlier had belonged — usually by birth and inexorably until death — to either the "haves" or the "have-nots," the latter group making life easier for the former. The social reversals of Christmas were discernible because one knew to which group one belonged; the introduction of a middle group or class mottled the social mix to the benefit of the society in many ways, but it had an effect on the social traditions of Christmas, which were facilitated by the identities of the gift-givers and the gift-receivers.

Moreover, the nineteenth century found children emerging as separate from other types of dependents, and the domestic entertainment of children with toys became part of the obligation of parents toward their progeny at Christmas time. From the standpoint of the liturgical year and the Christian tradition, however, the exclusion of the poor and needy removed the initial social impetus for the feast, and the domestic celebration with children at the center, though perhaps desirable for other reasons, had no independent precedent in the ritual traditions of Christmas.

Remnants of the older social and economic ministrations are still reflected in the Lectionary for Christmas, particularly in the first readings. The social reordering of Christmas for centuries was not simply for the day itself, but was characteristic of some church traditions generally throughout the span between December 25 and January 6. In fact, one of the keenest remnants of social reversal during this Christmas-Epiphany span marked the celebration of the Feast of the

---

59. Stephen Nissenbaum, *The Battle for Christmas: A Cultural History of America's Most Cherished Holiday* (New York: Vintage, 1997): 22.

Holy Innocents, December 28, a day celebrated as such from the early church, even, perhaps, older than the celebration of Christmas itself.

Here in the United States there was a need to find the ritual symbols of St. Nicholas, Santa Claus, and the Christmas tree with its lights in "ancient" traditions of the Netherlands and Germany. But at best such European practices were very local in those places, not nearly as universal as periodical literature in the nineteenth-century United States would have led people to think. About the tree, for example:

> There is a belief among those who care about such things that the Christmas tree was spread throughout American culture by German immigrants. There is some truth to this. But, much like the notion that Santa Claus was brought to these shores by the Dutch settlers of New Amsterdam [New York], such a belief also conforms to our desire to see our Christmas customs as rooted in something old-fashioned and authentic, in ancient folkways untainted by the marketplace. But Christmas trees became widely known in the United States during the mid-1830s, almost a decade earlier than any broad-based immigration from Germany can be said to have occurred.[60]

The truer reality was not that the custom came from the German immigrants, but from U.S. writers who had traveled in the local German places where the tree was a custom. These writers romantically described the traditions of German culture at Christmas and inspired the U.S. inculturation of Christmas earlier than did any German people practicing such rites in their new homeland. *Reading* about the Christmas tree through the eyes of a journalist who had been abroad was much more likely to have been the source of the decorated tree than *witnessing* the custom first-hand would have been. The tree customs were relatively new in German culture when they began to make their way into the American tradition of Christmas.

The change in the U.S. celebration of Christmas from one with *social* influence to one with merely *familial* warmth would not have been so inherently problematic if indeed the Gospels of Christianity were so inclined toward family. The values of the infancy narratives seem to have less and less support in the customs of Christmas as time goes by. There are remnants of the older theology of the feast, but — quite surprisingly — these adhere to relatively non-liturgical denominations, like the Salvation Army, whose tintinabulators can be found on streets

---

60. Ibid.: 177.

and at supermarkets collecting from the haves for the needs of the have-nots.

Much of this history of society and Christmas is more aptly taken up in the disciplines of economics, sociology, and theology, but because the exigencies of rich-and-poor in society have traditionally been reflected in the scriptures readings, hymns, preaching, and prayers of Christmas, the bearing of this deep tradition for the liturgy cannot be ignored.

Part Three:
The Theology of Christmas

Christ's Birth Today

The theology of Christmas has always emphasized the birth of God's Son in the present tense, and the church's liturgies on the feast have maintained this focus on the present with the pervasive use of the word "today" in its prayers and hymnody. This theology is captured in the responsorial antiphon sung frequently for Christmas, "Today is born our Savior, Christ the Lord," as well as explicitly and repeatedly in the Propers. In fact the very first word of the church at the Vigil of Christmas is "Today," as it appears in the entrance antiphon in the Sacramentary: "Today you will know that the Lord is coming to save us, and in the morning you will see this glory."[61]

The key word from the early church is also "today," *hodie* in Latin, a word that punctuated sermons on the solemnity of Christmas from its earliest years. So, too, in the Prefaces of the Eucharistic Prayer, the theological emphasis on the birth of Christ today and the use of present tense verbs is transparent, as in the Second Preface for the Eucharistic Prayer at Christmas:

> Father, all-powerful and ever-living God,
> we do well always and everywhere to give you thanks
> through Jesus Christ our Lord.
> Today you fill our hearts with joy
> as we recognize in Christ the revelation of your love.
> No eye can see his glory as our God,
> yet now he is seen as one like us.
> Christ is your Son before all ages,
> yet now he is born in time.

---

61. Entrance Antiphon, Christmas Vigil, in *Vatican II Sunday Missal: Millennium Edition* (Boston: Pauline Books and Media, 2001): 66.

He has come to lift up all things to himself,
to restore unity to creation,
and to lead mankind from exile into your heavenly kingdom.
With all the angels in heaven
we sing our joyful hymn of praise:
Holy, holy, holy Lord.[62]

Like the Christmas prefaces, the text of solemn blessing for Christmas deftly captures the simultaneity of God's favor in the historical past and in the present moment — today, *hodie* — while drawing on the major scriptural metaphors for the solemnity and the season:

When he came to us as man,
the Son of God scattered the darkness of this world,
and filled this holy night with his glory.
May the God of infinite goodness
scatter the darkness of sin
and brighten your hearts with holiness.
R. Amen.

God sent his angels to shepherds
to herald the great joy of our Savior's birth.
May he fill you with joy
and make you heralds of his gospel.
R. Amen.

When the Word became man,
earth was joined to heaven.
May he give you his peace and good will,
and fellowship with all the heavenly host.
R. Amen.[63]

Such texts challenge the church to awaken in its members a new appreciation of Christmas in the broadest sense — past, present, and future — as it was in the theology of St. Leo, when he instructed the church of Rome in the fifth century and continues to instruct the church now: "Today the sacrament of the Lord's birth shines brilliantly before our eyes."

Sun and Light in Christmas Prayers

Though in the northern hemisphere the sun appears only briefly in the sky at the time of Christmas, for the shortest day of the year precedes

---

62. Ibid.: 650–651.
63. Ibid.: 681–682.

the feast by just a few days, light and the sun are primary symbols for the feast. The beautiful metaphors of light and darkness accompanied the liturgical prayers of Christmas from the very start, and they are still very deep in the tradition. They are seen clearly in the prayers, such as in the collect at the Midnight Mass, for example, as the church prays:

> Father,
> you make this holy night radiant
> with the splendor of Jesus Christ our light.
> We welcome him as Lord, the true light of the world.[64]

And at the Christmas Mass at Dawn:

> Father,
> we are filled with the new light
> by the coming of your Word among us.
> May the light of faith
> shine in our words and actions.[65]

This imagery was linked to a particular verse from a relatively unknown book at the end of the Old Testament, the Book of Malachi: "[F]or you who fear my name the sun of righteousness shall rise" (4:2a). After the verse was translated into Latin by St. Jerome at the end of the fourth century, the key phrase taken up in preaching for centuries was that of the rising "sun of righteousness," or "sun of justice," *sol iustitiae*, applied to the Savior, Jesus Christ, as the feast of his birth was being inculturated widely in the last quarter of the fourth century, linking the day and its season, as before, to the balance of justice in society.

The ritual traditions of the church for Christmas through the centuries have been drawn from metaphors of light, particularly in those places where the light of day is at it shortest in the year. Images of light and darkness have been at the heart of the readings proclaimed at Christmas for centuries. Most poetic is the opening of the first reading at the Midnight Mass, from the prophet Isaiah (9:2):[66]

> The people who walked in darkness
>   have seen a great light;
> those who dwelt in a land of deep darkness,
>   on them has light shined.

---

64. Ibid.: 73
65. Ibid.: 78–79.
66. The RSV numbering here differs from most Bibles following the Hebrew numbering. In other translations, the verse is numbered as Isaiah 9:1.

The Gospel reading from John at the Mass during the Day also reflects this image of the Son: "The true light that enlightens every man was coming into the world" (1:9).

This confirms the strength of the history-of-religions hypothesis about the origins of Christmas, for the light imagery taken up in the natural time of the year when daylight is short supplies a fitting metaphor for the gift of the Son in the world.

Incarnate Word

The moral tradition of Roman Catholicism finds one of its fundaments in the life-mediating gift to the world in the incarnation, in God's advent into humanity as the Word made flesh. Yet because much of the life-supporting rhetoric of the church is negative and punitive — that is, not encouraging people toward the experience of what is good and holy about God's manifestation in human flesh but merely chastising them for what is prohibited and sinful — the theology of Christmas and of God's manifestation in human life is weakened. With the encouraging theology and the incomparably beautiful narratives of the Christmas Gospels, the solemnity would be a wonderful time for preachers to speak not only about the sanctity of God's presence in his Son, Jesus Christ, but also about the presence of God manifest in the flesh of baptized human beings in the church today.

As married Christians might be encouraged to sexual intimacy on Sundays,[67] Christmas coupling might occasion the advent of the bump in the birth rate in September and October that had once been noticeable. As the Lord's Day could be a celebration of the incarnation in marriage within the seven-day week, according to God's promise and gift in the post-resurrection narratives, so might Christmas be a time and season when the Son's coming could be joyfully and inventively celebrated in marital coupling and intimacy, a sign of God's restoration of humanity, a restoration captured well in the Third Preface to the Eucharistic Prayer for Christmas:

Father, all-powerful and ever-living God,
we do well always and everywhere to give you thanks
through Jesus Christ our Lord.
Today in him a new light has dawned upon the world:
God has become one with man,
and man has become one once again with God.
Your eternal Word has taken upon himself our human weakness,

---

67. See Volume 2, Chapter 1, "Sunday."

giving our mortal nature immortal value.
So marvelous is this oneness between God and man
that in Christ man restores to man the gift of everlasting life.
In our joy we sing to your glory
with all the choirs of angels.[68]

In God's love, of course, there is no change, and no time is better
than another for the human response to God's wonder and power. Yet,
though God's love for humanity does not change, the church marks
out the seasons of the liturgical year because humanity, weighed down
as it is with its inherited burden of original sin, cannot understand
or appreciate the fullness of God's gift in Jesus Christ except in the
sacraments ordered in time.

The "eternal Word of God," as used in the Preface above, refers to
the being of the second person of the Trinity throughout the ages, the
Son who existed from the beginning of time and will be with humanity
to its end. This Word is the gift of the Holy Spirit, for it is by the word
of the Spirit that the Son came to dwell in his mother, Mary. That
this incarnate presence is explicitly in the power of the Holy Spirit is
clear from the Gospel of Luke, where the angel Gabriel says to Mary,
"The Holy Spirit will come upon you, and the power of the Most High
will overshadow you" (1:35). This theology of manifestation is also
reflected in the Gospel proclamation from the Mass during the Day of
Christmas:

> In the beginning was the Word, and the Word was with God, and
> the Word was God. He was in the beginning with God; all things
> were made through him, and without him was not anything made
> that was made.

We know from this prologue of the Gospel of John (1:1–18; here at
1:1–3) that the Word of God existed before any other created thing,
and so at Christmas the church announces the eternity of the Word as
that Word is still proclaimed and celebrated in the sacraments by its
custodian, the people of God, the church.

Believers ever look to that relatively brief period of the life of the incarnate Jesus of Nazareth from his conception to his birth and infancy,
when he had "taken upon himself our human weakness," as in the
Preface of Christmas. Though this incarnate life is indeed God's gift,
for which the church continually offers thanks to the Giver, that is, the
Father, too often Christians understand the solemnity of Christmas to

---

68. *Vatican II Sunday Missal:* 651.

be only about the incarnate life of the Son in Bethlehem, Nazareth, the Decapolis, and Jerusalem, ignoring its link to the other manifestations that have continued unabated in the church from that graced moment in the manger. Such a narrow appreciation of the incarnation impoverishes the feast and distracts the community of faith from recognizing and celebrating God's gifts to humanity and the church at all times.

Christmas and Baptism

The baptized are God's people not because they deserve to be so, nor because they have earned their place in God's favor, but because of God's ever-effusive love and gift of his Son, made present in the first family long ago and continuing in the community of faith and its worship. The liturgies of Christmas remind us that the church is constituted and manifest "by the washing of regeneration and renewal in the Holy Spirit" (Titus 3:5b).[69]

Ministers of the liturgy and of the word, priests, and preachers work together to have the assembly of faith celebrate not just the memory of the infant Son in swaddling cloths, but the enduring life of the Savior today. This message and work will be efficacious by the power of the Holy Spirit in the church, and in the vibrancy and life of this community the forsaken and prodigal will find themselves restored and the broken will be made whole. God loves all of humanity, and the baptized are a sign of the bounty of that love. Christmas reminds the faithful that God's love is greater than human sinfulness. Baptism binds the people of God together, but such a bond is not without responsibility. Decisions about our lives are recast so that they no longer benefit just the individual, but the church and its sacraments.

Understanding the world of Palestine at the time of Jesus' birth, and seeing how improbable were the circumstances in which God's generosity was manifest, should be reflected in sermons that help people prepare for the advent of God in the most unlikely of times and places. Moreover, the precarious and complex evolution of the celebration and theology of the solemnity of Christmas confirms this improbability by merely human measures. Christmas is not only the expression of gratitude to God for the gift, but the humorous appreciation of how little humanity can do to earn God's love. That love might then flow into good works among the people in whom God's gift can be celebrated, but those works have no impact on the well-being of God.

The reading from the Letter to Titus proclaimed at the Midnight Mass of Christmas reflects the nuance of this shift:

---

69. Christmas Mass at Dawn, Second Reading.

[T]he grace of God has appeared for the salvation of all men, training us to renounce irreligion and worldly passions, and to live sober, upright, and godly lives. (2:11–12)

Moreover, the prayers of Christmas make the ever-present birth of Christ by the grace of the Father apparent. From the prayer after communion at the vigil Mass, the church prays:

> Father,
> we ask you to give us a new birth
> as we celebrate the beginning
> of your Son's life on earth.[70]

Christmas Hymns and Carols

The theology of remembering Christ's birth in the past so that the church can be alert to his birth today is well reflected in Christmas hymns ancient and new. The quality of hymns varies, as always, as does the well- or ill-suited relation between the implicit theology of the music and the explicit theology of the lyrics, but the popularity of the solemnity and the universality of its reception throughout most of the Christian world has resulted in a breadth of selection for this day and the season that follows it.

Even though Christmas was not a strong part of the Christian tradition and calendar in the United States before the nation's battle for independence from England, the feast, as recounted in the history above, did grow in strength in the nineteenth century. As a result, the most popular Christmas songs in the United States have been from the hands of Protestant composers and lyricists before the mass immigration of Catholics. Roman Catholic churches have integrated the Protestant hymns seamlessly, and this can be done because the texts have tended to draw from poetic elements of the infancy narratives of Matthew and Luke.

As with the prayers of the day, the hymns tend to reflect the theology of Christ's birth *today,* though in the spectrum of the theology of the hymns some have a stronger sense of Christ's birth in the church at prayer than others. More problematic are hymns with an already-but-not-yet theology, which teaches that God was present in the birth and manifestation at Bethlehem and will be present again at the end of time, but that humanity languishes in the vast interim between, a theology that betrays the sacramentality of God's gift throughout time

---

70. *Vatican II Sunday Missal:* 72.

and the incarnation of the risen Christ in humanity as a whole and the church as the elected remnant reflecting that humanity.

A Christmas hymn in which the theological component is strong — though perhaps not well complemented by the music that accompanies it — is "O Little Town of Bethlehem."[71] Written in the middle of the nineteenth century by Phillips Brooks, an Episcopal priest who lived in Philadelphia, and performed in his parish for the first time in 1868, the hymn's as-then-so-now quality is not didactic but subtle and formative, as in the liturgical texts examined above:

> O little town of Bethlehem!
> How still we see thee lie,
> Above thy deep and dreamless sleep,
> The silent stars go by.

The difference between it and many starry-eyed remembrances of the manger in Bethlehem in other hymns for Christmas is the author's combination of the first-person plural and the present tense, "How still we see thee lie," by which singers find themselves at the scene of the Savior's birth in their imaginations without depreciating the manifestation of God in the flesh today:

> Yet in thy dark streets shineth
> The Everlasting light;
> The hopes and fears of all the years,
> Are met in thee tonight.

The shining "dark streets" are a part of the world in our times as is the "Everlasting light," the metaphor that appears throughout the readings and prayers of the Christmas season:

> For Christ is born of Mary,
> And gathered all above,
> While mortals sleep the angels keep
> Their watch of wondering love.

The social upheavals named and the coming of justice proclaimed in Luke's birth narratives were as much a part of Brooks' Philadelphia in 1867 as they are today:

> Where children pure and happy
> Pray to the blesséd Child,

---

71. Phillips Brooks, "O Little Town of Bethlehem," in *The Hymnal of the Protestant Episcopal Church in the United States of America 1940* (New York: Church Pension Fund, 1940, 1961): #21–22.

> Where misery cries out to thee,
>   Son of the mother mild;
> Where charity stands watching,
>   And faith holds wide the door,
> The dark night wakes, the glory breaks,
>   And Christmas comes once more.

As the time of antiquity and the present are joined, so too singers today are joined to the heavenly host of angels who witnessed that earlier birth.

> O holy child of Bethlehem!
>   Descend to us, we pray,
> Cast out our sin and enter in,
>   Be born in us to-day.
> We hear the Christmas angels,
>   The great glad tidings tell,
> O, come to us, abide with us,
>   Our Lord Emmanuel!

As the church does in the celebration of the death and resurrection, so in the celebration of the birth of Christ: It does not merely remember, but celebrates, proclaims, and indeed experiences the reality of God-with-us in and through its members in their own place and time. Indeed, the best hymns do not suggest that the birth of Christ now is any less a gift and miracle for the motley crew assembling year after year than it was for the motley crew of parents, shepherds, animals, and magi at the manger in antiquity.

Liturgy at Home: The Tree and the Manger in the *Book of Blessings*

There are not many days or seasons of the liturgical year for which the church supplies rites for celebrations away from the church, yet Christmas is one for which there is an "Order for the Blessing of a Christmas Manger or Nativity Scene" and an "Order for the Blessing of a Christmas Tree." Although history highlights the consumerist impulse that has shaped Christian piety in the United States, and by it colored the use of the Christmas tree in the culture, as a symbol the Christmas tree is deeply and perhaps inexorably embedded into the feast and can be ennobled by the rites around it in Christian homes.

In the "Rite of Blessing of a Christmas Manger or Nativity Scene," the social circumstances of the family of Jesus are recalled toward the realization of salvation and justice as God-is-with-us in the world today. The introduction to the Order rightly points to the thirteenth-century holy man who popularized the tradition: "In its present form the custom of displaying figures depicting the birth of Jesus Christ owed its origin to St. Francis of Assisi who made the Christmas crèche or manger for Christmas eve of 1223."[72] In the rite of blessing, the general intercessions and prayer of blessing offer a powerful theology of God's providence in creation and family life:

Let us ask for God's blessing on this Christmas manger and upon ourselves, that we who reflect on the birth of Jesus may share in the salvation he accomplished.

R. Come, Lord, dwell with us.

For the Church of God, as we recall the circumstances surrounding the birth of Christ, that we may always proclaim with joy his gift of new life for all people, we pray to the Lord.

R. Come, Lord, dwell with us.

For the world in which we live, that it may come to recognize Christ who was greeted by the angels and shepherds, we pray to the Lord.

R. Come, Lord, dwell with us.

For our families and our homes, that Christ who was laid in the manger may dwell with us always, we pray to the Lord.

R. Come, Lord, dwell with us.

For parents, that their love for their children may be modeled on that of the Virgin Mary and St. Joseph, we pray to the Lord.

R. Come, Lord, dwell with us.

Then after the intercessions, the prayer of blessing is said:

God of every nation and people,
from the very beginning of creation
you have made manifest your love:
when our need for a Savior was great
you sent your Son to be born of the Virgin Mary.
To our lives he brings joy and peace, justice, mercy, and love.

---

72. *Book of Blessings* (Collegeville, MN: Liturgical Press, 1989): 583.

Lord, bless all who look upon this manger;
may it remind us of the humble birth of Jesus,
and raise up our thoughts to him,
who is God-with-us and Savior of all,
and who lives and reigns for ever and ever.
R. Amen.[73]

The introduction to the "Order for the Blessing of a Christmas Tree" offers sober catechesis: "The use of the Christmas tree is relatively modern. Its origins are found in the medieval mystery plays which depicted the tree of paradise and the Christmas light or candle which symbolized Christ, the Light of the world."

The introduction also indicates how the tree is suited to the liturgical year, marking it quite distinctly from the U.S. culture in which the trees appear after Thanksgiving: "According to custom, the Christmas tree is set up just before Christmas and may remain in place until the solemnity of Epiphany," followed by instruction on the tree's use in the home and in the church: "Although the primary place for the Christmas tree is the home, at times one or more may also be placed in the church. In such a case, the decoration of the trees should be appropriate to their use in the church, and care should be taken that they do not interfere with the requirements of the liturgical space." Moreover, "the lights of the tree are illuminated after the prayer of blessing."[74]

Preparing for the blessing of the tree, the minister addresses those present: "My brothers and sisters, amidst signs and wonders Christ Jesus was born in Bethlehem of Judea: his birth brings joy to our hearts and enlightenment to our minds. With this tree, decorated and adorned, may we welcome Christ among us; may its lights guide us to the perfect light."[75] The second of the two prayers of blessing makes the link in salvation between the tree and the cross:

Lord our God,
we praise you for the light of creation:
the sun, the moon, and the stars of the night.
We praise you for the light of Israel:
the Law, the prophets, and the wisdom of the Scriptures.
We praise you for Jesus Christ, your Son:
he is Emmanuel, God-with-us, the Prince of Peace,
who fills us with the wonder of your love.

---

73. Ibid.: 583–592.
74. Ibid.: 593–600.
75. Ibid.: 594.

Lord God,
let your blessing come upon us
as we illumine this tree.
May the light and cheer it gives
be a sign of the joy that fills our hearts.
May all who delight in this tree
come to the knowledge and joy of salvation.
We ask this through Christ our Lord.
R. Amen.

Or:

Holy Lord,
we come with joy to celebrate the birth of your Son,
who rescued us from the darkness of sin
by making the cross a tree of life and light.

May this tree, arrayed in splendor,
remind us of the life-giving cross of Christ,
that we may always rejoice
in the new life that shines in our hearts.
We ask this through Christ our Lord.
R. Amen.

Abbreviated versions of these rites are included in *Catholic Household Blessings and Prayers.*[76] For these rites in the home, the planner and presider will likely need some practice because the times of the liturgical year are few when rites of the church are bolstered by rites for the household. Catechesis in the parish to encourage households to use the domestic rites and to appreciate the link between the presence of Christ in the church and in the home is needed frequently because parishioners are often not aware of the existence of the resources or of how to use them in the sacred seasons of the liturgical year.

Conclusion

The motion picture *Love Actually* was released shortly before Christmas in 2003, appropriately so, for the narrative is set in the weeks leading up to the day. The movie captures a theology of Christmas and

---

76. The Bishops' Committee on the Liturgy and the National Conference of Catholic Bishops, *Catholic Household Blessings and Prayers* (Collegeville, MN: Liturgical Press and St. John's Abbey, 1988): 113–120.

the inculturation its narratives evoke in local communities. In an early scene the sister of Britain's Prime Minister (played by Emma Thompson) is chatting with her daughter, Daisy, about some rumblings at school:

KAREN [mother]: So — what's this big news then?

DAISY: We've been given our parts in the Nativity play. And I'm the lobster.

KAREN: The lobster?

DAISY: Yes.

KAREN: In the Nativity play?

DAISY: Yes. First Lobster.

KAREN: There was more than one lobster present at the birth of Jesus?

DAISY: Durr... [77]

The exchange mimics the tension between historical-Jesus scholarship and cultural expressions of popular piety, and with Christmas the piety is as expansive as historical criticism can be circumscribing. Yet the inventiveness of the evangelists in the infancy narratives is inviting, and so around the world the crèche is depicted in an infinite variety of ways, all derived from the manifestation of God's Son to humanity and the infancy narratives that, on this side of the equator, in the liturgy bring people together in celebration at the darkest time of the calendar year.

The opening scene of the film has the voice of the Prime Minister (played by Hugh Grant) as he offers a reflection on the state of the world. His opening monologue expresses a poignant theology of the manifestation of God's presence in the world as the revelation of love wonderfully set in the Christmas countdown, since love and its nativity ever reflect the dazzling brilliance of God's life in humanity. So the initial voice-over of Britain's P.M. at the outset of the story:

Whenever I get gloomy with the state of the world, I think about the Arrivals Gate at Heathrow Airport. General opinion's starting to make out that we live in a world of hatred and greed — but I don't see that. Seems to me that love is everywhere. Often

77. Richard Curtis, *Love Actually* (New York: St. Martin's Press, 2003): 14–15.

it's not particularly dignified, or newsworthy — but it's always there — fathers and sons, mothers and daughters, husbands and wives, boyfriends, girlfriends, old friends. Before the planes hit the Twin Towers, as far as I know, none of the phone calls from the people on board were messages of hate or revenge — they were all messages of love. If you look for it, I've got a sneaking suspicion you'll find that love actually is all around.[78]

As that monologue opens the film, the scene shows countless people arriving at the airport, engaging images of the full-bodied, magnetic embraces by people who have not seen one another over a long distance, at least, and perhaps over a long time as well, unions in the flesh of people who love one another.

Although the movie is set within the weeks leading up to Christmas, from one perspective one might think that there is little explicitly Christian theology in the cinematic narrative. Yet one notices its interwoven narratives of Christmas are a reflection of the omnipresence of love in the world and of the variety of particular manifestations of love as it always is, by necessity, expressed in the coming together in the flesh of people of all different shapes, sizes, colors, ages, and states. Whether in the church or not, these comings together are God's gift most generously manifested in human life by the power of the Holy Spirit. The church's traditions, narratives, symbols, and liturgical expressions provide a perfect means for appreciating and celebrating and sharing this gift, and Christmas is the deep pivot in the expression of God's love in the church.

As they are formed toward incorporation into the church before, at, and after baptism, Christians celebrate God's manifestation, and Christmas is an imperative feast of this gift to humanity in the Son of God. Since the risen Christ is experienced when two or three or more baptized are gathered (Matthew 18:20), and since the fruits of that experience is new life, what greater or more engaging narrative could one find in the scriptures than that of the infant Jesus come to the world as a baby? This baby came to change the world, as the incarnate individual, Jesus of Nazareth, and as the risen Christ he still comes, constituted and incarnate in the church and the world, and the celebration of Christmas exercises the ability of believers to find him where he is least expected, in twenty-first-century counterparts to that first-century feeding trough.

---

78. Ibid.: 9.

Since Christmas is the time of the liturgical year when the wonderful story of birth is proclaimed, the solemnity captures and celebrates the knitting together of solitary and fragile human lives so that they may be God's ongoing gift of presence in community — surprisingly perfect, still incarnate, and dependably eternal. Faith is the response to this gift of the ever-living, ever-giving God, accessible only with the embrace of the church wrought by baptism and appreciated over time. God's generosity does not change with human aging, but human ability to see God's presence in the utterly unexpected seems to deepen and widen with age and experience in relationships. Though physical abilities are constricted as we grow older, it seems that human appreciation of God's surprising and effusive ways — as a result of faith and the community on which the faith is founded — expands with age, a realization expressed poignantly in Mark Doty's *Heaven's Coast:*

> I can feel how large, how essential this moment is as it's happening; that is what I have come to love about being an adult, to the extent that I can claim that title: that one knows more about how good things are, how much they matter, as they're happening, that knowledge isn't necessarily retrospective anymore. When I was younger, I missed so much, failing to be fully present, only recognizing the quality of particular moments and gifts after the fact. Perhaps that's one thing that being "grown-up" is: to realize in the present the magnitude or grace of what we're being offered.[79]

Although Christmas is often popularly considered a celebration for children, human appreciation of the theology of Christmas is deepened by experience, and so the liturgies of the solemnity coax the complacent into opening their old eyes to see new things. This perplexity of human living is one of the many mysteries of God's love, uniting those brought forth by the work of the Holy Spirit, a union that captures the mystery of Christmas, the mystery of love..

Though for many people, life in the world and its societies too often serves up only hatred, greed, revenge, and violence, these are not the final word, even in a culture and time fueled by the anxieties of war, and even during the omnipresent depression of shopping mania in the weeks leading up to the celebration of God-made-flesh. Fact is that the church's celebration of Christmas bears a strong and engaging witness

---

79. Mark Doty, *Heaven's Coast* (New York: Harper Perennial, 1997): 90.

to God's love in the world, a love that was, is, and ever will be the first and last word in all human life, indeed in all living beings, from aardvark to zebra, mosquito to solar system.

Christmas celebrates love given to humanity and lived out day by day in the love of God toward the world and in the immeasurable bounty manifested for Christians in the story of the birth of Jesus in the humble circumstances of a feeding trough in Bethlehem two millennia ago. This manifestation was indeed a human and divine event different from the gift of the incarnation. That feast — the Annunciation, on March 25 — narrates and marks the message of the angel Gabriel to Mary or — another name for the phenomenon of the union of the divinity and humanity of God's Son in the womb of Mary — the incarnation, God made flesh, *carne.*

What is proclaimed at Christmas is not the point at which God became flesh in Mary, but the point at which the Son incarnate — in the flesh — was manifest and perceived by creation and by the human peers of Jesus of Nazareth in Roman-occupied Palestine of the early first century. Christmas is foremost a Christian reality, expansive in time and ever-deepening in gravity, the human reckoning of the graced moment that revealed the full intersection of heaven and earth in the taking on of flesh in God's Son Jesus, the moment when the Blessed Virgin Mary brought forth her Son Jesus.

Christians tend to identify Christmas as merely the remembrance of the birth of Jesus to his parents, Mary and Joseph, but the manifestation celebrated at Christmas includes much more. Although there is necessarily some identity, some continuity, between the first appearance of Jesus and the appearance of the risen Son today, each moment of God's manifestation in the Spirit is for the up-building and uplifting of humanity, and these moments include those of the Son revealed as the Word of God, as the incarnate Jesus of Nazareth, as the risen Christ proclaimed at the tomb, as the risen Christ in the church, and as the great King and Judge, the sorter of the living and the dead now and at the hour of our death. All these moments are swept up into the mystery of the revelation of God's Son in Jesus Christ yesterday, today, and tomorrow.[80] Any celebration that excludes any of these manifestations does not reflect fully the mystery of Christmas, of the Word made flesh then, now, and in the future.

This is the gift of Christmas, the great kindness of God in the appearance of the Savior, a gift mediated to the church in the "water of

---

80. See Volume 1, Chapter 1, "On God and Time," on Pope Benedict XVI.

rebirth," baptism, and in the "renewal by the Holy Spirit," who brings
believers together — strangers, neighbors, aliens, "fathers and sons,
mothers and daughters, husbands and wives, boyfriends, girlfriends,
old friends"[81] — as the body of the risen Christ. The wealth of salvation is a gift completely unearned, yet this is the greatest gift of the
season, for Christmas is the time when we recognize, celebrate, and
thereby give thanks to God for the state of being smothered in God's
love, which is, actually, all around.

---

81. "Love Actually," as in note 77 above.

Chapter 4

EPIPHANY

Bessie Popkin

At the start of Isaac Bashevic Singer's story "The Key," the protagonist prepares to leave home, a freighted feat for an elderly widow in New York City:

> Going out was connected with many difficulties, especially on a hot summer day: first, forcing her fat body into a corset, squeezing her swollen feet into shoes, and combing her hair, which Bessie dyed at home and which grew wild and was streaked in all colors — yellow, black, gray, red; then making sure that while she was out her neighbors would not break into her apartment and steal linen, clothes, documents, or just disarrange things and make them disappear. . . . Bessie had long ago realized that no means were adequate against those determined to be spiteful — not the metal door, the special lock, her letters to the police, the mayor, the FBI, and even the president in Washington.[1]

The day as she planned it, however, was diverted when she returned to the apartment after the errand, where

> She put in the key and turned it. But woe, the key broke. Only the handle remained in her hand. Bessie fully grasped the catastrophe. The other people in the building had copies of their keys hanging in the superintendent's apartment, but she trusted no one — some time ago, she had ordered a new combination lock, which she was sure no master key could open.[2]

So by her own design and strategy for survival, her life was without options or people to turn to in such a bind, so she ventured back out into the street, where

---

1. Isaac Bashevic Singer, "The Key," as in John Updike and Katrina Kenison, eds., *The Best American Short Stories of the Century* (Boston: Houghton Mifflin, 1999): 493–502, here at 493.
2. Ibid.: 496.

It occurred to Bessie that the eyes of the onlookers gleamed with an uncanny satisfaction. They enjoy other people's misfortunes, she thought. It is their only comfort in this miserable city. No, she wouldn't find anybody to help her.[3]

Only after she'd fallen asleep outside on some steps and awoken did the situation seem to shift:

> Her head, which rested against the wall, felt as heavy as a stone. Her legs had become wooden. Her ears seemed to be filled with water. She lifted one of her eyelids and saw the moon. It hovered low in the sky over a flat roof, and near it twinkled a greenish star. Bessie gasped. She had almost forgotten that there was a sky, a moon, stars. Years had passed and she never looked up — always down. Her windows were hung with draperies so that the spies across the street could not see her. Well, if there was a sky, perhaps there was also a God, angels, Paradise....
>
> For the first time in years, Bessie felt the need to recite a prayer. The Almighty would have mercy on her even though she did not deserve it. Father and Mother might intercede for her on high. Some Hebrew words hung on the tip of her tongue, but she could not recall them. Then she remembered, "Hear, O Israel."[4]

Singer's chronicle of Bessie's awakening is the tale of an epiphany, a reordering of world and society that reveals the pure, undeserved gift of new life from on high, after which the world and its inhabitants can never again appear as they had before. Various Christian biblical narratives reflect transformations like that seen in Bessie's new world: Paul blinded and fallen from a horse (Acts 9:1–9); Peter's vision convincing him that non-Jews should be admitted to the church (Acts 10:9–39).

For Bessie, an ordinary event occasioned the epiphany, the breaking of a key, after which the world was reborn: "She felt as if she had awakened from a long sleep. The broken key had opened a door in her brain that had shut when Sam died,"[5] and once she moved over the threshold occasioned by the epiphany, society and world were new, exciting, unprecedented:

> No, not all in this neighborhood were gangsters and murderers. One young man even nodded good morning to Bessie. She tried to smile at him, realizing she had forgotten that feminine gesture

---

3. Ibid.: 498.
4. Ibid.: 498–499.
5. Ibid.: 499.

she knew so well in her youth; it was almost the first lesson her mother had taught her.

She reached her building, and outside stood the Irish super, her deadly enemy. He was talking to the garbage collectors. He was a giant of a man, with a short nose, a long upper lip, sunken cheeks, and a pointed chin. His yellow hair covered a bald spot. He gave Bessie a startled look. "What's the matter, Grandma?"

Stuttering, Bessie told him what had happened to her. She showed him the handle of the key she had clutched in her hand all night.

"Mother of God!" he called out.

"What shall I do?" Bessie asked.

"I will open your door."

"But you don't have a passkey."

"We have to be able to open all doors in case of fire."[6]

The man who had earlier "only waited for her downfall" became her rescuer by the transformation occasioned by the meanest of objects, a door key: " 'Next time, if something like this happens, call me. That's what I'm here for.' "

Thomas Merton

Bessie's transformation was keenly imagined and written by Singer, yet the human subject of such a tale is not unique, for by God's grace people are always called to consider their world and society through new lenses. Bessie brings to mind other people and characters, real and invented, biblical and extra-canonical, who have been so transformed. Thomas Merton's intimate confessions of a complicated life in the Christian faith have occasioned epiphany upon epiphany for believers in the decades since his early death. "My life and my death are not purely and simply my own business. I live by and for others," he wrote in *Conjectures of a Guilty Bystander* — a work filled with epiphanies like that of Bessie Popkin — "and my death involves others."[7]

Again and again in *Conjectures* one finds Merton rightly reflecting on the necessary transformations and epiphanies in any Christian's life of faith: "One has to doubt and reject everything else in order to believe firmly in Christ, and after one has begun to believe, one's faith itself must be tested and purified. Christianity is not merely a set of forgone conclusions," he wrote, reflecting on the unpredictability of

6. Ibid.: 500–501.

7. Merton, *Conjectures of a Guilty Bystander* (Garden City, NY: Image Books, 1977): 225.

healthy Christian faith from within the predictability of monastic embrace, enclosure, and routine — weighty words from one of the most well-known cloistered monks of all Christian history. Such a disposition of openness to the unexpected precipitated Merton's continual conversion, realized in many aspects of this life.

Though he left the cloister of Gethsemane infrequently, *Conjectures* also has his reflection on a moment of transformation when he was away from the monastery:

> In Louisville, at the corner of Fourth and Walnut, in the center of the shopping district, I was suddenly overwhelmed with the realization that I love those people, that they were mine and I theirs, that we could not be alien to one another even though we were total strangers.

Akin to Bessie, Merton felt the change, as he wrote: "It was like waking from a dream of separateness, of spurious self-isolation in a special world, the world of renunciation and supposed holiness. The whole illusion of a separate holy existence is a dream."[8] This wonderment, the reckoning of one's connection to others in a new way, plunges one more deeply into the life of humanity and the life of God incarnate there:

> It is a glorious destiny to be a member of the human race, though it is a race dedicated to many absurdities and one which makes many terrible mistakes: yet with all that, God Himself gloried in becoming a member of the human race. A member of the human race! To think that such a commonplace realization should suddenly seem like news that one holds the winning ticket in a cosmic sweepstake.[9]

The joy celebrated at Epiphany is that one does not covet God's election as one's own, but shares and celebrates that election with all humanity. We are not privileged by our electing God but by his choosing us, not for the salvation of individuals, but for the redemption gained for all humanity — all "member[s] of the human race," past, present, and future — in the life and death of Jesus of Nazareth, the Son of God:

> I have the immense joy of being *man*, a member of a race in which God Himself became incarnate. As if the sorrows and stupidities of the human condition could overwhelm me, now I realize what we all are. And if only everybody could realize this? But it cannot

---

8. Ibid.: 156.
9. Ibid.: 157.

be explained. There is no way of telling people that they are all walking around shining like the sun.

As Merton realized, the social cohesion of humanity as a living body is a fruit of God's generosity. Yet this dawning is by revelation received in faith, and so there is no way of awakening humanity as a whole to it, or of awakening individuals to it, apart from a community of faith, with its canons of language, symbols, and behaviors. It can be passed along from blessed person to blessed person only as each finds the source of the gift outside themselves. The life of God is manifest in their life together but only if they can yield to an epiphany outside themselves, in the apartment building super for Bessie, and in the Louisville crowd for Merton. Our very being—breathing and gasping for breath, walking and standing still, eating and drinking, hungering and thirsting, bathing and getting dirty again—has a source apart from ourselves.

The solemnity of Epiphany does not occasion epiphanies of life anymore than the sacraments themselves constrain the presence of God, so that he no longer has autonomy over those or upon what he chooses to be present. The church discerns from the tradition when and where God is present and to be celebrated, but the presence of God is ever wider and wiser than the church's teaching, its feasts, or sacraments. So the solemnity of Epiphany celebrates God's illuminating, quirky, animating, and transforming presence in human life at all times, not only on the one-in-three-hundred-sixty-five-days when the feast appears in the liturgical year. The feast exists not to occasion epiphany but to celebrate it, or them. It embraces those moments — liturgical and extra-liturgical — as God's gift and presence to humanity.

As in the solemnity of Christmas in the last chapter, so it is in the solemnity of Epiphany here, when — as the small sphere of Bessie Popkin's New York life broadened to recognize that her deadly enemy might not be so unto eternity — the church encourages, embraces, and celebrates all times when ordinary, predictable endings are shaken up and set right to reveal surprises, transformations, and new endings. By God's grace and humanity's reception of it, the broken, prodigal, and forsaken are whole, found, and loved.

Part One:
The Origins of Epiphany — East

At its origins the celebration of Epiphany did not have three wise men as the main characters of the Gospel for the day; rather, the narrative of Epiphany, at its early third-century appearance, was the baptism of the Lord. Though the narratives of Bessie Popkin and Thomas Merton might at first seem quite distinct from the celebration of baptism, they are not so far apart, for, even before baptism had found its place in the liturgical year at the Easter Vigil, baptism was always the celebration of social transformation. The rite indeed marks people coming to the faith and reconfiguring their worlds as members of a new society, sharing new values with those who had before been strangers.

There are a number of aspects to the celebration of Epiphany in the early church that supply some understanding of the gravity it bears in the tradition and in the social changes it evokes in the church and believers. The first evidence of Epiphany as the celebration of the baptism of the Lord comes from Egypt. The historical development of the feast begins there and in other regions of the Eastern church.

Egypt

The earliest evidence comes from the *Stromateis* of Clement of Alexandria. Writing in or about 215, Clement was not describing the tradition of his own church, but that of the Basilidians, a Gnostic group who celebrated the birth and baptism of Christ on January 6. Clement's main point was calendrical, aiming to demonstrate that Jewish traditions of dating were more ancient than those of the Greeks and Romans. To this end he starts listing the various Caesars and how their births relate chronologically to the birth of the Christian Savior, and this is followed immediately by his description of those who are as attentive to the date of Christ's baptism as others are to his birth:

> There are some people who are more meticulous about the Savior's nativity and adduce the day as well as the year, the twenty-fifth day of Pachon in the twenty-eighth year of Augustus.[10]

> The followers of Basilides also celebrated the day of his baptism, spending the previous night in readings. They place it in the fifteenth year of Tiberius Caesar, on the fifteenth (or according to others the eleventh) of the month of Tubi.[11]

Though much has been written about the calendrical indications in this passage, the two days that he mentions as the fifteenth and

---

10. From note 671 in John Ferguson, *Clement of Alexandria: Stromateis*, Books One to Three (Washington: Catholic University Press, 1991): 132: "Pachon is the ninth Egyptian solar month (varying by our calendar from year to year) placing the birth on 20 May. The Armenian Church celebrated it on 6 January. The festival on 25 December dates from the year 336. There is no month in which the birth had not been placed."

11. PG 8: 888; trans. John Ferguson, *Stromateis:* 131–132.

eleventh of Tybi correspond, respectively, to January 10 and 6 in the Julian calendar.

The Basilidians were a group who believed that Jesus became the Son of God at his baptism, and later references to the "birth" narrative of the feast might not have been to the infancy stories but to the advent of divinity into humanity on the occasion of Jesus' baptism. Clement's description is supported by the antiquity of the evidence, for, even though the four Gospels were written long before Clement's tract, they were not brought together as a canon of inspired and authoritative scriptures a bit later. In fact, at the start of the third century, there were many more than four Gospels in circulation in the churches of Christianity. Moreover, the birth narratives of Jesus from the Bible are from the Gospels of Matthew and Luke, and even in those Gospels the infancy narratives are thought to be later additions.[12] Clement's reference to the Basilidians does not indicate the narrative of a particular Gospel proclaimed for the feast.

In addition to the narrative possibilities regarding the early third-century reference to Epiphany in Clement, January 6 would have coincided with the annual flooding of the Nile River. This great flowing body of water had flooded before the emergence of Christianity in Egypt, of course, so, as with other feasts, the calendar took advantage of cosmological and natural phenomena as catechetical tools. The symbol of water, so prevalent in Egypt at the beginning of January, was tied to baptism, so it is not surprising that the earliest story from the life of Jesus associated with Epiphany is the story of his baptism in the Jordan River at the hand of John the Baptist. For believers in ancient Egypt, the simultaneity of the flooding of the Nile River and the marking of Jesus' baptism ennobled the two events, for the natural waters were given symbolic, narrative, and religious meaning when the consecration of water and the celebration of baptism were marked at the time of the river water's yearly rise.

Even in this early evidence, there is the start of what will become common in the testimony about this narrative, countering the embarrassment some of the fathers felt at the Savior needing to be baptized. Jesus' baptism at the hand of John suggests, of course, that something was deficient in the Savior and needed to be rectified by the washing in the Jordan. Beginning the tradition of justifying why the Savior submitted to baptism, Clement asked:

---

12. Raymond Brown, *The Birth of the Messiah: A Commentary on the Infancy Narratives in Matthew and Luke* (New York: Doubleday, 1977). For the relation of the infancy narratives to the rest of the narratives, on Matthew, see pages 48–50; on Luke, 239–253.

On that day when Christ was reborn, was he already perfect,
or — a very foolish question — was he defective? If the latter,
then he needed to add to his knowledge. But since he is God, it
is not likely that he needed to learn even one thing more. No one
can be greater than the Word, nor can anyone teach him who is
the one and only teacher. But if he is perfect, then why was [he]
baptized? This is what happens with us, whose model the Lord
made himself. When we are baptized, we are enlightened; being
enlightened, we become adopted sons, we are made perfect; and
becoming perfect, we are made divine.[13]

The link between the natural overflow of the Nile and the baptism of
Jesus was aided by the narrative of Jesus' baptism (Matthew 3:1–17;
Mark 1:2–13; Luke 3:1–22), which itself took place in a natural context, the Jordan River — a comparably modest stream relative to the
Nile, but great in the Gospel narratives as the locus for the baptism
of the Savior. Though the scriptures do not offer such a theological
interpretation of the narrative, the fathers of the church will explain
the enigma they faced in explaining why the Savior underwent baptism, and they did so by offering the event as a chance for the Savior
to sanctify the waters of the world: not that he needed anything from
the rite performed at the hand of the Baptist, but that the world itself
needed the sanctification occasioned as his body touched the waters of
the Jordan River.[14]

Later testimony about Epiphany in Egypt comes from a father of the
Latin tradition, John Cassian (ca. 360–430), a monk from the Roman
province of Scythia. In Cassian one finds the custom of announcing at
Epiphany the date of the proximate Easter, as evident in the paschal
letters of Athanasius of Alexandria. According to Cassian,

In the country of Egypt this custom by ancient tradition observed
that — when Epiphany is past, which the priests of that province
regard as the time, both of our Lord's baptism and also of his
birth in the flesh, and so celebrate the commemoration of either
mystery not separately as in the Western provinces by one the
single festival of this day — letters are sent from the bishop of

---

13. *Paedagogos* 6:25–26; PG 8: 280–281; trans. by Simon P. Wood, *Christ the Educator*,
FC 23 (Washington, DC: The Catholic University of America, 1954).

14. See, for example, Hymn 9 for Epiphany from Ephraem of Syria, NPNF, second series, volume 13, part 2 (Grand Rapids: Eerdmans, 1983). For a comprehensive study on the
treatment of the baptism in the Fathers see Kilian McDonnell, *The Baptism of Jesus in the
Jordan: The Trinitarian and Cosmic Order of Salvation* (Collegeville, MN: Liturgical Press,
1996).

Alexandria through all the church of Egypt, by which the beginning of Lent, and the day of Easter are pointed out, not only in all cities, but also in all monasteries.[15]

The paschal letters of Athanasius span the years from 329 to 371, covering nearly the time from soon after the Council of Nicea (325) to the Council of Constantinople (381), a period during which there were tremendous change in theology and worship.[16] Among the changes would be the narrative content and theological significance of Epiphany.

Yet another fourth-century church leader, Epiphanius of Salamis (ca. 315–403), wrote of the celebration of Epiphany in Egypt. A Palestinian by birth, Epiphanius was an enthusiast of monasticism and founded a monastery in Judea, in Eleutheropolis. In his most famous work, *The Refutation of All Heresies*, he took up some of the calendrical concerns of his day, and among these was Epiphany, in particular his concern about pagan ritual practices associated with the day. Epiphanius was nothing if not a polemicist: "Those who guilefully preside over the cult of idols are obliged to confess a part of the truth, and in many places deceitfully celebrate a very great festival on the very night of the Epiphany, to deceive the idolaters who believe them into hoping in the imposture and seeking the truth." He continues by detailing what was done at the pagan celebration in Egypt:

At Alexandria, in the Coreum, as they call it, there is a very large temple, the shrine of Core. They stay up all night singing hymns to the idol with a flute accompaniment. And when they have concluded their nightlong vigil torchbearers descend into an underground shrine after cockcrow and bring up a wooden image which is seated naked <on> a litter. It has a sign of the cross inlaid with gold on its forehead, two other such signs, [one] actually [on each of] its two knees — altogether five signs with a gold impress. And they carry the image itself seven times round the innermost shrine with flutes, tambourines and hymns, hold a feast, and take it back down to its place underground. And when

15. Merja Merras, *The Origins of the Celebration of the Christian Feast of Epiphany: An Ideological, Cultural and Historical Study* (Joensuu, Finland: Joensuu University Press, 1995): 110–111.

16. See *S. Athanase: Lettres Festales et Pastorales en Copt*, ed. L.-Th. Lefort, Scriptores Coptici 19–20, Corpus Scriptorum Christianorum Orientalium 150–151 (Louvain: Imprimerie Orientaliste, 1955). Of the two volumes, the Coptic is in the first with a French translation of the same in the second volume.

you ask them what this mystery means they reply that today at this hour Core — that is, the virgin — gave birth to Aeo.[17]

From his description one can see why, once Christianity was the dominant religious tradition in Egypt, the nativity narrative found a home there, for its pagan precedent also had a virgin birth, and it is not unknown that church fathers often tried to draw pagans to the Christian faith by appropriating non-Christian symbols into the Christian narratives. The nativity content was not apparent in the early third-century mention of the feast by Clement of Alexandria, but at the time of Epiphanius the nativity appears as an integral aspect of the celebration of God's manifestations to humanity and the world.

Epiphanius also mentioned the virgin birth and its pagan precedent as part of a rite celebrated in Arabia similar to that of Egypt: "This also goes on in the city of Petra, in the idolatrous temple there. [Petra is the capital city of Arabia, the scriptural Edom.] They praise the virgin with hymns in the Arab language and call her Chaamu — that is, Core, or virgin — in Arabic. And the child who is born of her they call Dusares, that is, 'only son of the Lord.' And this is also done that night in the city of Elusa, as it is there in Petra, and in Alexandria."[18] He also demonstrated that the date of Epiphany was being contested, and, among other narratives, he incorporated here a mention of the magi, whose story would become the proclamation for the day in those places where the birth narrative was received and celebrated according to the newly promulgated Roman date, December 25. He continued:

> I have been obliged to prove this with many examples because of those who do not believe that "the Epiphany" is a good name for the fleshly birth of the Savior, who was born at the eighth hour and manifested, by the angels' testimony, to the shepherds and the world — but he was manifested to Mary and Joseph as well. And the star was manifested to the magi in the east at that hour, two years before their arrival at Jerusalem and Bethlehem, when Herod asked the magi themselves the precise time of the star's manifestation, and they told him it was no more than two years before. And this very word gave the Epiphany its name, from Herod's saying, "the manifestation of the star."[19]

---

17. Section IV.22.8 of *The Panarion of Epiphanius of Salamis: Books II and III (Sects 47–80, De Fide)*, trans. Frank Williams (Leiden: E. J. Brill, 1994): 50–51.

18. Ibid., IV.22.11; parentheses in translation by Williams.

19. Epiphanius, *Panarion*, IV.22.12; see Matthew 2:7.

The churches of Egypt resisted taking the Roman date of the nativity at least into the fifth century. John Cassian, writing about the Egyptian calendar in his *Conferences*, mentioned (sometime between 418 and 427) that the old custom was still maintained (*mos iste antiqua traditione servatur*).[20] There is evidence that a Christmas sermon was preached in Alexandria by one Paul of Emesa in the year 433, so by then the Western date of the nativity had been received in Egypt, or at least by a community in Alexandria.[21] From then onward the inclusion of the birth as one of the manifestations celebrated at Epiphany would decline in Egypt.

Though the excision of the birth narrative from the "day of the epiphanies," *dies epifaniorum*, might appear minor historically — for it was only one of a number of narratives associated with the day — the theological implications of the excision call for some theological reflection. The celebration of baptism at the Easter Vigil, in the embrace of the Three Days — with its Gospel narratives of footwashing, passion, and empty tomb — is strong and warranted, the loss of the link between the birth of Jesus in history and the birth of Christ in the newly baptized was (and still is) great. The Western preaching rhetoric of Christmas has never matched the depth of the preaching of the Eastern fathers who waxed wonderfully on the two births, of Jesus and of the baptized. For them the association had saving significance for humanity and cosmic significance for the world in which humanity dwells.

On Sunday,[22] all Christian unions — of spouses, of members of communities to one another, of churches praying together in ecumenical initiatives — bear fruit in a richness of God's life, which is a gift to humanity as individuals come together in love or churches come together in reconciliation. By God's grace and in the power of the Spirit, the whole — of society and human relationships of love — is indeed greater than the sum of its parts, but the realization of that whole, in the union of the parts, always comes with loss and sacrifice, as in the sacrifice of parents whose physical expression of love bears fruit in the birth of children and the countless sacrifices parents make for the well-being of their offspring.

---

20. John Cassian, PL 49:820–821.
21. Cyril Martindale, "Christmas," *The Catholic Encyclopedia*, volume 3 (New York: Robert Appleton, 1908). The article refers to an appendix to the acts of the Council of Ephesus, yet its reference is to Mansi, IV, column 293. There is no reference in that column to Christmas, and the council in that column is North African, years before the Council of Ephesus.
22. See Volume 2, Chapter 1, "Sunday."

In terms of the development of the liturgical year, one great loss in the joining of calendars of the local time-keeping traditions of East and West was the church's loss of rich theologies of birth and baptism from the preaching of Eastern churches. Perhaps the loss was necessary for the communion of West and East, but it cannot be ignored that this was a consequential loss of *theological* depth for the whole of the church since today theologies of baptism draw much more from images of death (and resurrection) than from images of birth (and resurrection). The richness of what was lost with the East's giving up the narrative association of birth and baptism is reflected in, among others, the nativity lullabies of the hymn-writer of Syria, Ephrem.

Syria

In the Syrian church, the nativity was celebrated on January 6, Epiphany, and in that tradition the birth of Jesus had cosmic consequences. The Syriac-writing Ephrem authored twenty-eight beautiful hymns on the nativity celebrated at Epiphany, and these capture the depth of the tradition lost when the Roman date of December 25 was received and the birth narrative cut away from the manifestations and from baptism. These hymns refer to the other narratives associated with Epiphany elsewhere — the magi coming to the holy family, the miracle at Cana — but the primary matter for Ephrem was that of binding the incarnation of the Savior to his birth and to the saving medium of baptism for the church.

The theological association of incarnation, birth, and baptism in Ephrem's work is astonishingly beautiful, as in these two long sections from the hymns:

Hymn 1

This is the night of reconciliation; let us be neither wrathful nor
    gloomy on it.
On this all-peaceful night let us be neither menacing nor
    boisterous.
This is the night of the Sweet One; let us be on it neither bitter
    nor harsh.
On this night of the Humble One, let us be neither proud nor
    haughty.
On this day of forgiveness let us not avenge offenses.
On this day of rejoicings let us not share sorrows.
On this sweet day let us not be vehement.

On this calm day let us not be quick-tempered.
On this day on which God came into the presence of sinners,
let not the just man exalt himself in his mind over the sinner.
On this day on which the Lord of all came among servants,
let the lords also bow down to their servants lovingly.
On this day when the Rich One was made poor for our sake,
let the rich man also make the poor man a sharer at his table.
On this day a gift came out to us without our asking for it;
let us then give alms to those who cry out and beg from us.
This is the day when the high gate opened to us for our prayers;
let us also open the gates to the seekers who have stayed but
        sought [forgiveness].
This Lord of natures today was transformed contrary to His
        nature;
it is not too difficult for us also to overthrow our evil will.
Bound is the body by its nature for it cannot grow larger or
        smaller;
but powerful is the will for it may grow to all sizes.
Today the Deity imprinted itself on humanity,
so that humanity might also be cut into the seal of Deity.[23]

HYMN 23

Blessed is your birth that stirred up the universe! . . .

[Too] small for You is the earth's lap,
but large [enough] for You is Mary's lap. He dwelt in a lap, and
        He healed by the hem [of His garment].
He [was] wrapped [in] swaddling clothes in baseness, but they
        offered Him gifts.
He put on the garments of youth, and help emerged from them.
He put on the water of baptism, and rays flashed out from it.
He put on linen garments in death, and triumphs were shown
        by them.
With His humiliations [came] His exaltations. Blessed is He
        Who joins His glory to His suffering! . . .
O Great One Who became a baby, by Your birth again You
        begot me.
O Pure One Who was baptized, let Your washing wash us of
        impurity.

---

23. Ephrem the Syrian, Hymn 1, from *Hymns*, trans. and intro. Kathleen E. McVey, CWS
(New York and Mahwah, NJ: Paulist, 1989): Hymn 1 at 63–74, quotation at 73–74.

O Living One Who was embalmed, let us obtain life by Your
   death.
I will thank You entirely in Him Who fills all.
Glory to You entirely from all of us![24]

Juxtaposed to the ordinary and expected stories historicizing the dire
circumstances of the holy family in Bethlehem at the end of a cold
December two millennia ago, such deeply theological and soteriologi-
cal reflections on the nativity in these fourth- and fifth-century works
from Ephrem are rich, if now absent from the church's nativity theology and preaching about baptism, Jesus' baptism or of those baptized
now. They remind believers that the saving work of God was revealed
in the humanity of Jesus Christ, but that this generous gift of salvation
is still revealed and celebrated in the experience of humanity.

The New Testament bears a variety of metaphors for a theology of
baptism — death (Romans 6), wedding (Ephesians 5), birth and rebirth
(John 3) — and within the scriptural embrace the tradition can draw
from these. When there were two main temporal poles for baptism —
with Easter emerging as the dominant time in the West, and Epiphany
as the dominant time for baptism in the East — these two theologies
of the sacrament were vibrant and interactive in Christian experience
and preaching. The loss of the birth narrative in the Epiphany context
might have been a necessary loss for the Eastern traditions as they
came into fellowship with the Latin tradition and accepted the Roman
date for the nativity. Yet too much was surrendered of the *theology*
of baptism that was drawn from the images of birth. In the West the
primary metaphor for a theology of adult baptism in the RCIA and the
liturgical year since Vatican II has been only death and resurrection,
with the main narratives for the theology Romans 6 and the proclamations of the empty tomb (in the synoptics). Natal imagery was diverted
from its primacy of place in time and experience when the Eastern traditions accepted the Roman date and when, not much later, Epiphany
ceased being a time for baptism. The Eastern churches, although still
connecting the practice of baptism with Epiphany, sacrificed a rich theology in giving up the nativity narrative. The strong social and unitive
theology of the ancient Eastern churches for Epiphany should not have
been forsaken simply because the date of January 6 no longer carried
the birth narrative. The hymns of Ephrem are but one of a number
of sources for this rich theology of baptism linked to birth, creation,

---

24. From Hymn 23, as in ibid.: 187–190, quotation here as at 189–190.

Adam and Eve in paradise, and heaven regained by the advent of the Savior, Jesus Christ.

In Ephrem's time Christmas was gradually being accepted by the Eastern churches, which — seeking communion with the Western churches — began to configure their ancient day of Epiphany so that it related to the nascent Western celebration of the nativity. Until the late fourth century, the December 25 date for the nativity was held only by Rome.[25] Although barbarian invasions of Rome, Italy, and, eventually, of the Roman Empire as a whole were near at hand, the church of Rome was itself actually growing in authority; therefore accepting the unique Roman date for the birth of the Savior was a sign of accepting and acquiescing to that church's authority. The acceptance or rejection of that date for the Savior's birth had nothing to do with historical veracity, but it had everything to do with church authority and survival.

Jerusalem

Writing his *Commentary on Ezekiel* in the year 411, Jerome — doctor of the church, translator of the Bible into Latin — remarked that the "day of the epiphanies" was the day when Eastern people celebrated Christ's "baptism, at which the heavens opened for Christ, and they do not think that he appeared in the flesh at Christmas."[26] In this he confirms the absence of any mention of Christmas in the travel diary of the Western pilgrim in the Holy Land, Egeria, who, though detailing much about the feasts and seasons of the liturgical year, said nothing of the celebration or commemoration of the birth of Jesus at Christmas. It appears, then, that like Egypt Jerusalem was resistant to accepting the Roman date for celebrating the birth of Jesus.

Cappadocia and West Syria

The sorting out of the dates, narratives, and customs for the feasts at the turn of the year and the winter solstice in the late fourth and early fifth centuries reveals a great deal about the relation of time-keeping and church authority, for even as Epiphanius was writing of the nativity at Epiphany in Egypt, the Cappadocians were already juggling dates, narratives, and theologies as they accepted the Roman date. Gregory of Nyssa, for example, preached at the funeral of his brother Basil the Great, who died just before January 1, 379. The younger brother's

---

25. See Part 1, Chapter 3, "Christmas."

26. PL 25:18: Quintam autem diem mensis adjungit, ut significet baptisma, in quo aperti sunt Christo coeli, et Epiphaniorum dies hucusque venerabilis est, non ut quidam putant Natalis in carne, tunc enim absconditus est, et non apparuit; trans. Connell.

funeral sermon makes it clear, as he recounts the holy days of that
time of year, that the nativity feast had just been celebrated, and two
of his sermons of 380 on the feast of St. Stephen also confirm the
reception of Christmas: "Christ has come to the world as its Savior,
and with him have the fruits of the church been brought forth," among
whom he counts Stephen.[27]

The confusion about the origins of Christmas in the East is complicated by the naming of the feast, for a sermon preached by Gregory
Nazianzus on *Theophany* — which was and remains the name of
Epiphany in a number of the Eastern churches — was likely delivered on December 25, 380.[28] The topic of his sermon on January 6
was on the "Day of the Holy Lights," and the theology of that Oration 39 is filled with some of the same imagery seen above in the
hymns of Ephrem of Syria, with the rhetoric of the new creation and
the new Adam.

The Oration does refer to the shepherds and the magi, but no less
present in the discourse are the themes of the baptism of the Lord,
illumination, and the splendor of the light brought in the mystery of
Christ's baptism.[29]

The chronology of the Eastern reception of the Roman date for
Christmas is evident in the fathers whose sermons reveal that the
nativity and Epiphany were kept as distinct liturgical celebrations;
among these preachers was Amphilochius of Iconium, a contemporary
of the episcopal brothers Basil the Great and Gregory of Nyssa. Distinct
from Gregory Nazianzus, Amphilochius preached on the birth without
either of the Eastern terms for the day, "Epiphany" or "Theophany."[30]

A few sermons of John Chrysostom signal the reception of Christmas on December 25 in the East, and in one sermon in particular,
preached in 386 by most reckonings, reveals that "the day has been
known to us for only ten years."[31] Elsewhere Chrysostom demonstrated how much time he had spent figuring out the calendrical
differences with the changes regarding when the year began and how

27. The sermons as are PG 46:701–721 and 721–736, the second with the clear reference
to the coming of Christ; see in particular column 721A; trans. Connell.

28. See PG 36:312.

29. Baptism and light, at PG 36:336, the displacement of the pagan gods at PG 36:337
and 340; illumination at PG 36:344 and 359; the conquering of the heretics, Sabellius and
Arius, in particular, at PG 36:348; the magi and shepherds at PG 36:349; baptism of Christ
PG 36: 349, 352, 354, 358, and 360.

30. See PG 39:35, "On the birth (*genéthlia*) of our great God and Savior Jesus Christ."
For more detailed interpretation of these sermons, see Jill Burnett Comings, *Aspects of the
Liturgical Year in Cappadocia* (New York: Peter Lang, 2005): 61–69.

31. PG 49: 351, trans. Connell; see K. A. Heinrich Kellner, *Heortologie* (Freiburg im
Breisgau: Herdersche, 1906): 97–98.

the months were named.[32] There he also stated that the gestation was of nine months and that the conception had taken place in the month of March, though he did not supply the exact date of the conception. His rhetoric reveals not only that his church had accepted the Roman date for the nativity, but some of his Epiphany sermons demonstrate that the variety of narratives for the day in the East had been winnowed down to the one advocated by Rome, the visit of the magi.

In summary regarding the Eastern traditions, it is clear that in the fourth through sixth centuries there was variety in how the two major feasts of this pole of the liturgical year were to be reckoned. Although the early third-century, Egyptian reference from Clement regarding the Basilidians is clear and uncontested, it is rather surprising that the reference antedates the next evidence of the feast by over a century and a half. This might be attributable to the circumstance that Clement wrote of a heretical sect rather than one in communion with the larger church in Egypt. The places that were in contact with the Latin churches most frequently and that sought communion with Rome, like those in West Syria, were those that accepted the Roman date of Christmas earlier, as early as any non-Roman churches in the West. Other places, such as Jerusalem and Egypt, resisted for some time, yet they eventually accepted the Western calculation and relegated the birth narrative to December 25. The Armenian church has never accepted the Roman date, and its theology of Epiphany includes the birth narrative and therefore is the only church whose theology of the day still maintains the theological link of baptism and birth.

Part Two:
The Origins of Epiphany — West

No extant testimony to Epiphany in the Latin tradition appears until the second half of the fourth century, yet the evidence soon after appears in abundance. Histories of the feast at its emergence in the West often circumscribe its narrative to the visit of the magi, which would eventually be the main narrative for the day. Yet the evidence of the fourth and fifth centuries, and even of the early Middle Ages, reveals that there are non-Roman remnants of narratives other than the story of the wise men from the Gospel of Matthew (2:1–12). Scholarship about the origins of Epiphany in the West has often tried to locate all references to the nativity in sermons and hymns about Christmas,

---

32. PG 49: 357.

but a close examination of the rhetoric of these sermons demonstrates convincingly that these were originally markers of Epiphany,
not Christmas.

Gaul
Emperor Julian
The third-century Egyptian evidence of Clement of Alexandria bears
witness to the existence of the day but without an indication of its theology. The earliest evidence for Epiphany in the Latin tradition does the
same. The source is secular, the journals of Ammianus Marcellinus,
describing an effort by the emperor Julian to be accepted by Christians
in Gaul:

> To gain the favor of all to him without any obstacles, he [Julian]
> pretended to belong to the Christian religion, which he had ear-
> lier secretly abandoned. He took a few as confidants in his secrets
> and gave himself up to divinations and predictions, and to other
> practices which worshippers of the gods always perform. And so
> that he might keep these things hidden for a while, on the day
> of the festival in the month of January which the Christian cel-
> ebrants call *epiphania*, he went into their church and departed
> after solemnly praying to the god.[33]

These machinations of Julian the Apostate took place in Paris near the
end of his reign, in the year 363. A much later recounting of the event
by the twelfth-century Zonaras refers to the feast of Epiphany in 363
as the "birthday of the Savior." If this was so, then the earliest record
of Epiphany in the West reflects the absence of Christmas near Paris
in the later fourth century, since Epiphany still embraced the Lord's
birth on January 6.[34]

Northern Italy
Ambrose of Milan
Regarding another early text that deals with this time of the liturgical year much has already been written, because a letter of Ambrose
of Milan would be the earliest non-Roman witness to Christmas, if it
had been so. A litany of historians of the liturgy and of the office of the
Roman papacy has wrestled with the following passage from Ambrose

---

33. Ammianus Marcellinus, *Ammianus Marcellinus*, Loeb Classical Library XXI.2.4–5;
volume 2 of 3 (Cambridge: Harvard University Press, 1935): 98–101.
34. See Volume 1, Chapter 3, "Christmas," on resistance to the reception of the Roman
date of the nativity; see also Botte, *Les origines*, 46; and, to the contrary, Thomas J. Talley,
The Origins of the Liturgical Year (Collegeville, MN: Pueblo, 1991): 141–142.

of Milan's *De Virginitate.* In this letter addressed to his sister Marcellina, Bishop Ambrose recalls for her the day on which she dedicated herself to virginity by "taking the veil" in the presence of Liberius, the bishop of Rome. Ambrose wrote:

> Because we have gone off track in what we have talked about in the two earlier books, holy sister, it is time now to turn again to the commandments of Liberius, of blessed memory, to look at those things that you used to discuss with me, because the holier the man the more graced is his word. For you marked your profession of virginity by a similar change in your clothing in the church of St. Peter on the birthday of the Savior. (What better day could there have been for this than that on which the virgin received her offspring?) Many daughters of the Lord were standing around competing with one another for your company.
>
> "You seek a good marriage ceremony, my daughter," he [Liberius] said, "You see what a great crowd of people has come together for the birthday of your Spouse, and has anyone gone away empty? This is he who, when asked, changed the water into wine at the wedding feast, so too in you he has conferred the sacrament of virginity, because earlier you were polluted with the vile elements of nature. This is he who fed four thousand people in the desert with five loaves and two fish. If there had been more, more would have been fed."[35]

Ambrose wrote this from Milan in the year 378, and in it he was recalling an event that had taken place almost a quarter century earlier, in Rome in the year 353 or 354. The passage is usually debated for one of two reasons, either by historians of the papacy because it is an indication of the supremacy of the bishop of Rome, here regarded with respect by another metropolitan bishop; or by historians of the liturgical year, because of the reference to "the birthday of the Savior." The latter is the issue of concern regarding the liturgical year.

In 353 or 354, at the time of his sister's veiling, Ambrose would have been about twenty years old; he would not be baptized a Christian until twenty years later, just a few weeks before his episcopal consecration in December 374.[36] Although there are words from the bishop of Rome in the passage, the words are likely to be those of Ambrose rather than of Liberius;[37] moreover, Ambrose never takes up the date of the feast,

---

35. Ambrose of Milan, *De Virginitate* 3.1.1 (PL 16: 219–220); trans. Connell.
36. Paredi, *S. Ambrogio e la sua età* (Milan: Hoepli, 1960): 157.
37. E. Casper, "Die Marcellina-Predigt des Liberius und das römische Weihnachtsfest," *Zeitschrift für Kirchengeschichte* 46 (1928) 346–355; see also Botte, *Les origins: 36.*

merely its significance as "the Savior's birthday." In this period when the calendar was being formed, the "birthday" to which Ambrose refers could well have been celebrated as December 25 in Rome and January 6 in Milan, or it is possible, too, that the birthday of the Savior was still being observed on January 6 in some churches in Rome and in Milan.

The evidence to support the date of this occasion as January 6 over December 25 is very strong. First, Ambrose makes references to the narratives of the Cana miracle and the multiplication of the loaves and fishes, both associated with Epiphany, not Christmas. Next, in the middle of the fourth century, the consecration of virgins was traditionally celebrated on any of the days of Epiphany, Pentecost, or the feast of the Apostles,[38] but there is no tradition for the consecration of virgins on Christmas. Also, because the phrase "birthday of the Savior" does not refer to a date but to a narrative that was celebrated on different dates in different churches, one looks to the other indications, and the other narratives of the passage are clearly those for Epiphany.

Illuminans Altissimus. Further support for the reference to Epiphany comes from a hymn written by Ambrose himself, *Illuminans altissimus*, "The Highest Light," referring to Jesus. The hymn of eight verses has indications of Jesus' baptism (verse 2), the birth from the virgin and the visit of the magi (verse 3), the changing of water into wine at Cana (verses 4 and 5), and the multiplication of the loaves and fish (verses 6–8), all narratives of the Epiphany.[39]

> Jesus, most high illuminator
> of the globes of the shining stars;
> peace, life, light, and truth,
> look favorably on those calling on you.
>
> and by a mystical baptism
> on this day you consecrate
> the flowing waters of the Jordan
> which turned back three times;
>
> and who by a star shining in heaven
> signaled the birth from the virgin
> and led the magi to the manger
> to adore you today.

    38. Mario Righetti, *L'anno liturgico*, Manuale di storia liturgica II, 3rd ed. (Milan: Ancorà, 1969): 66; *Storia liturgica:* 66, note 9.
    39. See Manlio Simonetti, *Inni* (Florence: Nardini 1988): 46–49.

and who infused the taste of wine
into the jars filled with water
the server drew it knowing
that he himself had not filled them.

Seeing that the waters were colored,
flowing with inebriation,
he was surprised that the changed elements
passed into other uses.

In the same way, while they divided the five loaves
for five thousand people,
the food increased in their mouths,
between the teeth of those eating.

The food was multiplied greatly
as much as was its distribution;
was anyone, seeing this, amazed
at the perpetual flowing of the sources?

The bread was supplied to overflowing
between the hands of those breaking it;
and the pieces that were not broken
escaped untouched by humans.[40]

Unwilling or unable to accept that Milan had not received Rome's Christmas over a half-century after its Roman appearance, some have argued that the hymn was for Christmas rather than for Epiphany, but the constellation of narratives indicates clearly that it was written for Epiphany and its complex of manifestations. Others have translated

---

40. Original Latin text taken from Ambrose, *Hymnes*, text, trans., and notes Jacques Fontaine (Paris: Cerf 1992): 335–359. Below is the stanza that has often been either misinterpreted or mistranslated, the third stanza of the hymn:

> *seu stella partum uirginis*
> *caelo micans signaueris*
> *et hoc adoratum die*
> *praesepe magos.*

An example of a translation that erases the birth from the stanza is from Daniel Joseph Donahoe, *Early Christian Hymns* (Middleton, CT: Donahoe, 1911): 22–23:

> The shining star of Bethlehem
> Guiding the Kings to thee this day,
> Be unto us as unto them,
> Thy guiding light upon our way.

the hymn to have readers miss the Epiphany meaning of the third stanza, rendering it as an explicit reference to the birth.

The last piece that mitigates attempts to find the letter to Ambrose's sister as a reference to a non-Roman Christmas in the middle of the fourth century is that Ambrose wrote a long commentary on the Gospel of Luke, and in that work there is not a single reference to the celebration of Christmas. There are references in the commentary to the magi (who do not appear in that Gospel) and to the feast of Epiphany,[41] but in a protracted commentary on a Gospel with very long narratives of conceptions and births, there is not a single reference to Christmas.

Chromatius of Aquileia

The earliest Latin sermon on Epiphany comes from Chromatius, bishop of the metropolitan church at Aquileia from 388 to 407, and his sermon is clearly linked to the earliest Egyptian testimony, in which the narrative of the feast of January 6 was the baptism of Jesus:

> Today [as we heard when the divine reading was proclaimed] our Lord and Savior was baptized by John in the Jordan, and for that very reason this solemnity is not small, but rather is great and indeed the greatest solemnity. For when our Lord deigned to be baptized, the Holy Spirit came upon him in the form of a dove, and the voice of the Father was heard saying: "This is my beloved Son, in whom I am well pleased."[42]

In Chromatius's sermon for Epiphany, there is no address to those to be baptized, but he does mark the occasion as that on which the Lord blessed the waters for the baptism of believers:

> Since therefore our Lord came to give a new baptism for the salvation of the human race and for the remission of all sins, he himself first deigned to be baptized, not so that he who had not committed sin might put sins aside, but that he might sanctify the waters of baptism to wipe away the sins of all believers born again through baptism. He was baptized with water so that we through baptism might be washed of all sins.[43]

---

41. *Expositio evangelii secundam Lucam* 2.43–44 (SC 45: 92–93).
42. Sermo 34.1, as in *Chromatii Aquileiensis Opera*, CCSL 9a, ed. R. Étaix and J. Lemarié (Turnholt: Brepols, 1974): 156; trans. Connell.
43. Ibid., 34.3; trans. Connell.

In addition to Chromatius calling the feast "the greatest of all solemnities," it is not unlikely that in Aquileia they were baptizing on Epiphany at the time, for the bishop continued:

> This is the true and one baptism of the church, which is given only once and by which someone is immersed only once, and that person is made both clean and new: "clean" because the stains of desires are put aside, and "new" because one rises into a new way of life, putting aside the old life of sin. For this washing of baptism makes a person brighter than snow, not in the skin of the body, but in the splendor of the mind and the purity of the soul. . . . Our Lord was baptized to sanctify the waters of baptism to wipe away the sins of all believers born again through baptism.[44]

Chromatius preached only about the baptism, but his episcopal peer Maximus of Turin mentioned the baptism narrative and the wedding feast of Cana. (There is no mention of the magi in any of Maximus's sermons at Epiphany.) Maximus is found explaining the meaning of the Greek word "epiphany" to his assembly, a sure sign that the feast was being introduced to the church at that time, another reason for assuming the fluidity of the feast in this Northern Italian ecclesial sphere.

Filastrius of Brescia

The excision of the nativity from January 6 was followed by a paring down of the various other narratives of Epiphany. This change started to appear in the late fourth and early fifth centuries, and here the churches of Northern Italy provide provocative testimony about the inculturation of the liturgical change. Indeed, the witness to follow shows that for some proclaiming a different story on January 6 was an issue of heresy, as revealed in this excerpt from a catalogue of heresies from Filastrius, bishop of Brescia, at the end of the fourth century; the work is the *Diversarum hereseon liber*, the "book of various heresies":

> There are certain heretics who have doubts about the day of the Epiphanies of our Lord and Savior, a day celebrated on January 6, saying that they must celebrate only the birthday of the Lord on December 25 but not the day of the Epiphanies.[45]

This reveals that in some places the newer feast is January 6, and some were maintaining that December 25 was to be celebrated but

---

44. Ibid., 34.2–3; trans. Connell.
45. See CCSL 9 (Turnholt: Brepols, 1957): 304; trans. Connell.

not Epiphany. Other were keeping the day, but, by his reckoning, not celebrating it correctly.

The name Filastrius assigns January 6, "the days of the Epiphanies," is curious because it reveals that there were *multiple* manifestations celebrated on the day, but the bishop turned around in the same section and argued against the possibility of more than one manifestation: "There are some who think that the day of the Epiphanies is the day of the baptism [of the Lord], and others who think it is the day of the transformation on the mountain," but Filastrius called these opinions heretical and maintained that the *only* proper narrative, contrary to the very name used for the feast, is the visit of the magi.

Peter Chrysologus

As in the church at Turin under its bishop Maximus, the word "epiphany" was also explained to the congregation of the metropolitan church of Ravenna in the sermons of Peter Chrysologus, bishop there during the second quarter of the fifth century. Here there is evidence of the celebration of Epiphany with three narratives, *trino modo*, in a "three-fold way," in his Sermon 157:

> On Epiphany the magi, bearing their spiritual gifts, confess their belief in Christ as God. . . . [46]

> On Epiphany Christ tasted the water turned wine at the wedding feast, so that he would be the Christ of power, not of desire, who would intervene at the wedding. . . . [47]

> And on Epiphany Christ entered into the river Jordan to consecrate our baptism, so that, being born again, he might raise up to heaven those whom he had taken up when he was born on earth. [48]

Another Epiphany sermon of Peter Chrysologus testifies to the narrative of the miraculous multiplication of bread, but that is not mentioned in the sermon about the "three-fold way" of Epiphany. The triple narrative seen here in fifth-century Ravenna is still extant in the tradition of daily prayer, for a remnant of the earlier sense of Epiphany as "manifestation" of God's presence in a variety of ways appears in the antiphons for the Gospel canticles at Morning and Evening Prayer, which in order are these:

---

46. *Sermo* 157.1, in CCSL 24b (Turnholt: Brepols, 1982): 976; trans. Connell.
47. *Sermo* 157.5, in ibid.: 978; trans. Connell.
48. *Sermo* 157.6, in ibid.: 978; trans. Connell.

Today the Church has been joined to her heavenly bridegroom, since Christ has purified her of her sins in the river Jordan: the Magi hasten to the royal wedding and offer gifts: the wedding guests rejoice since Christ has changed water into wine, alleluia.

Three wonders mark this day we celebrate: today the star led the Magi to the manger; today water was changed into wine at the marriage feast; today Christ desired to be baptized by John in the river Jordan to bring us salvation, alleluia.[49]

Although various sermons and sacramentaries in the Latin tradition of the early Middle Ages recognized and celebrated such a triple narrative of Epiphany, eventually the one to survive for the Mass was that of the visit of the magi, from the Gospel of Matthew. The preference for this narrative was probably the result of infancy stories gravitating toward that pole of the year, civil and liturgical, once the birth of Jesus had been fixed to December 25 and those of Jesus' suffering and death fixed in the spring.

North Africa

Augustine

Although the visit of the magi to Bethlehem is the primary narrative behind Augustine's sermons on Epiphany, his rhetoric does take up the issue of social transformation that was seen in the theology of some of the sermons from the Eastern churches. Epiphany for Augustine was commemorated as the celebration of the admission of non-Jews into the church and into the reign of God. He preached about the light of the star leading the Gentiles to the Messiah. He also related this revelation to the Gentiles to the feast of Christmas celebrated twelve days earlier:

On the day of this birth, our Lord was manifested to the shepherds aroused by an angel, and on that day, too, through the appearance of a star he was announced to magi in the distant East, but it was on this day that he was adored by the magi. Therefore, the whole church of the Gentiles has adopted this day as a feast worthy of most devout celebration, for who were the magi but the first-fruits of the Gentiles?[50]

---

49. *The Divine Office: The Liturgy of the Hours According to the Roman Rite*, I: Advent, Christmastide & Weeks 1–9 of the Year (London: Collins, 1982): 318–319 and 327.

50. Augustine, Sermon 199, On the Epiphany of the Lord, in *Sermons on the Liturgical Seasons*, trans. Mary Sarah Mudowney (New York: Fathers of the Church, 1959): 59–81, here at 71.

To those present for his Epiphany sermons, Augustine repeatedly explained the meaning of the word "epiphany" and its origins in the Greek tradition, revealing its relative novelty to their calendar.

Gaul

Sedulius

A lesser known writer of the late-antique piety of Christmas and Epiphany is the poet Sedulius, most famous for the *Carmen paschale*, or "Easter poem," a five-book, metrical summary of salvation, with the first book from the Old Testament and the following four from the life of Jesus. The little we know about Sedulius comes from spare notes about him in two Latin authors, Isidore of Seville and Gennadius of Marseilles. Their information suggests for him the location of Gaul, though neither mention his place in their remembrance.

In spite of the minuscule amount known about him, Sedulius contributes unique literary evidence to the history of Christmas and Epiphany in the West, for he wrote an alphabetical poem of twenty-three stanzas, originally called the *Paean Alphabeticus de Christo*, the "Alphabetical Hymn about Christ." Each of the twenty-three stanzas begins with a letter of the alphabet, A, then B, then C, and so on. (There were only twenty-three letters in the Latin alphabet at the time.) Such works are sometimes called "abecedarian," and in this structure the alphabetical format reveals the evolution of these two feasts at the turn of the year, for the order of the composition testifies to the original union of the birth narrative and the feast of Epiphany in the Latin tradition.

Later, in the Middle Ages, the poem would be split into two parts with the introduction of December 25 as the day of the nativity, yet even after the cleavage the two parts remained popular in the tradition for centuries.[51] Once the poem was split, the stanzas from A through G became a Christmas hymn, whose first line, by which it is known, is *A solis ortus cardine*, "From the rising of the sun." The first two stanzas are enough to display how the literary form manifested the theology of the new feast:

> *A solis ortus cardine*
> *Adusque terre limitem*
> *Christum canamus principem*
> *Natum Maria virgine.*

---

51. The hymn was included in the new edition of the Roman Breviary published after the Council of Trent, during the papacy of Urban VIII in 1632.

From the rising of the sun
to the ends of the earth,
let us sing of Christ the Prince,
born of the Virgin Mary.

Beatus auctor seculi
Servile corpus induit,
Ut carne carnem liberans
Non perderet, quos condidit.

The blessed creator of the world
put on a servant's body,
so that, liberating the flesh through taking flesh,
he would not lose what he had made.

The other part of the hymn — which picks up at H, following the other's final G — is also known by its first line, *Hostis Herodes impie, . . . quid times?*, "Why, unholy Herod, are you afraid?," as a reference to the king's ordering of the slaughter of the innocents in a effort to kill the Messiah (Matthew 2:13–18). Although some of its earlier twenty-three verses would be excised over time and the exigencies of the changing liturgical year, the first four stanzas that survived for centuries each reveal one of the narratives of Epiphany — in order, the nativity, the magi, the baptism of Jesus, and the wedding feast at Cana:

Hostis Herodes impie,
Christum venire quid times?
Non eripit mortalia,
Qui regna dat caelestia.

Why are you afraid, unholy Herod,
That Christ is coming?
He who offers the heavenly realm
Does not destroy mortality.

Ibant magi, quam viderant,
Stellam sequentes praeviam:
Lumen requirunt lumine,
Deum fatentur munere.

The wise men went
Following the star that they saw;
They sought the light by the light
And with their gifts put their faith in God.

*L*avacra puri gurgitis
Caelestis Agnus attigit;
Peccata, quae non detulit,
Nos abluendo sustulit.

> When the heavenly lamb
> touched the pure cleansing pool,
> he, whom sin did not touch,
> removed it from us by washing.

*N*ovum genus potentiae,
Aquae rubescunt hydriae,
Vinumque iussa fundere
Mutsvit unda originem.

> A new kind of power
> That caused the springs of water to blush,
> So that wine came forth,
> Changing its original stream.

The popularity of the two Latin hymns lasted more than a millennium beyond their unified composition by Sedulius, for Martin Luther translated both of them from Latin into German for worship at Christmas and Epiphany in the reformed tradition: *Christum wir sollen loben schon* and *Was fürchtst du Feind Herodes sehr.*

Part Three:
The Middle Ages

Western Remnants of the Eastern Traditions

Although the narrative of the magi became the primary gospel reading for Epiphany in the Latin tradition and has remained so until today, there were occasional traces — like the announcement of the date of Easter — of the Eastern traditions that were maintained in the Latin churches for a few centuries. It is also as likely that these were not exclusively Eastern customs for Epiphany, but there is no Latin evidence before the historical chronicle of the emperor Julian's Epiphany visit to Paris, and so the more dependable hypothesis is that the Eastern traditions were carried to the West and found their place in some of the calendars and liturgies of non-Roman churches. Below are a few more of the remnants of baptism from the medieval evidence for Epiphany in the Latin tradition.

Early Medieval Conciliar Decrees about the Proximate Date of Easter

In the Egyptian traditions there was the custom of a paschal letter being sent out from the patriarch of Alexandria announcing the date of Easter a few months away. The complex calculation of the date of Easter after the Council of Nicea, in addition to the variety of configurations of the calendar from place to place, led to the need for the promulgation of the date of Easter so that all churches would observe the greatest annual solemnity on the same day. Eventually, the celebration of Epiphany became the time for such an announcement.

In the writings of Ambrose of Milan, the bishop did not mention the announcement of the date of Easter, but in his Commentary on the Gospel of Luke he detoured into a mention of the ritual enrollment of the candidates for baptism at the coming Easter Vigil. His mention reveals that this enrollment of the candidates traditionally took place on January 6, as he wrote in Book IV:

> I also know, Lord, that it is night for me when you do not guide me. No one has yet written his name; it is still night for me. I have cast the spear of the word for Epiphany and as yet I have started nothing; I have cast through the day.[52]

Though he does not say that this was also the occasion for announcing the date of Easter, it is not unlikely that the ceremony of enrollment would also have been the occasion for announcing the date to the faithful assembled in church for Epiphany. If so, then the church of Milan in the fourth century would have been unique in witnessing a tradition that was manifest in other non-Roman Latin churches only in the early Middle Ages.

The Fourth Council of Orleans. One of the councils that demonstrates the tradition of announcing the date of Easter on the feast of Epiphany was the fourth council of Orleans, which met in (or around) the year 545. The very first canon of the council says that there was a concern that "holy Easter" be observed by all priests (or bishops) at the same time (*ab omnibus sacerdotibus uno tempore celebretur*).[53] The sacred event was to be announced on Epiphany "by the metropolitan [bishop] from the apostolic seat," *per metropolitanos a sede apostolica*, lest there be any doubt about when Easter was to be kept.

---

52. 4.76: *et ego, domine, scio quia nox mihi est, quando non imperas. nemo adhuc dedit nomen suum, adhuc noctem habeo. misi iaculum uocis per epifania et adhuc nihil cepi* (CSEL 32–IV: 177; SC 45: 181); trans. Connell.

53. *Concilium Aurelianense IV*, canon 1, in Mansi IX: 127–140 for the whole of that council, this canon at 129–130.

The Fourth Council of Toledo. To the southwest of the continent, and, tellingly, distant from the jurisdiction of Rome, the canons of a Spanish council, the Fourth Council of Toledo, reveal a similar regulation, namely, that three months before Easter the metropolitans would announce the day of the "Easter festival," the "day of the resurrection of Christ," so that in their various regions Easter would be celebrated at the same time, *uno tempore celebrandum annuntient.*[54] This particular Council of Toledo was convened in (or around) the year 633.

Gregory of Tours and Eugene of Carthage. In his *Books of Miracles,* Gregory, bishop of Tours (ca. 538–593), wrote of a woman of Jericho who had been caught in adultery. In the narrative the bishop described the custom for the holy day of the Epiphanies, *dies sanctus Epiphaniorum,* when "all would go down into the river Jordan to bathe the wounds of the body."[55] This reflects the earliest of the Eastern traditions, in which the narrative of the Lord's own baptism was proclaimed, not because he needed the baptism, according to the rhetoric of the fathers of that time, but because humanity longed for the sanctification of the waters of the world so that those coming to the faith by baptism would be cleansed in the water sanctified by the Savior's baptism.

A different story, but with similar links to the baptism narrative of Epiphany in the East, was captured in an exchange between the Vandal king Huneric of North Africa and Bishop Eugenius of Carthage. Eugenius was trying to walk the fine line between helping his church survive in the context of the non-orthodox faith of the Vandals and not assenting to their errant Christology. In a response to Huneric, bishop Eugenius described an incident that happened in Carthage, where he was the bishop.

In the city was a blind man named Felix, who was visited by the Lord during that night, and told that the "day of the Epiphanies" would bring light: "Get up," the Lord told the man, "and go to my servant bishop Eugenius, and tell him that I have directed you to him. And at the hour when he [the bishop] used to bless the font — so that those coming forward would be baptized into the faith, he will touch your eyes — your eyes will be opened, and you will see light." And it happened as the Lord had foretold.

---

54. Mansi X: 618.
55. PL 58:213.

Byzantines and the Blessing of Water

A ritual element that retains some of the original baptismal content of
Epiphany from its origins in Egypt (as in Clement of Alexandria on the
Basilidians) and even from its earliest Latin sermon (on the baptism of
the Lord, from Chromatius of Aquileia) is the solemn blessing of water
in remembrance of the Baptism of the Lord. The feast of the Baptism
of the Lord in the lectionaries of most Western churches has remained
proximate to Epiphany, for as December 25 was received as the date of
the birth of Jesus and as the story of the magi became the sole Gospel of
the day, the other narratives of Epiphany were relegated to succeeding
Sundays of the year. (In particular, the Baptism of the Lord is the last
Sunday of the Christmas season — coincident with what would be the
First Sunday in Ordinary Time or First Sunday after Epiphany — in the
current taxonomy of narratives in the year.) Yet the solemn blessing
of water on Epiphany not only was maintained within the Byzantine
(Greek) tradition, but was translated into Latin in the Middle Ages and
manifest in the eighth to eleventh centuries.[56]

Rupert of Deutz

Echoes of the earlier tradition of celebrating the baptism of the Lord lin-
gered in the tradition. One of the early works that supplied a theology
of the liturgical year was from the hand of Rupert of Deutz (ca. 1075–
1130), a colorful and contentious monk of the early twelfth century.
Rupert lived in exile with his abbot for three years during the crisis
over the Investiture Controversy, and wrote theological works on the
origin of evil against his fellow monk Anselm of Laon, defending the
Benedictine life against the emerging new orders of the Cistercians
and canons regular. His *Liber de divinis officiis*, or "Book about the
divine rites" — written in or near the year 1111 — interprets the calendar primarily with allegory, though it occasionally revealed traces of
the development of the theology of a feast, as it does for Epiphany.
The triple narrative of the feast is supplied in the first line of Rupert's
commentary:

> The holy day of Epiphany, which is celebrated for three reasons,
> for the day on which the Lord was worshiped by the magi,[57]

---

56. For a study of an early manuscript with this rite, see D. P. DePuniet, "Formulaire Grec
de L'Épiphanie dans une Traduction latine ancienne," *Revue Benedictine* 29 (1912): 29–46.
The Latin manuscript transcribed in DePuniet's work explicitly identifies itself as from the
East, for it begins, *Benedictio anquarum sanctarum Theophaniarum secundum ordinem
orientalium aecclesiarum.*

57. Rupert used the word *Chaldaeis*, or "Chaldeans," for the magi, a common appellation
for them in the Latin tradition.

and similarly in the beginning, thirty years later, when he was baptized by John, and at the start of the year when the water was made wine at the wedding feast, when, it is said, it is celebrated as a primary solemnity of the divine rites for these three reasons.[58]

The magi were accorded primacy of place, but much more of Rupert's commentary focused on the baptismal tradition. For this Rupert cited a long passage from the letter of Leo the Great to the bishops of Sicily. After the citation of Leo's epistle, Rupert continued to explain that the foundation of baptism was not in the baptism of the Lord but in the blood and water that flowed from the side of the Lord, according to the passion of John (19:34). Nearly all that Rupert wrote about baptism was from Leo, yet in the second section he expounded at length on the magi. In this he continued the message of social change that accompanies the presence of the Lord at Epiphany, as earlier, zeroing in on the admission of the Gentiles to salvation, "Jews and Gentiles joined together as one people."[59]

The sign at Cana (John 2:1–11) is the third narrative of Rupert's commentary, and he related it to its place in the chronology of the life of Jesus, namely, that it took place at the beginning of his ministry as the baptism had been. In his construction, as in all interpretations of scripture in his age, he brought together the synoptic and Johannine traditions together, here seeing the sign of turning water to wine at Cana as a sign for the church to break the fast of forty days during which the Spirit had led the Lord into the desert, where he was tempted and he did not eat. He drew from two passages of the Gospel of John, the blood and water from the side of Jesus and the wedding at Cana, and then constructed a chronology of Jesus with the synoptic tradition's baptism of Jesus and fasting in the desert and with frequent mentions of the "thirty years" (Luke 3:23) — a marker of Jesus' age that appears only in Luke — and with diversions to geography from the ministry in Galilee and the rejection at Nazareth (Luke 4:14–30, *passim*).

Rupert provides these details as a way to explain the Vespers antiphon for the day: "We worship on the holy day of Epiphany adorned with the three miracles, as we sing":

---

58. Rupert of Deutz, *Liber de divinis officiis*, ed. Hrabanus Haacke (Turnholt: Brepols, 1967): 98–102, here at 100; trans. Connell.

59. Ibid.

Today the star led the magi to the manger,
On this day Christ was baptized by John,
And on this day he made water into wine at the wedding feast.

These are the three manifestations by which "true divinity was made known in the flesh," *quibus uera per carnem diuinitas innotuit.*[60]

Part Four:
Epiphany in the Work of Thomas Talley

In his *The Origins of the Liturgical Year* Thomas Talley proposed that the four narratives found in the various traditions for Epiphany had been single narratives in communities that had once proclaimed from a single Gospel.[61] He introduced this hypothesis regarding Epiphany and the beginning of the year with a demonstration using the fourth Gospel:

> We may suppose... that within that major portion of the year there was a point at which the reading of the gospel of John was begun, a course reading that would bring the liturgical community to the passion narrative at the following Passover. That reading might at the outset have begun in the autumn, influenced by *Simhat Torah*, which began the reading of the Law in the synagogues following the feast of Tabernacles; indeed some have suggested that the gospels were shaped in relation to the course reading in the synagogues. Nonetheless, whenever the reading of the gospel of John began, it began with the proclamation that, "In the beginning was the Word... and the Word was made flesh and dwelt among us." It would speak of the baptism of Jesus and of his first miracle at the wedding feast in Cana, that "beginning of the signs" in which he "manifested his glory."[62]

While this possibility has some of the appeal of a simple answer to complex evidence, I think there are serious problems with the suggestion.

First, although it is true that the Jewish year — in some places and at some times — began at the autumnal feast of Tabernacles (*Sukkot*) that

---

60. Ibid.
61. Part Four will examine closely Thomas Talley's hypotheses regarding Epiphany and its place in the calendar as he presented these in *The Origins of the Liturgical Year* (Collegeville, MN: Pueblo, 1986). For readers who have not read or been influenced by the work of Talley, Part Four can be skipped for the argument continues uninterrupted with the theology of Epiphany in Part Five.
62. Ibid.: 131.

concludes with the festival of *Simchat Torah,* during which the scrolls are rolled back to the beginning of Genesis, there is no accounting for the shift of the start of the year from autumn to Epiphany in Talley's reckoning, nor is there even one witness to confirm the hypothesis that Epiphany, the festival of the "manifestations," was a time in the year when a course reading through a Gospel would commence, or, more accurately perhaps, through *the* Gospel, since the hypothesis hinges on each community having had *one* narrative that would later be shared and admitted to the canon of *four* Gospels.

Talley continued to argue the proposal:

> Then, given the association of his birth and baptism with January 6 by "orthodox" and heretics alike, it seems more than possible that the beginning of the course reading of the gospel fell on that date in the second century, first in Asia but quickly adopted as the beginning of the year in neighboring churches also, in Syria, Palestine, and Egypt. In some other places as well it would be the point from which the reading of the gospel began, although not that of John.[63]

Here the problem with Talley's construction is the selection of places. By the second century, the Christian faith was not circumscribed to the four places he seeks to emphasize to further his argument: Asia Minor, Syria, Palestine, and Egypt. The faith and its scriptures had been promulgated and transported to many, many other places throughout the Mediterranean world and beyond.

So why did he choose these four places in particular? Because they would be places where he could find a ritual life that drew primarily from one of the four Gospels of the New Testament, as he continues the argument:

> Jerusalem's tenacious commitment, in the fourth century and later (and still among the Armenians), to the celebration of the nativity on the Epiphany is probably rooted in the antiquity of the local tradition, for which the beginning of the reading of Matthew made the nativity alone the theme associated with January 6.[64]

So his argument has here engaged the particulars, and, as expected, the readers find Talley's hypothetical construction being realized by his interpretation of evidence leading to one place = one Gospel; in this case, Palestine = Matthew. What might slip by is that the theory

---

63. Ibid.: 131.
64. Ibid.:131.

attributes the confluence of Epiphany narratives to the second century, but the supporting evidence he used to support the particular manifestation of this regarding Jerusalem and the Gospel of Matthew is from the *fourth* century. He then moved southward from Palestine for the place of the next Gospel's contribution:

> In Egypt... the baptism seems to be the original theme, "the beginning of the Gospel of Jesus Christ" according to Mark, the evangelist who gave his name to the see of Alexandria and to its liturgy.[65]

At this point the reader has found the Gospel of John ascribed to Asia Minor; the Gospel of Matthew to Jerusalem, in Palestine; and the Gospel of Mark to Alexandria, in Egypt. What about Luke?

> We are unable to assign the gospel of Luke to any particular church, and it is the only gospel that presents itself as addressed to an individual, and sort of "first epistle to Theophilus," by contrast with the more liturgical appropriate proclamatory openings of the other gospels. Nonetheless, the Byzantine tradition, which now begins its course reading of Luke from Holy Cross Day (September 14), earlier began that cursus at the beginning of the civil year, September 23. The tenth-century typikon of Hagia Sophia [in Constantinople, in present-day Turkey], we noted above, still indicates that date [September 23] as the "New Year" and begins its reading of Luke on that day.[66]

He ends with a caveat, but one that will supply support for an argument he makes toward the end of the book: "It is not possible to see a more primitive course reading of Luke, but this beginning of the course reading at the beginning of the year does conform to our hypothesis, if it does not support it." In other words, regarding the Gospel of Luke, Talley's theory of the year is viable only if one accepts the following conditions:

---

65. Ibid.: 133. Though it is not a major point, the opposite is true: There is no accounting historically for the evangelist giving anything to the church in Egypt, though it may have been that the church or churches of Egypt did proclaim the Gospel of Mark. And, though it slides by as an aside, the baptism as a Markan narrative is not established here. Talley sought to find a narrative at the beginning of each gospel that could be allied with a particular place in the early period, but nowhere in the evidence is there an accounting for the baptism narrative of Epiphany being the narrative from the Gospel of Mark.

66. Ibid.: 133–134.

- *If* the author can hypothetically move the start of Constantinople's year forward three and a half months, from September to January, and

- *If* the proclamation of the Gospel of Luke can be attributed to Constantinople centuries before there is any indication that this was so, and

- *If* we can believe the author's later suggestion that the Gospel of Mark, with the Gospel of Luke, was *also* favored at Constantinople.

If those unlikely conditions can all be set as the foundation of his hypothesis, *then* the theory conforms to the evidence and supports his engaging hypothesis.

In Talley's reckoning of the Gospel narratives for Epiphany and the beginning of the year, the baptism narrative would have been from the beginning of the Gospel of Mark, proclaimed at the start of the year by a community that used that Gospel in its worship. The birth narrative would have come from the beginning of the Gospel of Luke, the visit of the magi from the beginning of the Gospel of Matthew, and the wedding feast from the beginning of the Gospel of John. His proposal is arresting in how it both explained the multiplicity of narratives for the feast, and because it is in accord with biblical criticism, which has come to see that each canonical Gospel was born from the narrative expression of a particular community of faith in the late first or early second century. The complexity of narratives for the feast of the manifestations at Epiphany was thus a simple explanation for the complex experience of churches in the eastern Mediterranean world, uniting and divorcing as they did in those early centuries according to theological or disciplinary ends, alternately adding or excising Gospels or parts of Gospels as they defined ecclesial communion and its narrative expression in worship and calendar. The proposal therefore also accounted for the anthropology of ritual experience, in which the communal experience of the risen Christ was manifested uniquely from one church to another as people in those communities gave narrative expression to their experiences of Christ in their midst.

Although these positive aspects of the Talley hypothesis exist, there still remain some grave issues that would need resolution for reception into the academy of liturgical history. First, calendars, secular and ecclesial, varied widely in antiquity, and it is not clear that January was universally accepted as the start of the civil year, or indeed the start of the liturgical year and thus the time when the beginning of the four Gospels would have been proclaimed. Elsewhere in the book, Talley had proposed that the start of the year was in the spring, when Passover and Easter were celebrated. Upon what sources does the Talley theory draw for establishing January 6 as the approximate start of the year in all of the localities in which those Gospels were proclaimed?

Also, although the narrative of Cana could only come from the Gospel of John and the visit of the magi only from the Gospel of Matthew, the narrative of the baptism need not have been born of a Markan community, for the Gospels of the Matthean and Lukan communities also have narratives of the baptism of Jesus. (The same is true of the narrative of the birth of Jesus, which could as well have been born of the infancy story in Matthew as of that in Luke.) Because he gives no evidence for linking the baptism of Jesus to a community from which the Gospel of Mark emerged, Talley himself seems to be the link.

Also, the magi, baptism, birth, and Cana narratives are not the only four celebrated on Epiphany in late antiquity, for there is strong testimony to the narrative of the multiplication of loaves and fishes, which appears in all four canonical Gospels, and, though less strong as an Epiphany narrative, to the transfiguration, which appears in all three synoptic Gospels. Talley's hypothesis of the four Epiphany narratives as the result of the union of churches that had previously had one narrative is compelling, but the evidence is far from secure.

Moreover, neither the multiplication nor the transfiguration appears near the start of a canonical Gospel, so what theological or calendrical explanation would account for the embrace of these other narratives at the start of the year?

Also, an important ingredient for the hypothesis was drawn from a non-canonical Gospel, the Secret Gospel of Mark, so if that narrative is within the embrace of the tradition for the period from which Talley drew, then by what method would he distinguish texts and narratives that were included for Epiphany and texts and narratives that were not?

Finally, another question raised by the Talley theory relates to the establishment of the canon of scripture. Although scholarship has established that the canonical texts were all written by the first quarter of the second century, it is far from established that the four Gospels were universally considered a canon such that a feast like Epiphany, emerging as it did at least in the beginning of the third century, would have had only four narratives in its embrace, or that these would end up, coincidently, being the four that would finally be elected as the only four in the New Testament.

Part Five:
The Theology of Epiphany

For all of Christian history until the reforms of Vatican II, Epiphany was celebrated on a fixed date regardless of the day of the week. Although there are no loud lamentations about the reforms, the transfer of the feast in the United States from January 6 to the Sunday between January 2 and 8 (inclusive) marked a drastic change. Perhaps because Epiphany is still a solemnity, a feast of high regard in the church, little critical thought has been given to this major calendrical alteration. Even apart from assessing the change by the criteria of larger attendance on Sunday or by the compatibility of the theologies of Sunday and Epiphany, the church cannot ignore that the solemnity had been kept on a fixed date from its first appearance nearly eighteen centuries ago until Vatican II.

The origins of the date of Epiphany are the same as those for the date of Christmas. In some ancient churches the incarnation (conception) and death of Jesus were both celebrated on the Jewish date of 14 Nisan. This lunar determination of the date for Passover was reckoned into different cultures in different ways, with some communities in the Latin West tending toward March 25 (and, hence, Christmas nine months later on December 25) and some communities in the East tending toward April 6 (with the birth feast marked on January 6). Since the *date* had been the determination of the feast for nearly two millennia, the transfer of the feast in the United States to a Sunday is not a small change.

In its present liturgical expression, the solemnity of Epiphany engages Christian imaginations (in the West) very little. At best it is one in the chain of narratives in the nativity span, with the late Advent Gospels of annunciation and conception; with the Christmas narrative of the infant Jesus' manifestation to humanity at his birth; with the slaughter of the Holy Innocents on December 28; and, at least for Catholics, with the Solemnity of Mary, the Mother of God, on January 1. That the feast and its date antedated all of these and that the feast was originally a baptismal feast in many churches of the Greek, Syrian, and Egyptian traditions is hardly known or missed. Does the profound history and former theology of Epiphany weigh in the balance lighter than the convenience that a Sunday celebration offers the members of the church? Is the pastoral advantage of a fuller church enough to have warranted such a break in the calendrical precedent?

Since the major reform of the liturgical year in 1969, a few feasts that had been celebrated on weekdays or on calendar dates that would year by year fall on different days of the week have been relocated temporally to Sundays. In the United States, Ascension Thursday has been relocated to the Seventh Sunday of Easter; the feast of the Most Precious Blood of Jesus, once kept on July 1, is now joined to Corpus Christi and this combined Solemnity of the Body and Blood of Christ is observed on the second Sunday after Pentecost. The feast of Epiphany is another of those that have been changed from dated feasts to Sundays. Maintaining feasts on fixed dates is a tradition of time-keeping quite different from the culture in which weekends are the times for celebrating. While church attendance is assuredly higher because of the habit of Sunday worship, liturgical time-keeping has been accommodated to the culture such that now Christian time-keeping is little distinguishable from the time-keeping of non-Christians.

The ancient connection between Christmas and Epiphany as feasts marking different reckonings for the date of Jesus' birth reminds believers that these dates are not of history but of church invention, an important recognition that the presence of the risen Christ in the church determined, and continues to determine, times for the liturgical marking of events in the life of Jesus, even when there is no extant data for determining their historicity. This recognition also helps weigh in the balance with academic efforts to find the historical Jesus. Such efforts may bring to light the world of first-century Mediterranean life for the benefit of historians, but have little pastoral efficacy. The dates are determined by the true experiences of God's presence mediated by communities of faith rather than by dates suggested or dismissed in the writings of historians.

Another change that observing Epiphany on Sundays introduced is the reduction in the awkward juxtapositions of the temporal and sanctoral calendars, the former a concatenation of Sundays through the liturgical year (for the most part) and the latter dependent on dates independent of the days of the week on which they occur. Yet, the rubs between temporal and sanctoral calendars make liturgical time different from year to year, and draw the church into actively participating in calendar-making, a process that calls on the community's active input and communicates that it is an ongoing process of faith rather than a process determined by hierarchy or history.

For Roman Catholics, between the solemnities of Christmas and Epiphany falls the Solemnity of Mary, Mother of God, on January 1. Mary has long been the subversive icon of social reversal and surprise. One of the options for the Preface for that day captures this: "Father, all-powerful and ever-living God.... All generations have shared the greatness of your love. When you looked on Mary your lowly servant, you raised her to be the mother of Jesus Christ, your Son, our Lord, the savior of all mankind." This is a fitting theology for the span between Christmas and Epiphany, echoing as it does Mary's song of praise: "For he who is mighty has done great things for me, and holy is his name" (Luke 1:49).

The Church at Prayer on Epiphany

The theology of Epiphany is revealed in the collects for the day. Each prayer emphasizes God's ongoing presence and manifestation in the church:

> Let us pray
> [that we will be guided by the light of faith]
>
> Father,
> you revealed your Son to the nations by the guidance of a star.
> Lead us to your glory in heaven by the light of faith.[67]

In this prayer, God's presence as light calls humanity toward the fullness of life:

> Let us pray
> [grateful for the glory revealed today through God made man]
>
> Father of light, unchanging God,
> today you reveal to men of faith
> the resplendent fact of the Word made flesh.
> Your light is strong; your love is near;
> draw us beyond the limits which this world imposes,
> to the light where your Spirit makes all life complete.[68]

Common to the theology of each prayer is the imagery of light — the "star" of the first, and "light" and "resplendent fact" of the second — and this is important as we see the metaphorical link to the light imagery of Easter and know that, in the process of initiation and in theology, the feast of Epiphany has links to Easter. In late fourth-century Milan, Ambrose lamented that on the feast of Epiphany he had called for the enrollment of candidates for initiation and no names had appeared. The light imagery in these prayers is linked to the baptisms that will happen at the Easter Vigil. In the RCIA sequence of rites today, many churches celebrate the Rite of Acceptance of Catechumens

67. *Vatican II Sunday Missal: Millennium Edition* (Boston: Pauline Books & Media, 2001): 114.
68. Ibid.: 114–115.

on the First Sunday of Advent and the Rite of Election or Enrollment of Names, often at the cathedral with the bishop, on the First Sunday of Lent. So the connection between the ancient catechumenal process is maintained, but the day of Epiphany has lost its more intimate connection with Easter in pastoral life.

Preachers would do well to consider these two prayers as the starting point for the theology of their message, for the usual inclination to dwell on the historicity of the event — "from what lands did the magi come?" — would be avoided if the present imperative of the prayers — "lead us to your glory," "today you reveal...the resplendent fact of the Word made flesh" — were taken more seriously. Preachers would be called to see the resplendence of God in the community of faith, would have to trust that God continues to reveal glory to people of faith, and would encourage the community to find God's light and love in their own place and time rather than occupying them with the enigmas of the Gospel account of the visit of the magi two thousand years ago. This theology of God's presence in the present is also strong in the preface for Epiphany at the start of the Eucharistic Prayer:

> Today you revealed in Christ your eternal plan of salvation
> and showed him as the light of all peoples.
> Now that his glory has shone among us
> you have renewed humanity in his immortal image.[69]

The prayers of the liturgy for Epiphany strongly suggest that God is still active in the people called into the church by baptism. Yet the preaching for the feast — as for all feasts — needs to highlight this activity of God since the metaphor and narrative of the magi bearing gifts, left by itself, might be strange enough to divert the community from this emphasis in the prayers.

The Liturgy of the Word

The three readings for Epiphany are Isaiah 60:1–6, Ephesians 3:2–3a, 5–6, and Matthew 2:1–12.

The fitting aspects of the reading from Isaiah are the potent theology of light and darkness, the theology of "manifestation" or appearance, and the traditions of the magi foreshadowed in this passage. The reading suggests the social reversal that will accompany the manifestation of God among us; God's city, laid waste in the past, will witness its vindication:

---

69. Ibid.: 652.

> Arise, shine; for your light has come,
> and the glory of the LORD has risen upon you.
> For behold, darkness shall cover the earth,
> and thick darkness the peoples;
> but the LORD will arise upon you,
> and his glory will be seen upon you.
> And nations shall come to your light,
> and kings to the brightness of your rising.
>   (60:1–3)

The theology of light has been characteristic of the imagery of this feast from the early church. Moreover, the celebration of baptism has long been wedded to the metaphor of light, and still in our own celebrations of initiation — RCIA, infant baptism, funerals — the Easter candle illumines the bodies of those whose transitions from death to new life are being marked and celebrated. This theology of light is most powerful in its use in the Gospel of John: "I am the light of the world" (8:12). Because in the early church Epiphany was a celebration of baptism in the life of the church and was also the occasion for remembering the baptism of Jesus, the theology of light in this reading from the prophet Isaiah is fitting.

Prominent also is the theology of "manifestation." The feast of the Annunciation, or the feast of the incarnation (as it is called in some traditions), is that on which the church remembers the Word of God becoming flesh, like us in all things but sin (Hebrews 4:15). But this was not contemporaneous with the manifestation and revelation of the Son to the world. The word and feast of "epiphany" is a celebration of the revelation of God's presence to humanity, to the church, to those being initiated and in those being initiated. When the words of the prophet are proclaimed, "the Lord will arise upon you, and his glory will be seen upon you" (60:2b), the church is awakened to the revelation of God's presence in the church and particularly in those who are candidates for the initiations that will be celebrated this year at Easter. The presence of catechumens reminds the church that the risen Christ is not just a memory but a living and active presence in the people with whom it celebrates and, most especially, in the people who, in vulnerability, are willing to seek membership and commit their lives to the gospel and the church proclaiming the gospel.

The most familiar aspect of the reading from Isaiah is the foreshadowing of the story of the visit of the magi. We hear in this passage, "nations shall come to your light, and kings to the brightness of your rising," and a "multitude of camels shall cover you. . . . They shall bring gold and frankincense" (60:3, 6). The response to the reading from Isaiah — from Psalm 72 — emphasizes the universality of the faith borne by the narrative of the magi's visit: "Lord, every nation on earth will adore you."

The second reading (Ephesians 3:2–3a, 5–6) also marks the universality of the faith, and it erases the impediment of time in realizing the presence of God in the church. The church is proclaimed as the "body," as the incarnate, revelatory presence of God in the world, like the incarnation in the "body" of Jesus of Nazareth. In the letter the author spoke to the newly embraced Gentiles, but in the proclamation of the reading today the community of faith hears that "it has now been revealed," and that you "are fellow heirs, members of the same body, and partakers of the promise in Christ Jesus through the gospel" (5–6). This reading is a foundation for the long-standing, socially transforming theology of the feast, as Christians associating with people with whom they had not previously associated bring them into the community of God's presence. This reading is a precedent for the Bessie Popkins and Thomas Mertons of all times and places, calling the people of God to step over the lines of constriction and judgment that curb the presence of God.

Matthew's brilliant and engaging story gives license to the Christian imagination — preachers, sculptors, painters, musicians, creators of stained-glass windows — by supplying a narrative of the infant Jesus and his parents that contained these "wise men from the East." The Greek word *magus* has the same etymological root as "magician" or "astrologer," and for this reason exotic couture and narratives embellished the brief story. So, even though these foreigners from the East appear only in one Gospel and in it play just a minor part, in the Christian imagination the space these three occupy is much grander than the space they do in the Bible.

From Matthew's Group to Three Individuals. One basic difference between the written Gospel narrative and the imagination-engaging tradition of the visitors from the East is that of numbering the visitors as only *three* magi. The story itself does not mention how many magi visited, but perhaps the three gifts — gold, frankincense, myrrh — themselves evoked three characters. Tradition has named them Caspar, Melchior, and Balthasar, but, again, creative imagination and tradition have supplied what the scripture narrative did not.

In examining a number of visual representations of the exotic astrologers, one sees that they have embodied an expansive place in which artists have imagined how people in other cultures have lived and dressed. The magi are often seen on animals that would have been strange in the places where they were depicted — camels, elephants, or at times even giraffes. Also, in most of the artwork there are suggestions of the former, pre-nativity lives of the three as fortune-tellers, star-gazers, crystal-ball-interpreters. And then there is also the issue of race, for often in artwork two of the magi are white, Caspar and Melchior, and one black, Balthasar.

The gifts they bear to the nascent savior are also in the order of the names, with Caspar bringing enough gold to make the greedy salivate, Melchior carrying enough frankincense to make one's nose tickle, and Balthasar bringing up the rear with the myrrh. Unlike the visual uniqueness of the magicians in Christian art, Matthew never mentions any one of them as an individual. They appear always as a group in the evangelist's presentation: "we have seen his star in the East, and have come to worship him," "Herod summoned the wise men secretly," "they rejoiced exceedingly with great joy," "they saw the child with Mary his mother," "they offered him gifts, gold and frankincense and myrrh," and finally, "being warned in a dream not to return to Herod, they departed to their own country by another way" (Matthew 2:2, 7, 10, 11, 12).

The attribution of gifts and races makes them individuals. Though the depiction of the group as two-thirds white, one-third black was not universal, it was fairly common for one of the three magi to have been depicted as African. Balthasar has gotten short shrift in the artwork over the centuries. One will usually find him at the back of a canvas, or with only his head peeping at the child over the shoulders of the fully depicted Caspar and Melchior. Priority of proximity to the savior child is accorded to the parents, then to the white fellows, and finally to Balthasar, whom one might find relegated at a distance farther away than the farm animals who had come to feed on the hay.

A well-known folk-song of the Christmas season in Argentina is *Los Reyes Magos*, the "magical kings," which opens like this:

> *Llegaron ya, los reyes eran tres,*
> *Melchor, Gaspar y el negro Baltazar,*
> *arrope y miel le llevaran*
> *y un poncho blanco de alpaca real.*

> They're already here, those three kings:
> Melchior, Gaspar, and the black Balthasar.
> They bring him grape syrup and honey,
> And a royal, white, alpaca poncho.

Any mention of *Los Reyes Magos* to native Argentines brings unsolicited choruses of the hymn, obviously a profound staple of traditional Catholic piety in Argentina. Yet in the lyrics there is an element of anti-black, pro-white racial bias. If in the song the first two were called *los blancos Melchor y Gaspar*, "the white Melchior and Gaspar," then the mention of Balthasar's race would not be a problem. Not only is the whiteness of the first two not mentioned, simply assumed, but Balthasar's negritude is juxtaposed to the "pure white alpaca poncho" given to the infant Messiah, a sign that, unlike the third magus, holiness was clearly accorded to white things and people.

The joy of the scripture narratives at Christmas time is that they are indeed spare, and they draw us in to imagine God's gifts as ever new and ever lavish. The Bible is an immutable rule of the Christian faith, but the local traditions drawn from the narratives are not immutable. They are meant to be inculturated according to the experience of the Catholic faith in each parish and family. In the prayers, music, decorations, and artwork of Christmas and the Christmas season, pastoral ministers need to consider expanding the boundaries of the story to incorporate some of those who would today be as scandalous and as holy as the negro Balthasar probably was centuries ago.

The scriptures are meant to be proclaimed as fuel for our imaginations, communal and individual. Our hearts, minds, and dreams are formed by the age-old tales. The Argentine inculturation of the story is captured in the hymn's gifts of grape syrup, honey, and the alpaca poncho, for these are not of the ancient Mediterranean world of the holy family of Joseph, Mary, and Jesus, but of the holy families of traditional Argentine life, families whose quotidian life would have known these three gifts.

Conclusion

The earliest narrative for the solemnity of Epiphany, the baptism of Jesus himself in the Jordan River, remembered and celebrated the medium of Christian social transformation, that is, the waters of baptism. By that event, the waters of the Jordan River were sanctified by the touch of God's Son, and by them, in turn, all the waters of the world were sanctified for baptisms in ages and places far from the Palestinian waters of Jesus' baptism. Those waters are the medium of sanctification because they bring people into a new society, that of the Kingdom of God. The quality of such social transformation embraced by the solemnity of Epiphany may have been why nineteenth-century

French novelist Victor Hugo set the raucous scene at the start of his *Notre-Dame of Paris* on Epiphany. Though written and published in 1830–1831, Hugo's opening scene was set in a mob on Epiphany centuries before his writing — on January 6, 1482. That time would have been a few decades *after* the invention of the printing press and a few decades *before* Martin Luther's posting of 95 Theses on the church door at Wittenburg, both events of unprecedented social and religious transformation on the continent. The Reformation was a cultural eye-opening for Christians in Europe, much like Bessie's personal eye-opening at the beginning of this chapter. The earliest lectionaries for Epiphany testify to the admission of the Gentiles to the church as one of the earliest of the readings associated with the feast. The unimaginable social change in the church of the first-century, with the shift of the church's populace from Jewish to Jewish and Gentile membership, led the tradition for the social changes that would be wrought by the narrative of the baptism of Jesus, and, from the fourth century on, by the narrative of the exotic magi from the East coming to visit Mary, Joseph, and their infant son.

In the late fifteenth-century opening scene of Hugo's novel the reader discovers Epiphany coincident with social melee and ecclesial disorder. After a huge cortege and procession of staid Catholic hierarchy and clergy has trod the streets of Paris, the street crowd enacts the antithesis of the somber religious scene as it elects the "fools' pope," the pope of the streets, Quasimodo, the "hunchback" of the popular, if not original, title of the book. Hugo's description of the scene includes many elements of religious and social mayhem: people dressed as pagan gods, particularly like Jupiter; descriptions of gender mix-ups and transvestism; depictions of apparent deformities of creation, like Quasimodo himself.

In a keen view of ecclesiastical upheaval on the day of Epiphany, the crowd seeks to dignify the poor, crippled beggar Quasimodo, but with predictable immutability church officials in attendance do not comply with their desire:

> The novelty of this remarkable scene evoked such wildness and merriment in the hall that it was not long before the cardinal became aware of the noise. . . . Outraged by such audacity [from Quasimodo], the cardinal exclaimed: "Palace bailiff, throw this scoundrel into the river."[70]

---

70. Victor Hugo, *Notre-Dame of Paris*, trans. John Sturrock (London: Penguin, 1978): 61.

The cardinal's wish is not obeyed, and the hunchback — called "his perfect ugliness," "as vicious as he's ugly," an "infernal man" by others attending — is raised up from his state. The street's assembly itself raises up church members and, in some cases, non-members whom it considered leadership material for its invented ecclesial society for Epiphany.

Hugo's *Notre-Dame* relates the story of this pope-for-a-day society, which had elected as pope sometimes a man, sometimes a woman; yet in 1482 it would be the crippled male protagonist of the well-known tale:

> All the beggars, manservants and cutpurses had joined with the students and gone in procession to the lawyers' wardrobe to fetch the fools' pope's cardboard crown and mock chimer. Quasimodo allowed himself to be dressed up without moving a muscle and with a sort of proud submissiveness. Then they seated him on a multicoloured litter. Twelve officers from the brotherhood of fools lifted him on to their shoulders, and a sort of bitter, disdainful joy spread across the face of this cyclops as he saw all those handsome, straight, well-made men's heads beneath his misshapen feet. Then the yelling, ragged procession got under way to make, as was customary, its circuit of the internal galleries of the palace before parading the streets and crossroads.... On this litter, resplendent in crozier, cope and mitre, was the new pope of fools, the bell-ringer of Notre-Dame, the hunchback Quasimodo.[71]

True to the topsy-turvy invention of Epiphany in its earliest manifestation in the tradition, which was likely begotten from a pre-Christian tradition of social upset at the turn of the year,[72] the tradition of stational processing throughout the city was a long-standing element of Parisian Epiphany.

The attention and fanfare were not unwelcome by the new pope, whose

> hideous and unhappy face had opened out to a degree hard to convey and now looked both proud and self-satisfied. This was the first taste he had ever had of the delights of vanity. Hitherto, he had known only humiliation, contempt for his condition and disgust for his person. And so, stone deaf though he was, he relished the acclamation of the crowd like a real pope, that crowd

---

71. Ibid.: 73, 88.
72. Clement A. Miles, *Christmas Customs and Traditions: Their History and Significance* (New York: Dover, 1976): 17–28, 161–186.

which he had detested because he felt it detested him. What did it matter that his people was a pack of fools, cripples, thieves and beggars, it was still a people and he its sovereign. And he took all the ironic applause and mock respect seriously, although it should be said that mixed in with it, among the crowd, went an element of very real fear. For the hunchback was strong; his crooked legs were nimble; his deafness made him vicious: three qualities that tempered the ridicule.[73]

Although the associations of Hugo's narrative of Paris in the late fifteenth century might seem quite distant from the feast of the Epiphany familiar to the church in the twenty-first century, Christians can recall that the very name of the solemnity means "manifestation," and the readings for the feast reflect the church's understanding of the day with that element as central to its theological significance. Hugo placed the cacophonous procession on the date of January 6 because the social customs traditionally attached to the feast gave him the intuition to set the scene on the particular solemnity at the beginning of the year when many social upheavals customarily occurred, perhaps from pre-Christian times.

The various narratives for the feast in the fourth and early fifth centuries — the birth of Jesus, the visit of the magi, the baptism of Jesus in the Jordan River, the water turned into wine at the wedding feast in Cana of Galilee, the multiplication of loaves and fishes, and the transfiguration — all had the element of change and surprise, and the theology of the feast as manifestation of God in the world delivers such expectations in church life. The association of the feast with the social mayhem of the procession in Hugo's story — with a deaf, misshapen hunchback as its pontiff and narrative keystone — can be held up in light of the Christian scriptural testimony to the social disruptions that accompany the advent of God at all times and in all places.

Again and again in the early tradition one can detect that God's reign was ever accompanied by surprises regarding who is included in the divine embrace. Recall the social expectations of the Gospel: "When you give a dinner or a banquet, do not invite your friends or your brothers or your kinsmen or rich neighbors, lest they also invite you in return, and you be repaid. But when you give a feast, invite the poor, the maimed, the lame, the blind" (Luke 14:12–13), that is, the Quasimodos of this world.

---

73. Hugo: 88.

Quasimodo Gentili Infantes

Because Hugo wrote the novel in only four and a half months — writing on average 1500 words a day — it does not seem likely that the author would have considered the history of the tradition of the feast in its Eastern and Western veins, yet, as the foregoing history of the day demonstrates, such research is necessary to unlock even just a fraction of the complexity of this feast's history. But perhaps the collective unconscious of church experience for the feast was incorporated into the impetus for setting his story on this day.

Central to unlocking the link between Hugo's narrative and the solemnity is the name of the protagonist, Quasimodo, in light of the ancient baptismal narrative of Epiphany and of the theology of surprise that accompanies the feast. Those familiar with the novel, or with a movie based on the novel, readily think "monster" or "hunchback" when they hear the tag "Quasimodo." But the author accorded this name to the cripple from its use in Christian worship, for it comes from the entrance antiphon of the liturgical day when, in the narrative of Hugo's novel, a handicapped child was abandoned by his parents and left in the church of Notre-Dame in Paris:

> Sixteen years prior to the events of this story, one fine Quasimodo Sunday morning, a living creature was deposited after mass in the church of Notre-Dame on the wooden bed set into the parvais on the left-hand side, facing the great image of St Christopher, at which the carved stone figure of Messire Antoine des Essarts, Knight, had been kneeling starting in 1413, when they took it into their head to overthrow both saint and worshipper. This was the wooden bed where it was customary to expose foundlings to public charity. Whoever wanted them could take them. In front of the wooden bed was a copper bowl for alms.
>
> The sort of living creature lying recumbent on this plank on the morning of Quasimodo in the Year of Our Lord 1467 seemed to be exciting the liveliest curiosity amongst the quite large group that had collected round the wooden bed. This group largely comprised members of the fair sex. They were nearly all old women.[74]

The women who come upon him in the pew of the cathedral consider him, alternately, "a sin to look at," "not a child," "a monkey gone wrong," and "a real monster of abomination." One declared, "I'd rather give suck to a vampire" than to him, and a final one exclaimed on

---

74. Ibid.: 155.

looking at him that "it would be better for the villeins of Paris if this little magician were lying on a faggot rather than on a plank of wood," that is, suggesting that the deformed infant would have been better burned than given support by the church.

Even though the novel opens in the context of Epiphany, the liturgical day when the women found the child was not Epiphany but Low Sunday, the liturgical day that the church now calls the Second Sunday of Easter. The Latin antiphon for the day was the source for the anonymous child's name. The entrance antiphon in the Roman Missal — at the time of the story's setting, 1482, and still at the time of Hugo's writing, 1830 — began with the Latin word that became the character's name:

> *Quasimodo gentili infantes, alleluia:*
> *rationabiles sine dolo lac concupiscite, alleluia, alleluia, alleluia.*

> Like newborn infants, Alleluia;
> Yearn for milk without guile, Alleluia, Alleluia.

Even if this name was the inadvertent result of Victor Hugo's hastily written narrative, the meaning of the antiphon and its baptismal associations are wonderfully reflective of the time of year, of the twelve-day span from Christmas to Epiphany. Minus the Alleluias added to the biblical text for the liturgical setting in the Fifty Days, the Vulgate verse comes from the First Letter of Peter, and this part of the text is addressing the newly baptized:

> You have been born anew, not of perishable seed but of imperishable, through the living and abiding word of God. . . . So put away all malice and all guile and insincerity and envy and all slander. *Like newborn babes*, long for the pure spiritual milk, that by it you may grow up to salvation; for you have tasted the kindness of the Lord. (1:23; 2:1–3)

This last sentence became the antiphon for the Second Sunday of Easter that prompted Hugo to name the character Quasimodo. (The meaning of the word *quasimodo* is simply the "like" that precedes "newborn babes," in the meaning of "as" or "similar to" or "in this way.")

In the Roman Missal of 1570 and perhaps for a while before that, the first line of the entrance antiphon (as above) is "like newborn babes," followed by the Alleluia, and the second line is the imperative, "long for the pure spiritual milk." (The Latin calls it "milk without deceit," or "without guile," perhaps, aptly linked to protagonist of Hugo's tale.)

Though the reading from First Peter is no longer proclaimed on a Sunday during the Fifty Days of the Easter season, the church can be content to know that the same entrance antiphon of Quasimodo's name — shortened to the nickname "Quasi" in the Disney version of the story — is still in place for the Second Sunday of Easter: "*Like* newborn children you should thirst for milk, on which your spirit can grow to strength, Alleluia."[75]

Regarding the feast at the center of this chapter's investigation, the key element of the antiphon is that it is addressed to those newly baptized, for it is still placed on the Second Sunday of Easter, an octave after the initiation rites of the Easter Vigil. But the theology of manifestation and surprise and social mayhem can still adhere to our theology of Epiphany and to the vocation of the newly baptized, who — "like newborns," neophytes, members of the body of Christ — will follow in the example of the Savior himself, whose vocation called him to upset the religious leadership of his time and place and to reverse so many of the social values and customs of first-century Palestine's culture and society.

Over the centuries since the earliest Latin testimony, the significance of this august feast has been in steady decline in the Roman Catholic tradition and the churches of the Reformation. Some of the churches of the Orthodox liturgical traditions have maintained the day's depth and breadth. The study of the feast's history and theology is important not only for an appreciation of a cardinal ingredient of the calendar, but because the evolution of Epiphany reveals a great deal about how narratives are related to the feasts they mark, about how and why liturgies change, and about the increments by which the calendar is formed, reformed, and put in jeopardy.

As described at length in the calendar reckoning between East and West, a primary loss to the Christian tradition regarding Epiphany was not the separation of birth from Epiphany as it was the separation of the narratives of birth and baptism, and Hugo's story reminds the church of the depth of the ancient connection. The First Letter of Peter contributed to the liturgical tradition that begot a name for Victor Hugo's crippled beast; as a text reminding the church of the significance of the baptism of the Lord and the baptism of new members of the church, the words of Peter are rich and wonderful. The Eastern traditions surrendered the nativity to Roman dating, yet there was no complementary maintenance of the theology of Epiphany — from Egypt and Syria, in particular — in the theology of initiation as it is now

---

75. *Vatican II Sunday Missal:* 114.

celebrated in most Christian churches. That loss of the feast's theology is greater than the juggling of dates and narratives in late antiquity. The New Testament embraces a variety of theologies of baptism, and the loss of the infancy and birth images in that variety contributes to the eclipse of the feast after Vatican II; let the church remember its tradition, as it sings:

Quasimodo gentili infantes, alleluia:
rationabiles sine dolo lac concupiscite, alleluia, alleluia, alleluia.

Chapter 5

CANDLEMAS

Prior to Vatican II, liturgical passivity marked the assembly gathered for worship in Roman Catholic churches. Anticipating the reform of the liturgy, bishops at the Council hoped baptized members of the church who had been inactive for their whole lives would recognize the dignity of their Christian initiation and begin to participate actively — bodies, minds, hearts — in the prayer of the local community and in the rites of the universal communion of the church's embrace. With such full participation — those who reformed the rites surmised — the members of the assembly would recognize that they realized the risen Christ when they gathered on the Sundays and feasts of the church year.

Such hope for reform sprang from the church's recognition that non-ordained, baptized laity had been ignorant and poorly prepared for worship during (at least) the four-century span from the Roman Missal of Pius V promulgated after the Council of Trent (1570) to the Sacramentary promulgated after the Second Vatican II Council (1969). The *Constitution on the Sacred Liturgy* called for the "full, conscious, active participation" of the assembly gathered at prayer (#14). Perhaps the Council's leaders were overly optimistic in expecting a sudden active participation of the major sector of the church — the laity — in rites that had found them static, uninvolved, and peripheral for nearly a half-millennium, or perhaps it will take a complementary four centuries of activity to counter the assembly's immobility between the Council of Trent (1543–1565) and Vatican II.

The liturgy, many thought as the reform was underway, had been too much "mindless ritual" — an oxymoronic phrase that in the United States is usually spoken pejoratively. In secular life, apart from the church, rote behaviors of "tradition" are often considered anathema. In the wake of the Enlightenment's exalting of reason and the French Revolution's call for the social participation of all — from the highest to the lowest-born — all were and are supposed to be informed, conscious, and responsible participants in their own societies and governments. The Roman Catholic church was indicted in and after the French Revolution (1789) as an institution that had formed many people in the

199

mindless rituals of its worship. During the Enlightenment the Roman Catholic church stood as anti-democratic in a democratically liberated and now secular society. By the middle of the twentieth century, the church recognized the need for reforming itself and its worship.

In the mid-twentieth-century reform the church took up some of the values of the movements that had earlier attacked it, the rationalism of the Enlightenment in particular, to emphasize understanding as a goal of the changes. As a charge for those who would work on the new rites, the *Constitution on the Sacred Liturgy* (#11) taught:

> In order that the liturgy may be able to produce its full effects it is necessary that the faithful come to it with proper dispositions, that their minds be attuned to their voices, and that they cooperate with heavenly grace lest they receive it in vain. Pastors of souls must, therefore, realize that, when the liturgy is celebrated, something more is required than the laws governing valid and lawful celebration. It is their duty also to ensure that the faithful take part fully aware of what they are doing, actively engaged in the rite and enriched by it.[1]

In the practical implications of such goals, the *Constitution* said: "The rites should be distinguished by a noble simplicity. They should be short, clear, and free from useless repetitions. They should be within the people's powers of comprehension, and normally should not require much explanation" (#34).[2]

To a great extent, such values were good ones to attend to as the liturgy was reconsidered and revised. But instead of moving the liturgical assembly from many mindless ritual actions to many mindful ritual actions, the reform generally moved from many to few ritual actions, virtually none in comparison with the engagement of the human body in the rites before the reform. Since Vatican II, the Sunday Mass has had far fewer processions, genuflections, signs of the cross, and bows for ordinary, non-ministering believers, and no more beatings of the breast at the "Lord, have mercy" and "Lamb of God."

The local church, as a resurrected people of faith — the reformers hoped — would be less penitent, less imitative of the suffering Jesus and more aware of the risen Christ. Though the death of Jesus of Nazareth won salvation for humanity, that death did not erase suffering from human experience. Both suffering and rising are aspects of

---

1. *Vatican Council II*, Volume 1: The Conciliar and Postconciliar Documents, ed. Austin Flannery (Northport, NY: Costello, 1998): 6–7.
2. Ibid.: 12.

who Christ is at all times: the suffering of the body of the church participates in the life of Christ, and through him in the life of God. The new theology and Christology expressed in the reform of the liturgy revised the rites to be celebratory, not penitential. Humanity continues as ever to be both saved and still sinful after the incarnation of Jesus of Nazareth in its midst two thousand years ago.

Consonant with the rational goals of the *Constitution on the Sacred Liturgy*, the faithful are indeed more aware of what takes place in the liturgy, but, though they may *think* about worship more than before Vatican II, they are *doing* a lot less. This does not represent a usual Roman Catholic anthropology. The body's participation should not be secondary in worship, and the church has come to recognize that participating with one's mind is lopsided without the participation of one's body. The people of God miss the assembly's frequent changes of posture, its processions, its incense and smells, its candles and lights. Leaders of the liturgical reform lament that contemporary youth seem more traditional, often longing for a return to the Missal of Pius V. Their longing, however, is not just retrogressive; underlying it is a hunger for having their senses and bodies engaged by the rites — which is why people miss things like statues and incense. Furthermore, older members of the church miss the pre–Vatican II norms for feasting, fasting, and enacting the church's rites in their homes and work lives. More might have been done in the reform to help local churches appreciate the incarnate Christ in world and community and celebrate that in the liturgy. In the absence of norms and rubrics about how the body might act in consonance with theology and catechesis after Vatican II, many people have sought a return to the church of the "old days."

Between Trent and Vatican II liturgical norms had been universal; if one local church was to do something during the year — fasting, feasting, processing, lighting candles — all would do it. In those centuries, uniqueness was discouraged; indeed, it was censured. The directives of Vatican II marked a great change in this regard, placing responsibilities on bishops and pastors, who would discern each local community's way of expressing its celebrating, fasting, feasting, and participating. The clergy, however, were not — and indeed, most still are not — trained to discern the Spirit's movement in the local assembly and give expression to this at worship. For centuries, norms were handed down in the Roman Catholic church, from the pope down through the bishops, who were, in this regard, merely the medium for transmitting and enforcing these norms. Discernment, invention, and creativity were not encouraged by the faithful or by the local bishops, and bishops are usually not chosen for inventiveness. Although the bishops of the Council might have hoped that the hunger of God's people for manifesting in their assembled body what God has given to humanity in Christ would quickly be fulfilled, most churches languished, and moved therefore from universal prescriptions before Vatican II to the stasis that is too commonly the celebration of the seasons and feasts of the liturgical year today.

This reflection is put at the start of this chapter because the reform of the feast of Candlemas is one of those that has fallen out of view for most believers. Instead of ascertaining how local churches might observe February 2 in an apt and perhaps prophetic way, bishops and pastors have allowed its complex and corporal rituals and deep traditions to languish. The call from some quarters for a retrieval of pre–Vatican II observances is not merely a yearning for the archaic, but a call to have the faithful bodies of the Body of Christ engaged in worship as they once were. The result is that, in many dioceses and parishes, the church has not moved forward in discerning how human ecclesial behavior would be recognizably different in the various seasons and particular feast days of the calendar.

Such considerations are warranted in studying Candlemas, or the Presentation of the Lord, for its ancient and medieval observances were unique and because it is not a day on which many stake a claim, whether conservatives or liberals. Before Vatican II — even with the useless repetitions that the Council wanted to eliminate, and even without the full awareness that the reform called for — the people of God participated in this feast with their bodies. Complementing the body's work with the mind's understanding was a laudable goal, but displacing the former with the latter has been the regrettable result of the reform in general.

The rites of Candlemas — as of all feasts and seasons — should be expressed in the body of Christ, the assembly of individual bodies brought together by God's grace and the Holy Spirit in baptism. Although the feast of the Presentation is an ancient and long-standing Christian feast, its august theology and complex development have waned in the last few decades, indeed, even centuries. Candlemas once signaled elaborate processions and candle-lighting, a poignant celebration at the near-end of winter. Its narrative has elements that recall the Christmas celebrations of six weeks earlier and some theological elements that anticipate the approaching passion on Good Friday. "Simeon took [the child Jesus] in his arms," the story in Luke reminds the church, harking back to the mystery of Christmas, and yet he says to Mary, the infant's mother, "A sword will pierce your own soul too," anticipating the passion that, with death, is the inevitable complement of life's joys (Luke 2:28, 35b).

Candlemas in a Monastery in the United States in 1943

Although the feast has diminished in importance, even more so than the greatly diminished Solemnity of Epiphany,[3] the Presentation still reverberates in the tradition from unexpected places. Thomas Merton (1915–1968), the well-known Trappist monk and prolific author and poet, wrote "The Candlemas Procession" not long after he entered Gethsemane Abbey in Kentucky, in 1941.[4] Merton had been baptized Roman Catholic only in 1938, in his early twenties. So, unlike most Catholics in the United States (then and now), who are baptized as infants and learn the ritual actions as they grow up, the rites of the liturgical year were relatively new for him when he wrote the following poem.

This was written still a few decades before Vatican II, so the scriptures were then proclaimed in Latin; the poem thus refers to part of the Latin text of the day's Gospel, *lumen ad revelationem gentium,* "a light of revelation to the Gentiles," a reference to the symbol of light placed on Simeon's lips by the evangelist Luke in his writing of the Gospel (2:32):

THE CANDLEMAS PROCESSION

Lumen
Ad revelationem gentium.

Look kindly, Jesus, where we come,
New Simeons, to kindle,
Each at Your infant sacrifice his own life's candle.

And when Your flame turns into many tongues,
See how the One is multiplied, among us, hundreds!
And goes among the humble, and consoles our sinful kindred.

It is for this we come,
And, kneeling, each receive one flame:
Ad revelationem gentium.

---

3. See Volume 1, Chapter 4, "Epiphany."
4. Thomas Merton, "The Candlemas Procession," *The Collected Poems of Thomas Merton* (New York: New Directions, 1977): 92.

Our lives, like candles, spell this simple symbol:

Weep like our bodily life, sweet work of bees,
Sweeten the world, with your slow sacrifice.
And this shall be our praise:
That by our glad expense, our Father's will
Burned and consumed us for a parable.

Nor burn we now with brown and smoky flames, but bright
Until our sacrifice is done,
(By which not we, but You are known)
And then, returning to our Father, one by one,
Give back our lives like wise and waxen lights.

Even as the scriptures were in ancient Latin, Merton apprehended the significance of the narrative and of the main elements of the Candlemas ritual itself, with its procession and its light — both elements that have been integral to the feast's celebration for more than a millennium.

The Lukan story captures, in part, the passion element of the Gospel's theology, recognizing the Savior's self-giving sacrifice manifest not only on the cross but also throughout his life, from conception to death. As Merton's poem relates, the church, then and now, is a procession of new Simeons and new Annas, of those who participate in the saving death and resurrection of the Savior of the world. This expression of the liturgical experience, written in mid-life — Merton died at fifty-three — glimpses how the candles of Christian ritual experience brought the community of faith together. Like the bread broken and wine sipped in the Lord's supper, one body though many parts, so the many candles in the feast's liturgy manifested the one light who is Christ, in the temple of the Presentation's narrative and in the body of Christ in the church. The symbol of the light of Christ is a sign that members of the community sacrifice some of what they are as individuals so that the whole of the church, the Body of Christ, may be greater than the sum of the parts — and so, as he wrote, "our lives" are "like candles," as the many candles are of the one light, the Light that is Christ.

The candle, the "sweet work of bees," embraces the strength that is the darkness-conquering light that is Christ, yet also reflects the vulnerability that is the flame. Each believer who has walked in procession with a lighted candle — at the Presentation, at the Easter Vigil, at the baptism of an infant, at the Dedication of a Church, at the Feast

of St. John Lateran — knows the strength of the sign and the vulnerability of the flame, precarious to keep lighted as one walks. Yet the
warming and brightening experienced in the life of the assembled is
itself a sign of our "sinful kindred," of the lot humanity shares by its
downfall occasioned by its selfishness and betrayal, instigated in the
"No" of humanity's first parents, Adam and Eve, and ever weighing
down, soiling, and impeding the realization of the grace of God. Merton's words imagine human beings as "wise and waxen lights," as new
prophets for a new age, as the risen Christ that celebrates its lot by
God's generous favor, as the baptized stand poised — between birth
and death, between Christmas and the Three Days — on Candlemas.

Always marking the year between Christmas and Easter, the feast of
the Presentation straddles the mysteries of Christ's birth into humanity and death for humanity. The celebration of Christmas in churches
of the United States often fashions its theology so that the joy over-
shadows any hint of pain, but the theology of the Lukan circumcision
narrative and of the feast itself has through the tradition captured the
balance of joy and pain, relief and horror, that is humanity's fate in
every age. Candlemas is, in this, not unlike the passion elements of
the nativity stories, as they work in both the Gospel of Matthew and
the Gospel of Luke.

The Presentation of the Lord proclaims a wonderful narrative of the
Gospel, with the infant Son bearing salvation to those who had waited
for him patiently for many years. In this the feast is one of the few
that is uniquely oriented to ministering to the elderly, those who have
been faithful to the tradition for most of their lives — indeed, those
who might remember when Candlemas actually had candles!

Part One:
The History of Candlemas — East

Origins

In "The Origin of Lent at Alexandria," Thomas Talley wrote that "the
fast of forty days had its origins at Alexandria where it followed immediately upon the celebration of Jesus' baptism in Jordan and where
it was concluded with the conferral of baptism in a celebration associated with one whom we know as Lazarus."[5] He suggested that the
period ended with a commemoration of the raising of Lazarus and

---

5. Thomas J. Talley, "The Origin of Lent at Alexandria," as in Maxwell E. Johnson, ed.,
Between Memory and Hope: Readings on the Liturgical Year (Collegeville, MN: Liturgical
Press, 2000): 183–206; here at 183.

that "a fully baptismal liturgy" was celebrated on a day "whose general outline is the same as that for the Epiphany."[6] But he did not offer evidence connecting a particular church with such a commemoration of Lazarus and a full baptismal liturgy celebrated together in the middle of February.

In one of the most important contributions of his work, Professor Talley explained that the post-Epiphany forty-day span was eventually grafted onto Holy Week, but with the key change that the span no longer *followed* a major feast, as it had originally followed Epiphany in Egypt. Rather, it *anticipated* a major feast — Easter — or at least anticipated yet another span, the one week leading to Easter, known as "Great Week" in Jerusalem and eventually in some churches of late antiquity. The earliest evidence of the forty-day span anticipating Easter is a paschal letter of Athanasius from the year 330.[7] Egyptian resistance to relinquishing its initiation traditions is clear from the late introduction of Easter baptisms there, appearing for the first time only at the start of the patriarchate of Theophilus of Alexandria (d. 412), in 385.[8] If Talley's proposal is accepted, then one can figure that perhaps the forty-day, pre-Easter period (now called Lent) resulted from the merger, on the one side, of this Alexandrian post-Epiphany forty-day span and, on the other side, from a pre-Easter span of a different, shorter length in other churches.[9] A puzzle about this evolution, which is why it emerges in a study of Candlemas, is what the earlier forty-day Egyptian span had anticipated. What was that day — as posited by Talley — that day dedicated to a full baptismal liturgy in the middle of February, at which was proclaimed the narrative *de Lazaro* from the Gospel of John?

In spite of the amount of evidence on this in Talley's work, there has been no reliable evidence offered regarding what took place at the end of the forty-day, post-Epiphany fast. Talley himself asked, "If... we are to think of that imitation of the fast of Jesus as immediately following the Epiphany, what is to be said of the time of baptism in such a scheme?"[10] A little further along, he confesses that though "there seems no way

---

6. Ibid.: 186.

7. Talley, *Origins of the Liturgical Year* (New York: Pueblo, 1986): 168: "Prior to Nicaea, no record exists of such a forty-day fast before Easter. Only a few years after the Council, however, we encounter it in most of the Church as either a well-established custom or one that become so nearly universal as to impinge on those churches that have not yet adopted it."

8. Ibid.: 195. It is odd that evidence for the span of the pre-paschal forty days appears in Egypt relatively early, but the paschal baptismal rite, evident in many other churches earlier, is received by Egypt half a century after these others.

9. Ibid.: passim.

10. Ibid.: 194.

to present a very coherent picture of all these developments, it does appear that in their totality they represent an attempt to harmonize two traditions, one that had known a fast of forty days after Epiphany and another that had, as early as 340, situated that fast before Easter."[11] Maxwell Johnson candidly highlighted another missing element when he asked: "How does this Alexandrian forty-day post-Epiphany fast become the pre-paschal Lent?" Like Talley, he answered, "For this there is no clear or easy answer."[12]

Below is the earliest evidence for the feast of Candlemas — now celebrated by the church forty days after Christmas, on February 2 — highlighting the scripture narratives of the Presentation and of the raising of Lazarus. Johnson is correct in his assessment that there is no easy answer, but the evidence might yield yet a little more, with a close look at the original scriptures from the evangelists Luke and John. With this, new questions are raised about what might have happened in the liturgy on the fortieth day after Epiphany.

Candlemas in Jerusalem in the Early Church

The first textual evidence of the Presentation, as with so many things about the calendar in the early centuries, comes from the diary of the pilgrim Egeria, who wrote in Latin and took a trip to the Holy Land in the late fourth century (ca. 381–384). She was in Jerusalem on the date when the narrative of the presentation of the infant Jesus was proclaimed, and she related:

> The fortieth day after Epiphany is indeed celebrated here with the greatest solemnity. On that day there is a procession into the Anastasis, and all assemble there for the liturgy; and everything is performed in the prescribed manner with the greatest solemnity, just as on Easter Sunday. All the priests give sermons, and the bishop, too; and all preach on the Gospel text describing how on the fortieth day Joseph and Mary took the Lord to the temple, and how Simeon and Anna the prophetess, the daughter of Phanuel, saw Him, and what words they spoke on seeing the Lord, and of the offering which His parents brought. Afterwards, when all the ceremonies have been performed in the prescribed manner, the Eucharist is then celebrated and the dismissal given.[13]

11. Ibid.: 220.

12. "Preparation for Pascha? Lent in Christian Antiquity," in *Between Memory and Hope: Readings on the Liturgical Year* (Collegeville, MN: Liturgical Press, 2000): 207–222; here at 218.

13. The translator suggests in note 314 that, by Egeria's phrase *hic celebrantur,* "celebrated here," this was not a feast known to the religious pilgrim from her liturgical traditions in

A question about the account of the celebration in Egeria's narrative is whether there might be some indications of initiation in her description that "everything is performed in the prescribed manner with the greatest solemnity, *just as on Easter Sunday.*" We do not know from what community Egeria took her sojourn to the East at the beginning of the penultimate decade of the fourth century, so we cannot know if her comparison of the Presentation feast to Easter confirms that baptisms were included in the description of the day's observances "just as on Easter Sunday," but it at least leaves the possibility open. This might seem like an odd suggestion, however, since the narrative of the Presentation hardly bears the gravity of the narratives that would usually have accompanied initiation rites.

Differences in Dating

With Egeria's reckoning in mind, calendrical arithmetic yields that the fortieth day from Epiphany, January 6, would have been February 14, the locus of the first evidence for *hypapante*, the "meeting," as the feast of the Presentation was (and is) called in Eastern traditions, or for the feast of the *occursus domini*, the "meeting of the Lord," as it was called in Latin churches. Soon after the time of Egeria's trip, many churches of the East began to accept the Roman date of the nativity (December 25), whereas the birth had earlier been one of the manifestations celebrated at Epiphany (January 6) in some churches of the East.[14] The backward shift of twelve days in reckoning the day of the nativity, from January 6 to December 25, accounts for the shift of the Presentation from February 14 to February 2, where it has been celebrated for a millennium and a half. In different places the change of dates happened at different times, as everything did before the mass medium of the printing press; Constantinople adopted the February 2 date only during the reign of the Emperor Justin (518–527), but soon, under Justinian (527–565), the date was officially changed so that it would fall precisely forty days after Christmas.[15]

---

the West; but it is at least possible that her emphasis was not in comparing the Jerusalem tradition in which the feast was celebrated to her home community in which it was not celebrated, but in comparing her community's relatively minor observance to the Jerusalem tradition where it was celebrated "with the greatest solemnity." George E. Gingras, trans. and notes, *Egeria: Diary of a Pilgrimage*, ACW 38 (New York: Newman Press, 1970): 96–97, 224–225.

14. See Volume 1, Chapter 4, "Epiphany."

15. Bert Groen, "The Festival of the Presentation of the Lord: Its Origin, Structure and Theology in the Byzantine and Roman Rites," in *Christian Feast and Festival: The Dynamics of Western Liturgy and Culture*, ed. P. Post, G. Rouwhorst, L. van Tongeren, and A. Scheer (Louvain: Peeters, 2001): 345–381; here at 351–352.

Regarding the story of the presentation of the child Jesus to Simeon and Anna in the Gospel of Luke, the "meeting" to which the name refers has been associated for centuries with the meeting of the old man Simeon, the aged prophet Anna, and the infant Jesus in that place, the Temple, to which the parents brought their son for circumcision (or, in the Middle Ages, to which Mary was brought for purification after childbirth). Although Egeria recounts that "the preaching on the Gospel text describing how on the fortieth day Joseph and Mary took the Lord to the temple," the Gospel of Luke does not mention such a forty-day span between the birth and the Presentation of the infant Jesus in the Temple.

The witness of Egeria is augmented by the testimony of a few others about worship in Jerusalem on the Presentation. Cyril, archbishop of Jerusalem for much of the second half of the fourth century (349–387),[16] reveals — in a sermon on "the *meeting* of our Lord and Savior Jesus Christ with Simeon, who took God in his arms" — that there were processions with lights and lamps; that Adam is exulted by the reception of Christ by Simeon; that the feast is linked to the narrative of Israel's crossing of the Red Sea; that, as Israel wandered for forty years, so the church waits forty days after the virgin birth to celebrate the Presentation; and, finally, that the heavenly spouse, Christ, returns with the virgin mother of God to the marriage chamber as he is presented in the Temple. The latest of these is a constant of the imagery for the theology of the Presentation, and it is captured in the antiphon in the Greek and then Latin traditions for the feast:

> Decorate the marriage chamber, Zion,
> and receive Christ the King:
> bow down to Mary, who is the gate of heaven:
> for she carries the King of glory in a new light:

As often with the calendar, the evidence is not unambiguous. An account of a riot that happened in 602 in Constantinople at the time of a grain shortage suggests that the king participated in a litany during which there was a procession (with bare feet). According to a study of the account of the riot — Martin Higgins, "Note on the Purification (and Date of the Nativity) in Constantinople in 602," *Archiv für Liturgiewissenschaft* 2 (1952): 81–83 — in that year, 602, the Nativity was still being celebrated on January 6, not on December 25, and the Presentation was still celebrated on February 14, with a vigil and a procession.

16. The sermon from which this comes has variously been considered spuriously and correctly ascribed to Cyril. Current scholarship — see the *Supplementum* of the *Clavis Patrum Graecorum* (Turnholt: Brepols, 1998): 197, no. 3592 — attributes the sermon to Cyril. An earlier volume — CPG, volume 2 (Turnholt: Brepols, 1974): 292, no. 3592 — had it listed as spurious. For the authenticity of the sermon in its Georgian version, see J.-M. Sauget, *Un Homéliare Melkite Bipartite: Le Manuscrit Beyrouth, Bibliothèque Orientale 510* (Louvain: Louvain-La-Neuve, 1988): 280, no. 40; on the Arabic version, see Joseph-Marie Sauget, *Deux Panegyrika Melkites pour la seconde partie de l'Année Liturgique: Jérusalem S. Anne 38 et Harisa 37* (Vatican II: Biblioteca Apostolica Vatican IIa, 1986): 71–72, no. 31.

the virgin carried the Son in her hands before the light-bearer:
about whom Simeon, holding him in his arms,
preached to the people that he would be
the Lord of the living and the dead
and the savior of the world.[17]

The nuptial metaphor of the wedding chamber appeared elsewhere for the Presentation. In his aforementioned homily, Cyril of Jerusalem proclaims that "Today the heavenly spouse, with the mother of God, returns to his wedding chamber, as he is presented in the Temple."[18]

Baptismal Narratives on the Feast of the Presentation

The Armenian Lectionary, testifying to worship in Jerusalem, confirms what Egeria describes, as it lists the meeting of Simeon and Anna with the virgin mother and her child. Yet the lectionary also lists Galatians 3:24–29 as the first reading on this day: "For as many of you as were baptized into Christ have put on Christ" (3:27).[19] (This very verse was and still is sung in the Coptic liturgy on the day of Lazarus, a point taken up later in the chapter.)

References to the first man, Adam, and to the first couple, Adam and Eve, abound in other Greek sermons for the feast. (The preachers of some of the sermons on the Presentation are, in many cases, uncertain, but as rhetorical pieces the juxtaposition of the theological elements on this day is the critical element, not the identity of the authors.) Even though there seems to be little reason to find a narrative or theological link between the second creation account and the Lukan story of the Presentation, such a connection appears in a sermon attributed to the Jerusalem presbyter Hesychius, in which he connected Adam and Eve to Simeon and Anna.[20] So too in a sermon ascribed to Modestus of Jerusalem one finds, uniquely, the primacy of place assigned to Anna rather than Simeon, as he preached about the redemption of the "daughters of Eve" in Anna's presence at the event.[21] The redemption

---

17. *Adorna thalamum tuum, Sion, / et suscipe Regem Christum: / amplectere Mariam, quae est caelestis porta: / ipsa enim portat Regem gloriae novi luminis: / subsistit Virgo adducens manibus Filium ante luciferum: / quem accipiens Simeon in ulnas suas / praedicavit populis Dominum eum esse vitae et mortis, / et Salvatorem mundi.* Liber Usualis Missae et Officii (Paris: Desclée, 1947): 1243–1244; trans. Connell.

18. PG 33:1189; the metaphor is evident also in the preaching of Amphilochius; Germanus, Archbishop of Constantinople (ca. 640–733); and of Theodotus of Ancyra.

19. See Kenneth Stevenson, "The Origins and Development of Candlemas: A Struggle for Identity and Coherence," *Ephemerides Liturgicae* 102 (1988): 316–346; here at 317; also published in *Time and Community: In Honor of Thomas Julian Talley*, ed. J. Neil Alexander (Washington, DC: Pastoral Press, 1990): 43–76.

20. "On the Presentation of our Lord and Savior Jesus Christ" (PG 93:1468–1478).

21. "On Hypapante" (PG 86: 3275–3278).

of Adam in the feast of the Presentation is also part of the content in a sermon ascribed to Sophronius, patriarch of Jerusalem.[22] Adam (or Adam and Eve) appear often in the rhetoric of sermons and prayers about baptism, for the progenitors brought original sin and baptism is the means for its removal as one is initiated into the body of Christ, the new Adam.

In addition to the prevalence of the creation accounts in preaching for the feast, in the Jerusalem sermons there are references to narratives of the Hebrew scriptures that were traditionally associated with initiation: Noah and the ark,[23] and Jonah and the whale,[24] both narratives heavy with water symbolism and both found in some lectionaries of initiation rites and in church mosaics elsewhere in the early centuries.[25]

So, though the narrative for the fortieth day after Epiphany is, at first sight, the Presentation story, which does not have strong baptismal indications, there are strong initiatory elements latent in Egeria's comparing the day to Easter; in the timing of the feast forty days after Epiphany (even without a warrant from the Lukan narrative); in many of the Old Testament narratives employed; in the theological emphases of the preaching for the day; in the ritual symbols, especially the light, highlighted in the preaching; and in the baptismal implications of the reading of Galatians 3:24–29, as in the Armenian Lectionary.

The Presentation in Other Eastern Churches

Nearly omnipresent in sermons on the Presentation are images of light. Sometimes the content is on the general word "light," but frequently on instruments of light, "candles" and "lamps," indicating that this was not just a theological metaphor but one connected to the ritual actions and objects of the feast in many communities. This prevalence of light imagery holds for the Jerusalem church, as in all the witnesses already mentioned, and for other churches in other Eastern and then Western traditions.

The metaphor of light and the use of candles is so pervasive for the feast of the Presentation that it appears in almost every ancient sermon, whether in Greek, Latin, or Syriac. Though one might think that

---

22. "On Hypapante or on the Meeting with the Lord" (PG 87/3:3287–3302; here at 3298–3299).

23. Ibid.: 3300–3301.

24. "On the Prophet Simeon, and on the Gospel Text 'Now let your servant,' and on the Blessed Virgin Mary" (PG 86:237–252; here at 252).

25. See, for example, Luigi Marcuzzi, *Aquileia: Geschichte-Kunst-Historiche Stätten*, photos by Mario Zanette (Sacile: Zanette, 1985): 42–45; G. Brusin, *Führer durch Aquileia* (Padova: Tipografia Antoniana, 1978): 25.

the Lukan narrative itself, with Simeon's canticle about a "light of revelation to the Gentiles," would evoke such omnipresence, the length
and depth of the reflections on light in the sermons seem to be much
heavier and more significant than the brief phrase about light in the
Lukan narrative would warrant. Nearly all of the early Eastern fathers
mentioned so far, plus a few more, preach about light, about candles,
or about lamps. Moreover, it was the ritual action with the lights, candles, and lamps, as well as the theological motif of illumination that
was taken up in the Latin tradition, in Ambrose Autopertus (d. 784),[26]
as well as in the ninth-century Regensburg Pontifical and in the ritual
book of New Minster (ca. 1070s).[27]

Other initiation symbols appear in the rhetoric from churches other
than Jerusalem. A link between the Presentation and baptism appears
very explicitly in the sermons of Amphilochius, the cousin of Gregory
Nazianzus and bishop of Iconium (373–395). Amphilochius preached
about baptism on this day, narrating how this child brought to the
Temple had opened the heavens for the flood of Noah, freed the an-
cestors from Egypt, led the nation through the divided Red Sea, and
brought the people into the land flowing with milk and honey.[28] In
this long sermon on the Presentation, Amphilochius even spoke of the
linen garment, the *sindona*,[29] in which the body of Jesus was wrapped
when it was taken down from the cross, a garment that is attested
as a baptismal garment explicitly (and as an altar cloth) in the Acts
of Thomas, the Gospel of Peter, and other sources.[30] So, as in Jerusalem, where the testimony is strongest, there were striking elements
in the celebration of the Presentation in other churches of Eastern
Christianity, and many of these elements have initiatory bearing.

In other churches the story of the Presentation was juxtaposed to
that of Jesus' entry into Jerusalem. Homily 125 of Severus of Antioch

---

26. Ambrosius Autpertus, *Sermo Ambrosii Autperti Presbyteri ad Monachos Monasterii Martyris Vincenti in Ypapante Sanctae Mariae*, as in *Ambrosii Autperti Opera*, ed. Robertus Weber (Turnholt: Brepols, 1979): 983–1002; see especially 993.

27. Franz Unterkicher, *Das Kollektar-Pontifikale des Bischofs Baturich von Regensburg (817–848) (Cod. Vindob. ser. no. 2762)* (Freiburg, Switzerland: Universitätsverlag, 1962): 93–97; *The Missal of the New Minster, Winchester, Le Havre: Bibliothèque Municipale, MS 330*, Ed. D. H. Turner, Henry Bradshaw Society 93 (1960): 69–72.

28. *Amphilochii Iconiensis Opera*, CCSG 3, ed. Cornelius Datema (Turnholt: Brepols, 1978): 11–73, here at 55.

29. Ibid.: 59.

30. See Frederick William Dander, *A Greek-English Lexicon of the New Testament and other Early Christian Literature*, 3rd ed. (Chicago: Chicago University Press, 2000): 924; G. W. H. Lampe, *A Patristic Greek Lexicon* (Oxford: Clarendon, 1961–1968): 1233. The *sindona* is later used in reference to the corporal (11th century), the towel used in the foot-washing rite, and the linen cloth for the altar; see Albert Blaise, *Lexicon Latinitatis Medii Aevi* (Turnholt: Brepols, 1975): 848.

(ca. 465–538), for example, shows that the narrative of the Presentation was a recent addition to the feast, which, though already evident in Jerusalem for over a century, was not yet being celebrated in Constantinople: "In this city of Antioch, as you know, this kind of feast is not known. And even in Jerusalem, this feast is not ancient, but it has been recently introduced." Severus continues that "one can say the same thing too about the feast known as '*Baïa*,' when a whole crowd, carrying palm-branches in their hands, accompany our Lord and Savior Jesus Christ, who is mounted on a small donkey and enters into Jerusalem."[31] Later traditions reveal that the palms and Lazarus eventually become a deep part of the tradition on the Saturday and Sunday before Easter, so Severus's preaching on *Hypapante* in Antioch on the novelty of the Presentation narrative as he talks about the entrance of Jesus into Jerusalem and the palms suggests that the Presentation narrative displaced the Lazarus narrative when the exchanges of traditions were being wrought between East and West. Moreover, the gravity of initiation indications in ancient Presentation sermons in the East and the brevity of these in the Lukan narrative about Simeon and Anna in the Temple suggest that the theology of the feast might have been deeper and older than the Presentation narrative that was finding a home on the feast in West Syria only in the early sixth century. Lazarus Saturday was for centuries traditionally paired with Palm Sunday at the beginning of the "Great Week," yet this sermon of Severus of Antioch links the new Presentation narrative with Palm Sunday. And, as already demonstrated in the chapters on Christmas and Epiphany, it was in this period that the narratives of Jesus' infancy — birth, slaughter of the innocents, magi — were moved toward December-January while narratives of the end of his life, such as Lazarus and the palm-bearers, were moved toward Easter, which would explain why the Presentation would have displaced Lazarus.

A link between the Presentation and Lazarus also appears in a sermon of Leontius, presbyter of Constantinople, who, in a sermon on Martha, Mary, and Lazarus, used the language of "meeting," *hypapante*.[32] In his sermon on the narrative of Lazarus, this day is juxtaposed to Palm Sunday, as he says, "Tying the palm branches, we approach the meeting with the Lord, crying out and saying, 'Hosanna, blessed is he who comes in the name of the Lord. To him be glory and

---

31. Severus of Antioch, *Les Homiliae cathedrals de Severe d'Antioche*, trans. Syriac Jacques d'Edesse, trans. French R. Duval (Paris: Firmin-Didot, 1906): 232–253; here at 246–249; trans. Connell.

32. See *Clavis Patrum Graecorum Supplementum* (Turnholt: Brepols, 1998): 310, no. 4639.

the kingdom forever."[33] So, even though the theologies of the narratives and the chronologies in the Gospels make them quite dissimilar, the Presentation and the palms are juxtaposed in a few places of the tradition.

This juxtaposition has more significance on recalling Talley's evidence. His theory hinges on the hypothesis about the forty-day period after Epiphany that might have culminated with "the conferral of baptism in a celebration with one whom we know as Lazarus."[34] Although there is a lacuna in the evidence about how the forty-day post-Epiphany period leading up to *de Lazaro* in mid-February came to be the forty-day pre-Easter period of preparation leading up to Holy Week, one is left with the question of whether the earlier baptismal feast at the end of the forty days had been one with the proclamation of the raising of Lazarus and whether the "meeting," *hypapante*, to which the feast refers might not have been the meeting between the holy family and Simeon and Anna.

On Luke 2, John 11, and the "Meeting"

Such questions and suggestions about the Lazarus story in February connected to a baptismal liturgy are supported by looking more closely at the scriptural narratives. First, a consideration of the vocabulary of the Lukan and Johannine narratives is warranted. The two words attached to the name of the Presentation feast in the Greek and Latin liturgical traditions, *hypapante* and *occursus*, do not appear in the Greek or Latin scriptural narratives of the Lukan pericope of the Presentation (2:22–38). Moreover, *occursus*, in verb or noun form, does not appear in the Latin of Egeria's description of the feast, even though she uses the word quite often in other parts of the diary.[35] There are five Greek words that might have been rendered into Vulgate forms of *occurrere*, "to meet," but none of these words — *apantaō, apantesis, katantaō, synantaō,* and *hypantaō* — are used in the Lukan narrative of the Presentation, though they are used more than thirty times elsewhere in the New Testament.

The vocabulary of "meeting" in the Johannine narrative is strengthened by Egeria's description of the community's observance at the Lazarium, that is, the place from which Lazarus came out of the cave:

---

33. Chrysostom, "On Martha, Mary and Lazarus"; PG 61:706. (Leontius's sermon was at one time attributed to Chrysostom.)

34. See note 5 above.

35. See D. R. Blackman and G. G. Betts, eds., *Concordantia in Itinerarium Egeria (A Concordance to the Itinerarium Egeriae)* (Hidesheim: Olms-Weidmann, 1989).

When it is getting to be dawn, at the first light on Saturday, the bishop officiates and offers the sacrifice at dawn on Saturday. Just as the dismissal is to be given, the archdeacon raises his voice and says: "Let us all make ready to be this day at the Lazarium at the seventh hour." And so, as it gets to be the seventh hour, everyone comes to the Lazarium, which is at Bethany, approximately two miles from the city. On the way from Jerusalem to the Lazarium, at about a half mile from that place, there is a church along the road at the very place where Mary, the sister of Lazarus, came forth to meet the Lord. When the bishop reaches this place, all the monks come forth to meet him, and the people go into the church, where a hymn and an antiphon are sung and the proper passage from the Gospel is read, describing how Lazarus' sister met the Lord.[36]

There is a clear emphasis here on various meetings, for the pilgrim stresses "the very place where Mary came forth to *meet* the Lord." She relates how "the monks coming forth to *meet* the bishop" to ritualize the event narrated in the Gospel, and she reiterates the proclamation of the Gospel's description of "how Lazarus' sister *met* the Lord." Unlike the absence of such a meeting in Luke's narrative of the Presentation, the Gospel of John describes two meetings in the account of the raising of Lazarus, and, of the five Greek words for "meeting" mentioned earlier, the one used in both places of the Lazarus narrative is *hypantaō*, which comes to name the feast on which the narrative of the Presentation eventually finds a home, *hypapante*.

Another indication regarding *hypantaō* in the scriptures is that two of its few *other* appearances in the New Testament are in the narrative of Jesus' entry into Jerusalem as a prelude to his arrest and crucifixion, and that in the Gospel of John the narrative follows the story of Lazarus. Yet unlike the Lazarus story, which appears only in the Gospel of John, each of the synoptics has a narrative of the entry into Jerusalem, but none uses *hypantaō* in the telling of the story. The verses with the verb in John are only five, and four of those five are in the stories of the raising of Lazarus and Jesus' entry into Jerusalem. In the latter the verses are 12:13 — "So they took branches of palm trees and went out to *meet* him" — and 12:17–18, which connects the narrative of the palms with the Lazarus story: "The crowd that had been with him when he called Lazarus out of the tomb and raised him from the

---

36. Egeria: 102.

dead bore witness. The reason why the crowd went to *meet* him was that they heard he had done this sign."

What of the light imagery, omnipresent in the Presentation sermons? The light in the Lukan narrative might be taken as a symbol of initiation, as in the canticle of Simeon: "Master, now you are dismissing your servant in peace, according to your word; for my eyes have seen your salvation, which you have prepared in the presence of all peoples, a light for revelation to the Gentiles and for glory to your people Israel" (2:29–32).[37] In Simeon's song, the light is connected to salvation, as it would have been in an initiation rite.

But the Gospel of John also often uses the contrasts of light and darkness for the presence and absence of God,[38] as also in the Lazarus story when Jesus says, "If any one walks in the day, he does not stumble, because he sees the light of this world. But if any one walks in the night, he stumbles, because the light is not in him" (11:9–10). Earlier in the Gospel, Jesus had identified himself as the "light of the world" (8:12), and the Gospel employs light as an indication of the presence of God and Christ. Of the two narratives, Presentation and Lazarus, both have light imagery, yet the Lazarus story carries a deeper theological interpretation of the light than the Presentation story, as does the Gospel of John as a whole.

Also prominent in the Lazarus account is its rhetoric about resurrection, for Jesus says, "Our friend Lazarus has fallen asleep, but I go to awake him out of sleep" (11:11); later in the story Jesus tells Martha, "Your brother will rise again" (11:23), to which she replies, "I know that he will rise again in the resurrection at the last day," but Jesus corrects her misunderstanding with one of the Johannine "I am" sayings: "I am the resurrection and the life; he who believes in me, though he die, yet shall he live, and whoever lives and believes in me shall never die" (11:25–26).

Another link between initiation and Lazarus comes not in Jesus' words but at the emergence of the once dead and decomposing Lazarus from the tomb: "The dead man came out, his hands and feet bound with bandages, and his face wrapped with a cloth. Jesus said to them, 'Unbind him, and let him go'" (11:44). The cloth is a *soudarion*, which appears only two times in the Gospel, here on the face of Lazarus (11:44) and in the empty tomb, where the body of Jesus had been

---

37. Unless otherwise noted, all scripture citations in this volume have been from the Revised Standard Version (RSV); this is from the New Revised Standard Version (NRSV), for its translation better suits the point and is warranted in the original.

38. See, for example, John 1:4–5, 1:7–9, 3:2, 3:19–21, 5:35, 8:12, 12:35–36, 12:44–46.

laid: Simon Peter "went into the tomb; he saw the linen cloths lying, and the *napkin*, which had been on [Jesus'] head, not lying with the linen cloths but rolled up in a place by itself" (20:6–7). This vesture common to Lazarus and to what was left in the empty tomb after the resurrection also brings initiatory imagery into the Lazarus story.

In summary, a tentative argument can be made that the main impetus for suggesting that the Presentation story displaced the Lazarus story at the end of the forty-day post-Epiphany span was that the scriptural narratives that had, until the middle of the fourth century, been unique to local traditions and regions were displaced by church and liturgical authorities. Part of the process of changing and assigning narratives happened as East and West met, and their ecclesial unions resulted in the addition and excision of the local traditions and scripture narratives of earlier times. This universalizing impetus happened in the most concentrated way during the fourth century as the general shape of the liturgical year emerged. After the Roman date for Christmas was, at first with resistance, gradually received by most churches, the infancy narratives moved toward that pole of the year. Moreover, even though the narrative of the Presentation says that the event took place eight days after Jesus' birth (Luke 2:21), the narrative was put in mid-February (at first) because of the Egyptian church's observance of the forty-day span after Epiphany. It seems that this had been a baptismal feast and that its original narrative had been John 11, the raising of Lazarus, a story filled with initiatory imagery and theology. When the forty-day span was moved toward Easter (or toward the "Great Week" before Easter), the Lazarus narrative stayed at the end of the span and was placed before Holy Week. The remnant of the originally post-Epiphany span was the feast of *hypapante*, the "meeting," on the fortieth day after Christmas, and that very name also suggests that its original narrative was that of Lazarus. The missing evidence that prevents this case being made simply or decisively is that there is no remnant of a full initiation liturgy on *hypapante*, forty days after Epiphany, at which the Lazarus story would have been originally proclaimed.

Part Two:
The History of Candlemas — West

As we turn from the Greek and Syriac sources of the Presentation to the Latin sources, there is a marked change in the weight of the feast and in the content of the preaching and liturgical prayers.[39] In quantity the sermons are far fewer and later than in the Eastern tradition, and the content is not as theologically deep, concentrating mostly on interpretations of the scriptural narrative as an event of the biblical past rather than on any revelation of God for the church assembled. Moreover, soon after its emergence in the West, the feast's focus moved from the child Jesus, Simeon, and Anna to Mary, the mother of Jesus. The title and rhetoric of the feast becomes the "Purification of Mary." By the time of the Latin sermons, Christmas (on December 25) had been universally received by Western churches, so the feast was no longer in mid-February but on February 2, where it has remained in the Latin tradition. The oldest Roman evidence is coincident with the Eastern churches changing the date of the festival from February 14 to 2. Though the day was called a "solemnity," some of the Latin preachers note that their assemblies do not recognize how important the feast is in the church's tradition.[40]

The earliest evidence of Candlemas in the West suggests that it was not introduced there until the middle of the seventh century, and, as in the East, its appearance shows that the feast involved a procession and lights. Some historians have suggested that the procession of the Christian feast in Rome might have been a way of attracting pagans to the rite, for there was a pagan rite of cleansing and penitence celebrated once every five years, and that occasion, called *Amburbale*, that is, "walking in the city," took place at the beginning of February. Unlike most scholars of the year, I am not inclined to attribute the emergence of feasts and seasons to a single cause, for in most cases I find the cause is the confluence of various factors. So, too, with the pagan procession at Rome; centuries before the Roman evidence, the Eastern sources reveal that the procession was integral to the feast. Its reception in Rome may have been supported or quickened by the pagan practice, but a one-to-one correspondence or displacement does not seem likely.

---

39. For a detailed chronology of the feast of the Purification of Mary, see I Deug-Su, "La festa della purificazione in Occidente (secoli IV=VIII)," *Studi Medievali*, 3rd series, 15 (1974): 143–216. Some study of the feast in the West has focused on its coincidence with the pagan celebration of *Lupercalia*. Though not part of this study, the primary source on the pagan origins is Pope Gelasius I, *Lettre contre Les Lupercales et Dix-huit Messes du Sacramentaire Léonien*, intro., text, trans., G. Pomarès (Paris: Cerf, 1959): 20–51, 161–189; also in PL 59:110–116. For secondary literature, see Pierre Battifol, *Études de Liturgie et d'Archéologie Chrétienne* (Paris: Lecoffre, 1919): 193–215; D. DeBruyne, "L'Origine des Processions de la Chandeleur et des Rogations a propos d'un Sermon Inédit," *Revue Benedictine* 34 (1922): 14–26.

40. Ambrosius Autopertus, "Sermon on the Hypapante of Holy Mary," *Ambrosii Autperti Opera*, ed. Robertus Weber (Turnholt: Brepols, 1979): 983–1002, here at 985.

Another uniquely Roman element that has been taken up in the histories of the feast is the former pagan feast of Lupercalia, a festival on February 14 that promoted fertility and cleansing. The evidence for this hypothesis is a "letter against Lupercalia" in the correspondence of Pope Gelasius I (492–496).[41] But a close reading of the letter does not reveal any elements about the Christian feast in Gelasius's rhetoric; the letter is primarily his effort to quash the popular pagan feast.

Some of the theological emphases for the Presentation in the West came from the Eastern traditions of the feast long after the circumcision story of Luke was the Gospel. The issue of the sin of Adam, for example, is common in the Purification preaching of the Venerable Bede (ca. 673–735). Also striking in Bede is that he quoted from the Lazarus narrative of the Gospel of John as he preached on the feast of the Purification of Mary: "I am the resurrection and the life; anyone who believes in me, even if he dies, will live; and all who live and believe in me will not die in eternity."[42]

As primogenitor, Adam appears not only in some of the rhetoric of the West for the Presentation, but he also appears in a sermon on Lazarus. One finds that, a few centuries before Bede, down on the eastern side of the Italian peninsula, Chromatius of Aquileia, who was the bishop in this metropolitan church from ca. 388 to 407, linked the narrative of Adam and that of Lazarus. In a sermon on the "resuscitation of Lazarus," Chromatius made the link between the question of the Lord to Mary and Martha, "Where have you put him?" (John 11:34), and the question of the Lord God to the primogenitor, "Where are you, Adam?" (Genesis 3:9).[43] Bede connected Adam to the Presentation, while Chromatius connected Adam to Lazarus. (The church at Aquileia manifested a number of elements in the calendar that it shared with the church of Egypt, perhaps an influence, generally, of its port of access to the Mediterranean or, more particularly, to the exile of the patriarch Athanasius there [ca. 345], an Egyptian church leader whose theology and Christology were welcomed and received.[44])

---

41. Gelasius I, *Lettre contre Les Lupercales et Dix-huit Messes du Sacramentaire Leonien*, intro, text, and trans. G. Pomarès (Paris: Cerf, 1959): 20–51, 161–189. The study of the letter is at 20–51, and a critical edition of Gelasius's letter at 161–189.

42. *Homilia 18*, in *Bedae Opera*, CCSL 122 (Turnholt: Brepols, 1955): 128–133, here at 131, quoting John 11:25–26; trans. Connell. The same homily is available, though not in a critical edition, in PL 94:79–83.

43. *Chromatii Aquileiensis Opera*, ed. R. Étaix and J. Lemarié, CCSL 9A (Turnholt: Brepols, 1979): 123–127.

44. See Volume 2, Chapter 3, "The Three Days."

While the theology of Candlemas in the West is generally less potent than what it had been in Jerusalem or other Eastern churches, it is striking that the Latin tradition of the Presentation maintains or takes up ritual practices that are linked to the initiatory content found in the East. Such practices, as described below, included the stational character of the feast, the rite of the blessing of candles, and even, in the late medieval period, the rubrics for a change of vestments in the Mass of the day.

Candlemas as Stational Worship

From its earliest evidence anywhere — Egeria's diary — the liturgy of the Presentation was stational, as Egeria recorded that "there is a procession into the Anastasis." Evidence of such processions emerges from many of the ancient sermons, and the processions continue even as the theology of the feast moves from East to West and changes significantly in the Middle Ages. In Rome, for example, the feast took hold, but by the time there is clear evidence of it there, in the ninth century, the celebration's character is more penitential.

The elements of the Presentation narrative emphasized in sermons shift from those concentrating on the presentation of the child Jesus to the purification of Mary. The theology built upon the issue of Mary's purification was the pastoral encouragement toward penance and purification, and the processional character reflected the journey of faith through penitence.[45] Yet this shift did not stem the stational character, as can be seen from the note about processions in the *Liber Pontificalis* of Pope Sergius I (687–701), wherein one finds "that on the days of the Annunciation of the Lord, the Falling-Asleep and the Nativity of the ever-virgin Mary, the Holy Mother of God, and of St. Symeon, which the Greeks call *Ypapante*, a procession should be made from St. Hadrian's."[46] (Except for the single and odd evidence of Pope Gelasius about Lupercalia in February, mentioned earlier, the note in the *Liber Pontificalis* is the earliest Roman testimony regarding the Presentation.) The description of the feast in the *Liber* also accords with the rite in the Ordo of St. Armand, which recounts, even with the penitential elements, that the people and the clergy processed with candles and sang, moving through the city of Rome from the church of St. Hadrian

---

45. Eventually the penitential aspect of the feast will appear in the East also; see Stevenson: 325, and the brief article of M. Higgins, "Note on the Purification (and Date of the Nativity) in Constantinople in 602," *Archiv für Liturgiewissenschaft* 2 (1952): 81–83.

46. *Liber Pontificalis*, 14; as quoted in Stevenson: 330.

to the Basilica of St. Mary Major.[47] As the traditions for the Presentation spread, the processions were inculturated and incorporated into the ritual traditions of religious communities and parishes.

The stational character of the day is also present in the two *ordines romani* that mention the Presentation, both of the eighth century, *Ordo XV* and *Ordo XX*.[48] Even though these appear just a short time after the first Western record of the feast, it is evident already that the focus has become the mother of Jesus, for in *Ordo Romanus XX* the rite is called "On the Purification of St. Mary." The other *ordo* has the same vocabulary found in the *Liber Pontificalis, "hypapante,"* perhaps indicative that this rite reflected an earlier level of the tradition of the feast.

Candles on Candlemas

As seen in Eastern testimonies to the Presentation, evidence of the use of lights, candles, and lamps was widespread.[49] So in the West, too, the tradition was adopted and taken up as the blessing of candles, which continued to accompany the rite even as the narrative theology of the feast moves from the presentation of Jesus in the Temple toward the purification of Mary, a theological concentration for the feast in the West for most of its history. The candle-blessing element appeared as an addendum to worship books in the ninth and tenth centuries,[50] but came to be received into the Latin tradition integrally within a few centuries. The various rites of the feast become more elaborate in the later Middle Ages, and some communities had remnants of a blessing of a "new fire," a provocative link with the fire in the development of the rite of the Easter Vigil in the Middle Ages.[51]

Vestment Colors at Candlemas

Although in the first millennium of the Christian faith evidence about the colors of vestments is spare, some of the earliest references are found in notes about liturgies for Candlemas. The eighth-century *Ordines Romani*, mentioned above, reveal that when the church gathered

---

47. Adrian Nocent, *The Liturgical Year*, volume 1, trans. Matthew O'Connell (Collegeville, MN: Liturgical Press, 1977): 328.

48. Michel Andrieu, *Les Ordines Romani du haut moyen âge III. Les textes (Ordines XIV–XXXIV)* (Louvain: 1961). The evidence for the Presentation appears at 113–114 for *OR XV* and at 229–236 for *OR XX*.

49. Kenneth Stevenson points out that the use of candles began in the middle of the fifth century, according to the witness of Cyril of Scythopolis, in his Vita Theodosii: "Then the blessed Mikelia, having practiced all manner of piety, was the first to introduce the celebration of our Lord with candles." See Stevenson: 316–346, here at 323–324.

50. Ibid.: 334.

51. Ibid.: 338.

at St. Hadrian's for Candlemas, the pope and the deacons put on black vestments, and thus dressed move to help with the distribution of the candles for the procession.

A half millennium later, one finds that black vestments are still a custom of the liturgy, though not for the whole rite. Apart from a smattering of bits and pieces here and there in the Latin tradition before this time, the third book of the *Rationale Divinorum Officiorum* — written by William Durandus, bishop of Mende, in the late thirteenth century — is one of the Christian tradition's earliest witnesses to the reasons for a scheme of colors to be used in the course of the liturgical year. Concerning February 2 Durandus wrote that "on the feast of *hypapante*, violet or black is to be used in the procession before Mass."[52] Then the color changed to white for the Mass. This change of color from the violet (or black) to white persisted in the tradition for centuries after Durandus.

Candlemas in the Roman Missal of Pius V

In the first printed Missal, promulgated in 1570 as the universal rite for all Roman Catholic churches in the world, Candlemas and Easter were the only days in the liturgical year when the liturgy started in purple vestments and changed to white. Harking back to the beginning of the chapter, where Egeria described the rite in Jerusalem for *Hypapante* as "just as on Easter Sunday," so in the sixteenth-century did these two days have ritual similarities. The change of vestments from purple to white reflected each feast's celebration as the terminus of a span of penitence.[53] The priest started the liturgy in a purple cope, but after the procession he was to put on white vestments for the Mass.[54]

That sixteenth-century Roman Missal named the day "The Purification of Mary," or *Purificatio B.M.V.*, more specifically the "cleansing of the Blessed Virgin Mary," solidifying for four centuries the Western shift in the early Middle Ages from a feast of the Lord, the "Presentation," to a feast of Mary, the "Purification." The prayers of the Mass spoke of the illumination and cleansing of those in attendance. The "wedding chamber" metaphor of the medieval rites is also present in the Roman Missal.

---

52. *Quidam etiam in festo Ypapantis, in processione que fit ante missam, utuntur violaceo vel nigro colore.* As from Michel Andrieu, *Le Pontifical Romain au Moyen-Age*, volume 3: *Le Pontifical de Guillaume Durand* (Vatican II: Biblioteca Apostolica Vatican IIa, 1940): 656–659.

53. With Hypapante the penitence might carry not only the echo of the span of forty days after Epiphany, for some churches observed the three-day Rogation span in February also. Rogation days, an observance in rural communities, were days of penitence and cleansing.

54. *Missale Romanum S. Pii V* (Regensburg, 1923): 498–502.

In the nineteenth-century worship book promulgated for small parishes, the *Memoriale Rituum* of Pope Benedict XIII, the rite for the day calls for two frontal pieces, *antependia* in Latin, to cover the main altar for the Presentation, a purple one over a white one, so that the purple can be readily removed after the procession when the Mass would begin.[55] Decorated even more than the altar-front were the clergy: amice, alb, cincture, stole, and purple cope for the main celebrant. They would remain so clad through the rite of blessing of the candles and their distribution, during which were sung the Canticle of Simeon and Psalm 43; likewise for the procession, with the antiphon, as had become traditional, *Adorna thalamum tuum, Sion,* "Decorate your marriage chamber, Zion," and a response.

When the Mass began, the priest would remove the purple cope and stole, and don — or "be donned by a second and third cleric," as the rubrics prescribe, even though it was written for *small* parishes — a white maniple, stole, and chasuble.[56] This change of vestments, seen first in William Durandus, in the thirteenth century, continued to Trent, then in the rites promulgated after Trent, and remained on the books until the reform of the liturgy after Vatican II. (In Durandus the color of the first vestments would be black or purple, but after Trent the color was only purple.) In addition to the rituals, theological issues persisted from the East in the connections to baptism and its images, to Adam, and to the resurrection of Christ, the new Adam, and the rites continued the use of candles, the procession, the stational character, and the image of the marriage chamber.

The Churching of Women in the Roman Tradition

Although it feels like a medieval rather than modern ritual practice, the rite of the "churching" of a woman forty days after she had given birth was still practiced in the Roman Catholic church until Vatican II and by churches of the Eastern traditions and by some Protestants also. This was quite a popular ritual tradition, an occasion for friends and family to celebrate the arrival of the newborn and the return to health of the mother in the weeks after she had given birth. The rite was quite likely an offshoot or imitation of the feast of the Purification of the B.V.M., but for centuries it was celebrated forty days after the birth of a child regardless of the time of the liturgical year. According to the teaching and understanding of the church, the woman was not

---

55. *Memoriale Rituum pro aliquibus praestantioribus sacris functionibus persolvendis in minoribus Ecclesiis Parochialibus* (Ratisbonae: Georgius Josephus Manz, 1862): 2.
56. Ibid.: 3–14.

able to receive the sacraments until she had been so "churched," or returned to communion after the impurities incurred during birth.[57]

Part Three:
Candlemas after Vatican II

Going back to the earliest theological traditions of the feast, the reformers of Vatican II reverted to the original christological focus of the feast when they named it the "Feast of the Presentation of the Lord," *Praesentatio Domini*. That name is confirmed by the prayers of the Mass, which also highlight the ancient meaning of the day, the "meeting" celebrated on that day. The meeting remembered in the Sacramentary of Vatican II is explicitly that of the child Jesus and Simeon and Anna, not the meeting, *hypapante*, of the narrative of Lazarus. So in the First Form of the rite of the blessing of Candles and Procession, the priest offers this invitation:

> Forty days ago we celebrated the joyful feast of the birth of our Lord Jesus Christ. Today we recall the holy day on which he was presented in the temple, fulfilling the law of Moses and at the same time going to meet his faithful people. Led by the Spirit, Simeon and Anna came to the temple, recognized Christ as their Lord, and proclaimed him with joy.
>
> United by the Spirit, may we now go to the house of God to welcome Christ the Lord. There we shall recognize him in the breaking of the bread until he comes again in glory.[58]

The remembrance of the meeting of the Lord in the temple of Jerusalem is the narrative that unites believers by the power of the Holy Spirit for meeting the Lord both in the liturgy of the day and in their daily lives.

The rubrics of the Sacramentary offer two forms for the start of the liturgy; the First Form is simply the "Procession," the Second form the "Solemn Entrance." The rubrics for the First Form prescribe these actions: "The people gather in a chapel or other suitable place outside the church where the Mass will be celebrated. They carry unlighted candles. The priest and the ministers wear white vestments. The priest may wear a cope instead of a chasuble during the procession." This

---

57. See A. J. Schulte, "Churching of Women," *The Catholic Encyclopedia*, vol. 3 (New York: Encyclopedia Press, 1913): 761.

58. *Vatican II Sunday Missal: Millennium Edition* (Boston: Pauline Books and Media, 2001): 1012.

instruction does carry forth some of the important elements of the traditions for the feast, with the prescription that the procession of the faithful should begin from a place outside the church.

After the sprinkling of the candles, the text sends those in attendance to celebrate the new presentation with the invitation: "Let us go in peace to meet the Lord." (The Latin rubric underlying this text, *Procedemus in pace ad occurendum Domino*, and other texts of the Mass uses a form of the word *occursus*, the Latin translation of the original Greek *hypapante*.) With the candles sprinkled, the priest takes a lighted candle and, as those assembled have their candles lighted, the procession moves toward the church where the Mass will be celebrated. On arriving at his chair, the priest "replaces the cope with the chasuble." The Mass then continues with the Gloria and the opening prayer.

Some of the texts of the liturgy continue the tradition of "purification," which had earlier been of the woman who had just given birth, namely Mary, but in the reform of the liturgy the texts focus on the cleansing and purification of the people of God so that they might recognize the Lord when they meet him. So the opening prayer:

> All-powerful Father,
> Christ your Son became man for us
> and was presented in the temple.
> May he free our hearts from sin
> and bring us into your presence.[59]

The first and second readings, Malachi 3:1–4 and Hebrews 2:14–18, have the same theological suggestion, with the second ending with the christological link to suffering: "For because he [Jesus] himself has suffered and been tempted, he is able to help those who are tempted."

The Gospel is the Lukan narrative (2:22–40) that has been proclaimed on the feast from its fourth-century Eastern origins, through the Middle Ages and Tridentine reform of the liturgy, until now. Although the narrative speaks of the Mosaic law for the purification of a *woman* after childbirth, the possessive pronoun of the original Greek of the Gospel — diverting from the gendered law and with some surprise — is a plural pronoun and is therefore most accurately translated: "When the days were completed for *their* purification according to the law of Moses. . . ."[60] This supports the relaxation in the rite from the

---

59. Ibid.: 1014–1015.
60. See Raymond Brown, *The Birth of the Messiah* (New York: Doubleday, 1977): 447–451.

former impurity attributed to women only and widens the purification
of the rite to the people of God generally.

A beautiful element of the Gospel narrative is the Canticle of
Simeon, which is very familiar to believers who celebrate Night Prayer
(Compline), for it has been lodged in daily prayer as the canticle for
the end of the day since the fifth century. Its Latin tag, *Nunc dimittis*, "Now you let go," is the briefest of the Gospel canticles of daily
prayer — with the *Benedictus* (Luke 1:68–79) as the canticle for Morning Prayer and the *Magnificat* (Luke 1:46–55) for Evening Prayer. The
deserved popularity of the Lukan tradition is evident in these three
canticles, coming as they do from the engaging infancy narrative of
the third Gospel. The dismissal of the *Nunc dimittis*'s rhetoric is from
the lips of Simeon, who in old age awaits God's revelation to the world
and the glory of its people, but that dismissal is also apt for the "dismissal" at the end of the day as believers entrust themselves to God's
care through the night.

While the prayers for the Mass for the Presentation are good, the ritual behaviors of the Mass — quite apart from the words and narrative
meaning of the liturgy — deliberately mark the feast as more distinct
in the liturgical year, an aspect of ritual life that has, for the most part,
been lost in the reform of the liturgy.

Lamentable in the reform is that the day continues to be oriented
backward to Christmas and its infancy stories with no anticipation
of the Easter spans coming. Though the Gospel narrative and ritual
elements for the day have plenty to link the day with the coming
Easter mysteries — the suffering of Mary, the use of holy water in
the sprinkling of the candles, and indeed the procession with candles
itself, which will next be done at the Easter Vigil — the reformers fashioned the rites for Candlemas as a liturgy linked with the others in
the Christmas nexus. Had the feast been revised as a bridge between
Christmas and Easter, the birth narrative would be ennobled by linking it to the rebirth celebrated in baptism at the coming Easter and
the celebration of Easter with the theology of birth that was lost when
the Western theology of Easter — as death and resurrection, from Romans 6 — overshadowed the link between birth and baptism that once
characterized the celebration of Epiphany.[61]

Even though the church ignored this potentially unitive temporal
aspect of the feast, the Easter elements remain in reflections on the
feast not written for worship, as in the Merton poem at the beginning
of the chapter and in the following contemporary poem:

---

61. See Volume 1, Chapter 4, "Epiphany."

CANDLEMAS

With certitude
Simeon opened
ancient arms
to infant light.
Decades
before the cross, the tomb
and the new life,
he knew
new life.
What depth
of faith he drew on,
turning illumined
towards deep night.

This poem, by Denise Levertov, is not far from the theology found in the poem of Thomas Merton, written about a half-century before.[62] The theology of the Merton and Levertov poems explicitly link humanity to the meeting of the Savior that is remembered in the Presentation narrative and experienced in the life of the baptized, one with the suffering Savior.

Merton wrote of "Our lives, like candles, spell this simple symbol: / Weep like our bodily life, sweet work of bees, / Sweeten the world, with your slow sacrifice," and ended with us, "returning to our Father, one by one," as he prayed to that Father, "Give back our lives like wise and waxen lights." So too Levertov's juxtapositions of "ancient arms" and "new light," of "the cross, the tomb / and new life," aptly capture the scriptural narrative that engages the imaginations of those worshiping in the devotion that unites them, yet also mention and anticipate the suffering and glory that the church shares with the life of the Savior it celebrates at Candlemas.

Conclusion

This chapter began with a reflection on the regard accorded ritual actions in the reform of Roman Catholic liturgy after Vatican II. Such a reflection might have been included in other chapters, but I include it here with Candlemas because the feast is virtually indistinguishable

---

62. Denise Levertov, "Candlemas," *The Stream and the Sapphire: Selected Poems on Religious Themes* (New York: New Directions, 1997): 11.

from other celebrations in the liturgical traditions of most parishes after Vatican II, even though the uniqueness of the day's procession and candles have been part of this feast's traditions for centuries, indeed for more than a millennium. The reflection at the opening of the chapter was on the reform of the liturgy in all places generally after Vatican II, but here let us consider the impediments to public rituals in the unique historical and cultural circumstances of church life in the United States.

The waning of Candlemas and its rituals demonstrate that in some places the church may have accommodated itself too much to earnest, mindful dedication to ritual texts without complementing that interiority with actions of the body at worship. Perhaps not for Protestants, for whom the body is less a theological locus of grace, but for Catholics living in a foundationally Protestant culture, the interior faith calls for a concomitant expression in flesh, but this complement was diminished in the reform of the liturgy and its calendar after Vatican II. Catholics need not be apologetic about the ritual foundations of their faith in corporal experience: the risen Christ is the body constituted by baptism by means of the assembly of individual bodies marked by the rites of the church and wedded to one another in the traditions of the faith.

Ritual Life in Western Christianity after the Reformation

Sixteenth-century reformers of Christianity — countering the Roman Catholic tradition into which they themselves had been baptized as infants and, for many, ordained as young men — indicted any theology that predicated grace on human action rather than on God's generosity, and much of Roman Catholic piety and preaching of the time did just that. Contradicting the Roman Catholic *status theologiae,* the reformers of northern Europe taught rightly that grace is a free, unearned gift. The indictments of Roman Catholic theology were not new even in the sixteenth century, for they had been levied in the fourteenth and fifteenth centuries by reformers like the Czech preacher John Huss (ca. 1372–1415, burned at the stake) and the English theologian John Wycliffe (ca. 1330–1384, exhumed and then burned at the stake). The powerful new ingredient that promoted the values of the reformers was the printing press. The Gutenberg medium for promulgating ideas and images enabled theological teachings to be read by individuals apart from a community of faith. Mindless rituals were excised from the reformed faith, and the most virulent anti-ritual and anti-body Christians were the Puritan founders of the United States.[63]

The call for reform in the middle of the twentieth century was born not from such theological errors but from the devastations of two world wars. Is this — church leaders and Christian theologians had to ask at mid-century, as they viewed the ravages of the war on their land and populations — the kind of life that Christian faith begets in the world? The mindless rituals of war rightly called all mindless rituals into question, but in spite of that righteous suspicion, not all rituals, not even all mindless rituals, are necessarily bad or pointed toward the indoctrination of evil.

The post–Vatican II emphasis on teaching and learning — on catechesis and consciousness of the faith and its traditions — came after centuries in which the baptized were merely peripheral and passive. Such a corrective was necessary, of course, but recent retrieval of pre–Vatican II rituals and objects demonstrate in part that the corrective had swung too far away from the fundamental and irreplaceable core of the faith in what is done by and to the human body in the sacraments. The Protestant culture from which this country was born was understandably suspicious of mindless rituals — in the Roman Catholic church and in the monarchical governing systems of Europe — that until the French Revolution had kept people poor, ignorant, passive, and quiet. The Christian tradition was rightly implicated by the revolutionaries who called for the separation of church and state so that all people, regardless of their social or economic state, would have equal voice and dignity before the government, before the law, in education and the economy. Yet the suspicion of mindless rituals has meant the loss of some of the customary rituals that can be dignifying, unifying in society, indeed strengthening for those who participate in them.

The United States is, generally, a culture in which the freedom of the individual, on the one hand, and national cohesion (particularly in times of war and strife), on the other hand, are both highly valued. Yet there is a limit to the goodness brought by an ebullient individualism, a solitary's sacramentalism, and a corporal Christology from the experience of one's own body apart from others. From the Enlightenment philosophies undergirding the founding of this country, individual Christian faith apart from a local community came to the

---

63. For a longer essay on this topic see my "On the U.S. Aversion to Ritual Behavior and the Vocation of the Liturgical Theologian," *Worship* 78 (2004): 386–404.

fore simply because — with the printing press and the abilities to re-produce the Bible for anyone who wants one — it *could* have such an existence for the first time in Christian history.

For centuries, at least until Gutenberg, liturgical texts were writ-ten large enough to be read and sung by a community. In those times scriptural and liturgical texts not only shaped one's mind and heart but one's body as well, or, more accurately, they were the instruments that made of the individual bodies present for worship the one Body of Christ, as the individual's was literally, sensorily, put into contact with a community. But once, after the printing medium, scripture and wor-ship were able to be separated from the church that produced them, religion forged its way ahead as a private or at least individual pursuit. The temperance movement's link with Christianity confirmed this anthropology as it moved individuals to heroic changes of life based on conversions of the heart and *personal* decisions accompanying conversions.

In the religious fervor of the very Christian nineteenth century, of which temperance was just a part, the influence of and formation by the church all but disappeared in religious rhetoric. No communal real-ization, manifestation, or incarnation of God's presence was needed to move a person to conversion, for God was present in the person with-out a church, its worship, or its ministers. Trusting in the immutable text of the Bible apart from the church's mutable members was char-acteristic of U.S. Christian piety of many kinds; for Protestants, this is most apparent today in rampant biblical fundamentalism, even when contrary to the most quotidian of scientific reasoning. In this way the culture begot a theology that flourishes without community, in which there is imagined to exist a Christ without a church, a *"personal* Lord and Savior."[64]

One can see how the Roman Catholic tradition in the United States poses a counter to the culture and how liturgical theologians need to be bold in their indictments of individualism, not toward the goal of converting those who are not Christians or of making Catholics of Protestants, but to pose alternatives to the extremes of individualism and nationalism, thereby opening up possibilities for healthier choices of life for Christian citizens.

---

64. It is lamentable that some Roman Catholic dioceses and parishes have adopted the rhetoric of "personal Lord and Savior" in their formation programs for the Sacrament of Confirmation, celebrated for many youths in their teenage years. This is unrecognizable language in the Catholic tradition, adopted, no doubt, without critical thought from evan-gelical theology. To this Roman Catholic author, the terms "personal" and "Lord and Savior" seem to have no point of contact or intersection.

The foundations of the Roman Catholic sacraments are not separate from the anthropological core of life. Humans wash and moisten with oil; eat and drink; order their societies according to skills, training, and natural talents; touch the sick and dying; commit themselves to lifelong intimate relationships and, yes, reproduce. Yet, too little preaching in the liturgy makes connections between the rites of the assembly performed in the sacraments and the actions of human life outside the church. Liturgical theologians — informed about the tradition and sensitive to God's presence in the world — can contribute in this regard by appreciating and teaching the intimate connection between life at worship and life outside the community of faith. The culture holds religion to be so private that the link between church life and society is often lost, yet when awake and attentive to God's presence in the world, liturgical theologians can demonstrate that there is a fundamental connection between life and liturgy.

The rites of the church (and of the liturgical year that gives structure to the rites) encourage members to wash, anoint, eat and drink, touch and make love to one another, as they are committed to one another by the Word and sacraments in the church. The rites demand that Christians be present to one another not as bodies of Christ, but as one bread and one body, as one cup and one blood of Christ, a presence made possible only "when two or three" — not one — "are gathered in my name" (Matthew 18:20). The Roman Catholic church in the United States seems to be the promulgator of an anti-body theology because it excludes women from orders and keeps families and parents out of leadership, yet the Roman Catholic liturgical tradition is in truth a contradiction to the direction of social life in the United States, which moves away from the body and toward communions without flesh.

The separation of church and state is a wonderful characteristic of the American experience, and the separation was to give breadth to religious experience so that people would be free to associate with those of like traditions. Yet greater freedom has heightened individualism, and religious communities have gradually become less demonstrably public, having themselves succumbed to cultural domination. Traditions and communities that had earlier communicated values to citizens have stopped having influence from the witness of those called to be preachers and prophets. When older Catholics reminisce about their experience of the faith as children, the most common things they mention are not things they learned but things they did — processions, genuflections, stations of the cross, adoration of the Blessed

Sacrament. Older Catholics are few who talk about how their lives were changed by a good sermon or a good catechism class. Many speak of the formation of their bodies, and that formation carried them to be good and sometimes disagreeable members of society, with expectations that God lives and acts in the world.

Retrieving the Rites of Candlemas

After an engaging investigation of the feast of the Presentation,[65] Kenneth Stevenson wrote "we need a feast that links Christmas and Easter together, and that is why the ultimate answer to the question, 'Where does it belong?,' must really be that this feast is a hinge that holds together the two main cycles of the liturgical year." And he prescribes that "a renewed Feast of the Presentation ought to remain on the fortieth day after Christmas, but there should be ways of making it point forward to Lent, Holy Week and Easter, not least because of the crucial second oracle of Simeon."[66] He did not overlook the complexity of the tradition of the feast but saw that the reform of the rite was too straitening:

> There is an unhappy tendency to make modern liturgy slick and manageable, and that can produce a piety that does not match up to life as many people experience it. Some of these ambivalences have been explored of old, and they need to be looked at again. With the archetypal symbol of light in darkness, perhaps this feast might gain some necessary depth, and point us at one and the same time to our sins — and the infinite mercies of God.

Stevenson's is a keen study of the tradition and observation about the reform. I would complement what he says about the meaning of the feast with the above reflection on the action of the feast, with a prescription that making sense need not be the only value reformers of the liturgy attend to. The engagement of the Body of Christ as an assembly of baptized bodies is a value lost particularly in the tradition of Candlemas and generally in many of the former traditions of feasts and seasons through the year.

The collective unconscious about Candlemas is still strong even though the feast has been in decline for a long time. Reformers of the calendar needed to consider how what believers did matched or did not match the theology of the feasts, but this need not have resulted in the

---

65. Stevenson: 316–346.
66. Ibid.: 343.

change from ritual action to ritual immobility, from the rites of the year with the assembly corporally engaged to rites in which the assembly is static and trapped in its pews. This anthropological value strengthens the complementarity of the social body and the community's soul, a complementarity that once did — and may yet again — characterize Roman Catholic theology and its liturgical year.

INDEX